NO MERCY

JOHN WALSH

WITH PHILIP LERMAN

NO MERCY

The Host of *America's Most Wanted*
Hunts the Worst Criminals of Our Time—
in Shattering True Crime Cases

POCKET BOOKS

New York   London   Toronto   Sydney   Tokyo   Singapore

POCKET BOOKS, a division of Simon & Schuster Inc.
1230 Avenue of the Americas, New York, NY 10020

ISBN: 0-671-01993-7

First Pocket Books hardcover printing November 1998

10 9 8 7 6 5 4 3 2 1

To crime victims everywhere
in their search for closure and justice

CONTENTS

Acknowledgments

Just as *America's Most Wanted* represents a collaboration among many, many people, both on our staff and out in the world, so does this volume.

I must first thank my partner, Lance Heflin, who has been the guiding force behind this effort, acting at various stages as initiator, cheerleader, editor, and mentor.

Phil Lerman has always brought to our program his dedication, his heart, and his sensitivity to the victims of crime: He brought all that to the long, hard process of creating this book, and I thank him for helping me make it the best it could be. I could not have done it without him.

Our researcher, Lydia Strohl, did an incredible job of pulling together an enormous amount of information. Eleanor Lerman, Donna Brant, and Cheri Nolan helped us tell our stories well, as did our sage, Emily Bestler.

Thanks to staffers and former staffers Sharon Greene, Lena Nozizwe, Michelle Hord, Wanda Witherspoon, Steele Bennett, Anthony Batson, Paul Sparrow, Susan Baumel, Margaret Roberts, and Gary Meyers for sharing your memories; and to the many, many more members of our team whose work, now and over the years, formed the basis for the tales told here. You are all, truly, heroes.

Thanks to all the Fox executives and staff who've supported us, helped us, and believed in us. Many crime victims have found justice because you had the guts to put us on the air and to stay with us when times got tough.

And, mostly, my thanks to all the crime victims and their families, the tipsters, and the law enforcement officers who shared their lives with us so that we may share their courage with you.

INTRODUCTION

Sometimes, we air a story on *America's Most Wanted* and we're all secretly thinking, we'll never catch this guy.

Like a fugitive named J. C. Giles—or, to be perfectly accurate, a fugitive *not* named J. C. Giles.

That was the name he gave himself. We knew it was an alias. And that's all we knew.

It was the last week of January in 1990; an old couple had placed an ad in the paper to sell their car. The husband, Jimmy Johnson, had just been diagnosed with cancer, and the couple had decided to sell the car, buy a van, and spend their few remaining months together, traveling the country side by side.

But when a man answered the ad identifying himself as J. C. Giles, a wealthy businessman from Atlanta, that dream disappeared. He went on a test ride with Jimmy Johnson—and never came back.

A week later, Jimmy's body was found by a tree crew on a remote section of road. He was handcuffed and bound in duct tape.

How could we catch his killer? The wife gave police a description, but the sketch they did was pretty awful. We had no name, no photo, no clues, nothing.

Just a woman who'd lost her life's companion, and who came

on *America's Most Wanted* with a plaintive plea: She wanted justice for her husband.

"Barring a miracle," one cop said, "we're not going to solve this case."

We aired the story on the third anniversary of the murder. Meaning the killer had a three-year head start.

But amazingly, someone was watching that night who could solve the crime.

She gave us Giles's real name: Juan Edwards.

She told us where to find him.

She told us she could testify against him at a murder trial.

There was a simple reason she knew all this.

She was his wife.

We kept the identity of our tipster a secret until Edwards was behind bars. But then we had to ask her: After keeping her secret all these years, what made her break the silence?

Her answer was simple.

For three years, as she read about the murder in the newspapers and heard her friends discussing it, she knew that her husband was guilty of the crime—among other things, she'd found the victim's wallet on her husband's dresser—but she had kept silent because she feared him.

She feared that he would kill her if she came forward.

But when she saw the victim's wife on our program, her heart was moved.

"When I saw it on television," she testified in court, "it was real."

That statement, so simple, so profound, so seemingly contradictory but so ultimately honest, is the center of everything we do at *America's Most Wanted*. Crime in America can seem so pervasive, so overwhelming, that people just want to turn away. They are numbed by the statistics, by the violence, by the yellow-tape-and-bodies-on-stretchers shots they see on the evening news. We believe that by telling crime stories in a different way—by giving the victims a voice, by letting people hear their eloquent pleas for justice—that the crimes become human, become real. And we have a real chance of solving them.

It is that voice, the voice of the victim, that has given rise to this book.

A long time ago, I was that victim, crying out on television for justice. When my son Adam was kidnapped in 1981, my world shattered into tiny, jagged fragments; when he was found, murdered, I knew I would never be able to make it whole again.

But I also knew that I couldn't let this beautiful six-year-old boy die in vain. His memory, his energy, led me down a path that I follow to this day.

It led me to Washington, where I fought—and still fight—for laws that make our children safer. It led me to *America's Most Wanted,* where, with the most dedicated staff of people I've ever known, we've been able to put more than five hundred dangerous fugitives behind bars, and bring twenty-three missing children home safely.

Behind those statistics, there are people. Real people.

Some of them are horrible, frightening, terrible people, the worst scum of the earth. They are the fugitives we profile, and we have hunted them down, each of them, to bring them to justice, to bring their victims closure and peace. We have done so with pride: We are not vigilantes. We are victims. But we are strong. And we will not let these animals prey on our families. We will fight back. As they showed no mercy to our loved ones, so we will show no mercy as well.

On the other hand, some of them are wonderful, kind, caring people: The tipsters. Like the woman who turned in the killer of Jimmy Johnson. People who know the hurt and the loss that the survivors are suffering through, and, against all odds, for no personal gain, and sometimes at great personal risk, say: I will help you. I will heal you.

Some are tough, dedicated people: The hunters. The law enforcement officials who help us bring all those fugitives to justice, who care enough to do their jobs very, very well.

And, finally, some of them are tender, inspiring souls: The victims of crime themselves, and the loved ones they leave behind. The ones who say, I am bowed, but I am not broken, I will survive; and who, in their strength, give strength to all crime victims everywhere.

When I tried to select the cases that we'd include in this book, I wanted to bring you all these people—the killers, the tipsters, the cops, and the victims alike. I wanted you to know how we do what we do at *America's Most Wanted,* so some parts of the book will take you behind the scenes at the program. I also wanted you to have a chance to get involved, just like our viewers do every Saturday night, so we've included some fugitive cases and missing children cases. In each one, there is a victim waiting for justice.

Ultimately, every crime case is not about the criminal but about the victim. I have always seen my work at *America's Most Wanted* as a tribute to Adam, and so it is the cases in which children are the victims that I become most deeply involved. The cases we selected for this book reflect that.

They also reflect, I hope, what the wife of that killer said way back when: What we portray is the reality of crime.

The truth.

I will say from the beginning that these stories are not for the faint of heart. I do not want to sugarcoat the horrors that these villains have wrought upon their victims. I want you to know exactly what happened. I want you, when you are done with this book, to be as angry as I am. Angry at the monsters who walk the earth, angry at the lawyers who help them get away with their evil deeds, angry at the judges who let them get out of jail, angry at the politicians who haven't got the courage to pass the laws that would keep them there.

I know that I am not alone in this.

There are many who have stared into the darkness, into the utter desolation that engulfs you after your world has been torn asunder.

Some return devastated, unable to see the light of day ever again.

Some return resigned to the pain and sorrow that is their life sentence.

Some get angry.

I got angry.

I stayed that way.

It is not an anger that destroys, but one that empowers. It is an anger that I use as my shield and wield as my saber.

Channeling that anger has helped me take part in what I believe is the most remarkable television program of all time, and has helped me work on more than fifteen hundred cases in eleven years.

Here are some of the cases that mattered to me the most.

CHAPTER ONE

The Demon Within

For such men are false apostles, masquerading as apostles of Christ. And no wonder, for Satan himself masquerades as an angel of light. It is not surprising, then, if his servants masquerade as servants of righteousness. Their end will be what their actions deserve.

—2 CORINTHIANS 11:13–15

Sometimes Satan comes as a man of peace.

—BOB DYLAN

It was not a typical Walsh family outing.

Translation: For once, I wasn't running late.

I was driving up the Florida Turnpike, headed into Orlando. I had one quick speech to make, but then I was meeting the family for a long weekend, and as I'm pulling off the highway onto the exit ramp, I'm thinking, let me make this a trip for the kids.

People tell me I can get awfully somber. When you deal with the world of death and violence and darkness, you always see the worst of humanity, and you get pretty morose about that without realizing it.

So whenever I get home, I try to tell myself: You'd better put that all behind you, and start thinking about soccer and lacrosse and cheerleading and Rugrats and all the things your kids want you to think about.

So that's what I'm trying to do on this trip. Keep it light. Get the speech out of the way, and try to turn back into a regular person for a while.

The gas gauge is low, and I know I'm going to forget about it once I get into town and get busy. I actually have a little time, so I pull off into a gas station. As I always do, I pick up the local paper. It's a habit I got into a long time ago—whenever I travel, I like to read the local papers. It gives me a feel for where I am, who the people are, what's going on in town.

And that's the first time I saw him.

Staring up at me, from the front of the local section of the *Orlando Sentinel*. There was something about his eyes—even in a black-and-white photo, you could make out that they were piercing blue, but behind that dull, mug-shot stare there was something more, something cold. After you've looked at a few thousand of these photos, you get to where you can read a lot into them. But there was something here I'd never seen before.

Then I looked over at the article, and saw what he'd done. And I gotta say, no matter how tough and macho you think you are; no matter how many people call you The Manhunter and tell you what a great asset you've been to crime fighting; no matter how many police reports you've read, how many forensic profiles you've studied, how many autopsy photos you've pored over—nothing prepares you for something like this. You become hyper-alert at these moments: The adrenaline starts pumping, you start sweating a little bit, your hearing becomes strongly attuned. You smell the gasoline on the asphalt, hear the hum of the motor of the ice machine next to the mini-mart's front door, notice the missing hubcap of the car at the next pump.

I don't want this. Not now.

But there was no way around it. The ugly, dark, dank world that *America's Most Wanted* inhabits had somehow insinuated itself into this brilliant, shining Florida morning.

As I was pulling away, I was turning over in my mind what I'd read.

The news article had one unusual fact: this vicious psychopath who had preyed upon an innocent family was no stranger to his victims. They knew him well, and until this moment, considered him a good friend.

From what I read, I knew that this guy was probably already out of the state, meaning the local cops had virtually no chance of catching up to him.

I knew that we had to hunt this guy down. And fast.

He was too dangerous to be out on the street.

And now that he'd committed this horrible, horrible act—possibly the most terrible act I'd heard of in my six years at *America's Most Wanted*—now that he had done this, he had nothing to lose.

■　■　■

He was born Edward James on August 4, 1961, in Bristol, Pennsylvania, a small river town outside Philadelphia, but from the time he could speak, he believed his name was Edward Matlack. It wasn't until he was ten years old and looking through some family photos that he realized the man who was raising him was really his stepfather. His natural father had disappeared when he was two.

But shortly before Eddie's twelfth birthday, his dad showed back up on the scene. That's the first bad break in this story.

Eddie wound up living with his dad for a while. While his mom kept a tight rein on Eddie, teaching him right from wrong, his dad was more of a party guy, trying to teach Eddie the ways of the world.

"That's when I was introduced to drugs," Eddie says. His dad "told me what was going on, let me experience it and see what it was like."

It started off simply, with Eddie sampling the marijuana he says his dad shared with him. "He showed me how to roll a joint. Basically, he showed me everything that was going on, so I'd be aware and I'd know what to be careful to talk about."

So with that twisted logic, Eddie says, his dad brought him into the world of drugs. And here's the sick irony: Eddie's dad was a drug counselor.

"He made a joke out of how he was a drug counselor and he did more drugs than the people he was counseling," Eddie remembered.

Very funny.

Eddie was dumped back on his mom, Nancy, after a while. But she had her own problems. With her current marriage hitting the skids, she moved to Florida to be near her mother. They stayed at her mom's in Winter Park for a while, then wound up settling in the Orlando area, near a town called Casselberry.

By now Eddie was in the ninth grade, and was having problems in school—problems like not showing up. And when he did, the school psychologist reported that Eddie said he was having blackouts.

"That's what he told them," said Nancy. "That he was having blackouts. I don't know if that's true. It would help me to think that he did have some mental problem, to tell you the truth. It would help me to believe that that led him to do what he did."

Nancy did all a mother could. She couldn't find a therapist to help her deal with her problem son—"When you don't have money, there is no place"—but begged and pleaded with a counselor at a local mental health clinic who agreed to see Eddie on the side, for free, twice a week. It did little good; Eddie kept getting more violent, more angry. His life by then was beginning to revolve around fighting and drugs. He'd graduated to angel dust—but what he wouldn't graduate to was the twelfth grade. When told he would have to repeat his junior year of high school, Eddie dropped out.

When he turned seventeen, Eddie entered the army. You'd think that maybe the discipline of the army would help him get his head on straight—but he was too far gone for that. He was stationed in Germany, in a town where drugs were easily accessible. For Eddie, it was a time to go wild. When someone would walk up to him and say, "Eddie, this stuff, can you get high off of this?" his standard reply was, "I dunno. Let me take some. Come back in an hour and I'll let you know."

It didn't take long for Eddie to earn a general discharge. The stated reason was "failure to conform." The admitted reason: drugs, alcohol, and fighting.

So Eddie was turned loose back on the streets of Casselberry, Florida. When he was straight and sober, he made friends easily, getting people to believe he was on their side in whatever little struggle the day presented. But when he was stoned, he was like a vicious, caged animal. The demons that welled up inside him were waiting to pounce, to strike out in pure rage.

Now, I don't want you to think for a minute that I'm telling you about Eddie James's background because I want you to feel sorry for the guy. Lots of kids grow up without a father, and some experiment with drugs, without becoming a psychopathic lunatic. It's just that when I come across an animal like Eddie James, I have to wonder: How did he get like this? How did he reach a point where he has no regard for human life, for his own life, for anyone around him? Sure, Eddie James had some tough breaks. So what? We all have. He had a bad role model at a crucial point in his life, but he was taken out of that situation, and was back with a mother who cared about him, tried to discipline him, and, within her abilities, tried to make all the right moves.

In the end, you have to put the responsibility back on the individual. Eddie James was turning into a monster inside. And he'd feed the monster that was growing inside him. He'd feed it alcohol, angel dust, then later LSD, and crack. And the monster would speak to him: It would say, it's not your fault, Eddie. It's them. All of them. It's all their fault. The hell with them. The hell with them. He'd feed the beast in his belly, and it would comfort him: It's not your fault, Eddie. They're all assholes. They don't deserve to live.

■　■　■

That summer, Eddie was talking about going into business with his friend Tim Dick—but there was a lot more talking than there was business. Eddie was a lot more interested in doing drugs and drinking than in looking for work, which is why their last business fell apart.

Tim was living at his mom's house: That summer there were lots of family barbecues there, and Eddie was always invited. It was a big, warm, extended family, and it opened its arms to envelop Eddie James.

The matriarch of this big family was Betty Dick. After her husband died, she packed up the kids and moved to Casselberry, settling in a nice, light-blue, one-story three-bedroom house, set a good ten yards back from the sidewalk, with four tall trees jutting up from a mottled but well-trimmed front lawn.

Betty had two of her kids and seven grandkids living just blocks away—Tim, of course, was still living at home—so on summer afternoons the house became a beehive of activity and laundry and laughter, always bustling with children running all over the place, screaming and horsing around and eating and squirting each other with hoses.

At the center of the action were two of Betty's grandkids, two beautiful blond girls: Wendi and Toni.

Wendi was about as sweet as a nine-year-old could be, the kind of kid you never had to tell things twice. She and Toni, who was a year younger, would fight, like any sisters do, and they'd cover up for each other, like any sisters do. They were inseparable: In the midst of all the chaos at Grandma Betty's, you'd look around for Toni and you'd find Wendi, and vice versa. Wendi was the more outgoing of the two; she was the mixer.

It was summer, but Wendi was already fretting about her birthday. She had every child's most dreaded birthday—December 24, which meant she always got shorted when it came to birthday and Christmas presents. One day she asked Grandma Betty if they could switch birthdays. Grandma, of course, said yes. She would do anything for her grandkids; something as trivial as this was nothing at all.

Toni was the shyer of the two, although she had a tiny streak of mischief about her: The lasting image in the home movies from those days is Toni laughing and pointing a finger at the camera. She loved to do that: laugh and point her finger at you. It was an impish, sprightly gesture, the kind of thing that an eight-year-old can do to melt your heart. Toni was the one who was most attached to her grandma; when Mom would take a long weekend at the beach, Toni was excited, because it meant the kids would stay at Grandma's and have her all to themselves.

Their mom, Lisa Neuner, did have to rely on Grandma Betty a lot for help with the kids (in addition to the two girls, she had two little boys, but no husband at the moment). But Betty didn't mind. In fact, she relished the job. She was a generous woman whose door was always open to her family; and that summer, her family included Eddie James.

Eddie, in fact, became a sort of uncle to the kids, especially to Toni. One neighbor remembers driving past the house and seeing Eddie softly brushing Toni's hair. "Me next," the neighbor called out, and Eddie laughed.

He was something of a frightening sight, if you weren't used to him: Eddie had fallen on a slide when he was nine, and his front tooth became broken and discolored. He never bothered to have it repaired or replaced. It was part of the eerie visage he presented, under his Mohawk-cropped blond hair and that frightening, disarming stare. But once you were used to him, his gap-toothed grin and wide smile made people comfortable. It certainly made the Dick family comfortable. Around the kids, and around the family, he was a gentleman. He was the guy who would fix your car when it broke down, baby-sit your kids when you needed to go to the store. He was also the class clown. He loved to draw attention to himself, and he loved to make the kids laugh.

But when he was on drugs, the clowning of the man who came to be known as Crazy Eddie and Caveman Eddie took on a strange edge. He would fill his mouth with butane, then exhale and flick a disposable lighter, so that big billowing flames appeared to be coming out of his mouth. Or he would start gnawing on the bark of a tree, like a crazed animal.

Everyone thought Eddie was funny. They couldn't know that the beast inside him was raging. That the last shreds of his humanity were falling away.

At night, the rage was more obvious. By now he had taken to petty crime: His rap sheet is a litany of assaults. He once stole a yacht in San Francisco, and once shot a man in what was later determined to be self-defense. But mostly it was fighting. Sometimes, when he was bored, he'd say to a friend, "Yeah, come on, let's go out to a bar and get into a fight."

But to Betty Dick and her clan, Eddie was family. In fact, at the end of the summer, Tim moved next door to live with his girlfriend, leaving a room open in Betty's house; and, since Eddie had nowhere else to live, Betty took him in.

"I felt close to them, like they were my family," Eddie said. "I was closer to them than I was to my real family."

When I think back on those words, on hearing Eddie James speak those words, I get a sick feeling in the pit of my stomach. To think that these people accepted him, made him feel like part of the family, is so tragic, so unfair. They could not have known what was coming. They did nothing to deserve what happened to them that warm late-summer night, as Lisa Neuner was heading back from the beach, and her four children were as safe as safe can be, having a sleepover with Grandma Betty.

■ ■ ■

It started earlier that day, September 19, 1993. Eddie was without work, and began the day with his new drug of choice, crack cocaine. He smoked quite a bit of it, then began wandering around the neighborhood. "I ran into some guys that had some downers, did that. To get off the jones-feeling of not having no crack no more. We started drinking beer, smoked a few joints, you know."

Evening began to fall, and Eddie found himself at the home of a friend, Todd. It was Todd's thirtieth birthday; Eddie arrived around 6:30 P.M. with a twelve-pack of Budweiser. Todd felt that, it being his birthday, he shouldn't have to deal with the barbecue; Eddie told him, relax, party, have a good time, I'll deal with this. He threw some chicken on the grill, and got the hamburgers ready, and the party wore on.

A photo remains from that moment. Eddie at the grill. We later took the photo into the lab and blew it up for use on the show. One of our producers said it was the most frightening face he had ever seen.

It is, quite simply, the face of the beast. Eddie's eyes are glowing and fierce; his snaggletoothed mouth is twisted into a hideous grin.

You have to understand how expertly guys like this can hide their true selves. How they rope their victims in. It is the most infuriating and frightening aspect of these predators: They are extremely adept at hiding their evil natures until it is much too late.

■　■　■

Eddie's wild day was beginning to wind down. Although it was only a little after 11 P.M., a dozen straight hours of drugs and drinking were about his limit. After finding and downing some gin, and smoking another joint, he headed home for the night, the home that Betty Dick had so graciously allowed him to share.

The front door of Betty Dick's house opened into the living room. Asleep on an overstuffed, three-cushion couch against the right wall were Lisa's girls, Toni and Wendi. An Indian-print rug hung on the wall above them, and another lay on the floor next to them. Between the couch and this rug slept Lisa's two young boys.

The wood-paneled wall that the couch rested against separated the living room from Grandma Betty's room. She was asleep in her waterbed when Eddie came home. He stumbled through the living room into the kitchen to raid the refrigerator. Wendi woke up when she heard Eddie; from her spot on the couch she could see the glowing red LED readout of the microwave in the kitchen, and noticed that it was eleven-thirty when Eddie headed off to bed. His bedroom was off the opposite side of the living room from Betty's bedroom. He walked down the hallway, passed the bathroom, and collapsed in his bed.

But he did not sleep. He was angry. In his warped, twisted way, he was angry at Lisa for leaving the kids with Betty. Angry for Betty that she had been taken advantage of. But that was just a momentary catalyst. The rage and fury that had replaced any shred of common human decency in Eddie James, the anger that he stored and fed and nourished, were finally ready to explode.

The monster was loose.

Eddie walked into the living room, and saw the two little girls asleep on the couch. He picked up little Toni, still asleep. Not the way you pick up a child: He picked her up by the throat. And shook her, like a rag doll.

Toni awoke in panic. Eddie held her up to his face, and for a moment, their eyes locked. This beautiful, wonderful, sweet child, who never hurt a soul in this world, was just a few feet away from the grandmother she knew would protect her, but with Eddie's hands around her neck she could only gurgle, staring into his frightening, fiery blue, soulless eyes.

He began to squeeze, tighter and tighter. Her eyes bulged, and her tongue swelled. Eddie thought, "You little bitch! You little bitch!" Then he began to say it out loud: "Die, you little bitch!" This poor, terrified girl, in the hands of a madman, heard her own neck begin to crack. There were small popping sounds, as her bones gave way to his massive hands.

And then this sick, demented excuse for a human being dragged the defenseless eight-year-old into his bedroom by the throat, undressed her, and raped her. I have seen the photos of what he did to this child, the condition he left her in, how mangled and torn her body was. And they leave me no doubt that this was the most vicious, cruel attack we have had to bear witness to in all the years we've been producing *America's Most Wanted*.

And I remember the words Eddie had used to describe his relationship with Toni: "You know, she was like a little niece to me. I sort of looked out for her if the other kids were picking on her. I looked out for all of them. Because there's sick people out in this world."

■   ■   ■

When he was done with his depraved act, Eddie James left Toni's body in the space between the bed and the wall. Later, he would say that he believed Toni was already dead when he raped her. "I can't believe I did something like that, but I remember thinking and it was, she was dead, and I figured, 'What the hell, why not,' you know, and I did what I did."

But Toni wasn't dead. She lived through the terrible nightmare, powerless to stop the terrible fear, the terrible pain. It wasn't until after he left her that this poor, crumpled child passed away.

Eddie walked into Betty's room—"to get me a grown woman," he was thinking—and saw her sleeping quietly on the waterbed. Above her head was a small crucifix; on the nightstand nearby was a large candlestick. Eddie picked it up, and brought it down, with all his might, on Betty's head, so forcefully that the candlestick broke in two.

As though drowning, Betty awoke gasping for air, struggling to understand what was unfolding before her, what was happening to her. Eddie looked in his hand; the candlestick was gone. In its place was a knife from the kitchen.

Eddie began furiously stabbing Betty, and pulling up her nightclothes; but by now there was so much blood around that he had lost interest in sex. And so he continued: With his left hand, he grabbed her by the throat. With his right hand he stabbed her, twenty-two times: eighteen times in the back, twice in the neck, once in the ear, once in the face. Through it all, Betty pleaded: "Why, Eddie? Why!" And Eddie shouted back, "Don't worry about it! Just give up the ghost!" Betty kicked at him, trying to push him away with her feet, putting up an enormous struggle to stay alive. Finally, for reasons we'll never know, Betty's thoughts turned to her baby, her youngest, her son Tim, who had moved next door; as the small figurine of Jesus on the crucifix above her head looked down upon her, she cried out, "Tim! I'm dying! I'm dying, Tim!"

Tim, of course, could not hear his mother's desperate cries.

But they did not go unheard.

A small figure in the doorway, wearing her mom's oversized T-shirt, bore witness to this horrifying scene.

It was little Wendi.

She had been awakened by Betty's screams, and stood motionless as Eddie stabbed her grandmother, as her grandmother pleaded for her life.

At that moment, Eddie turned around and saw the little girl.

He let go of the knife.

He let go of Betty's throat.

He turned and moved toward Wendi.

The child, frozen, could not move.

Eddie grabbed her by the neck, and violently threw her into the living room. She smelled the beer on his breath as he dragged her toward the same room where her sister lay, disfigured, on the brink of death.

And then, for some reason, he stopped short.

He dragged Wendi into the bathroom next to his room, tying her hands with a sock. And then he took off the bloody shirt he was wearing and tied her feet with it.

With astounding composure, Wendi asked Eddie to turn on the light, which he did. She then asked if he was going to hurt her little brothers: He said he wouldn't, because they were asleep.

And then he gagged her with a pillowcase, tying it around the back of her head, so she could ask no more questions.

Eddie then went into the kitchen and grabbed another knife. An eight-inch butcher knife. He went back to Grandma Betty's room, and plunged it into her back.

Because he wanted to make sure that she was dead.

Then he rolled her over, onto her back, and thought, "Let's see them figure this one out."

■　　■　　■

Eddie James, having raped and killed an eight-year-old girl, having stabbed a woman twenty-three times as she pleaded with him for her life, having tied up and gagged a young girl and left her on the bathroom floor to consider the carnage she had witnessed, proceeded to take a shower.

Afterward, Wendi, still tied in the bloody shirt, poked her head out of the bathroom to see Eddie James rifling through her grandmother's room, taking her keys, her wallet, and her purse. She could not see him going to her grandmother's bloody body and removing the rings that her husband had given her, or taking the bracelets her husband had given her, but Wendi did notice Eddie wearing all these things on his left hand as he exited the room. He looked at Wendi as he headed for the front door, and said, "I'll be back."

It amazes me, in retrospect, to think of the courage and strength of this little girl in that moment. She didn't panic; she didn't freak out; she calmly watched what was going on, and tried to figure out what she was going to do next, to save herself and her two little brothers, who, astoundingly, had slept through the entire ordeal, and who still lay curled up on the floor next to the couch.

She didn't have much time. After she heard Eddie leave in Betty Dick's car, she struggled in vain against her restraints. About five minutes later, she heard a car pull up.

Eddie walked back in the front door.

He was carrying a cup of coffee.

He looked down at Wendi on the floor.

He pointed his finger at her.

And he laughed.

Then he walked out the front door, and drove away.

■　■　■

Hours passed, and Wendi was alone, unable to free herself, unable to do anything but contemplate the horrors she had witnessed. This was probably the first time in her nine years that she had been alone in a house for more than a few minutes. And now she was alone with her sister dead in one room and her grandma dead in another.

The next thing she heard, at about 5:30 A.M., was another car pulling up in the driveway. Incredibly, she recognized the sound: the loud, muscle-car rumble of a Pontiac Firebird, like the one her Aunt Brenda drove. I'm saved! Wendi thought. Aunt Brenda is here!

Brenda, Lisa's younger sister, was at the front door with her two children, whom she dropped off every morning on her way to work.

Brenda knocked; one of the children, imitating Mom, copied the same knock, but more quietly.

Wendi wanted to call out: I'm here! I'm here! Come get me!

But she could not call out at all.

She had not been able to loosen the gag from her mouth.

Brenda, puzzled, loaded the kids back in the car and drove off.

Wendi thought, now what?

Somehow, perhaps through the excitement of hearing her aunt at the door, Wendi found new strength, enough to wrestle her hands free. She then undid the restraint around her legs, and pulled the gag out of her mouth and down around her neck. It was still dark out, and she was afraid: the fear that any nine-year-old would have alone in a house in the wee hours of the morning, multiplied a thousand times by the shock of what she'd seen, the trauma of what she'd been through, and the inexplicable terror of knowing that, at any moment, Eddie James could walk through that front door again.

Still, she managed to keep her cool. She thought Eddie might still be out front, and so she unlocked the back door and tried to climb the backyard fence. From there it would be a fifty-yard-dash to the house where her uncle Tim was living with his girlfriend, Nicky.

She made it over the fence, and ran like she'd never run in her life. She could see her uncle's house, on the corner.

She could also see a car, coming up the block.

And she thought it might be Eddie James.

But the car passed. And breathless, barefoot, exhausted, and covered with blood, she made it to her uncle's door.

And, in her own words: "I 'bout broke down the door from knocking on it so hard. And then Nicky goes, 'Who is it?' and I go, 'Hurry up! Unlock the door!' and then Uncle Tim goes 'What's going on?' and I go, 'Grandma's dead.' And he goes, 'Nuh-uh. Are you telling me a lie?' and I go, 'No, you can go over there, and look.'

"And he ran over there and looked.

"She was cold."

■   ■   ■

At first, as Tim looked down at the child at his door, he thought that the blood was from his dog. The dog was just about to have puppies, and his mind hit on that as an explanation for the blood that covered this little girl. Certainly that's it, he thought. The dog had her puppies in Grandma's bed, and Grandma was asleep, and Wendi woke up in the night and saw the blood, and figured that Grandma was dead. Poor child.

He tried the front door, but it was locked, so he went around to the back, and entered through the kitchen. First, he saw the two little boys, asleep, without a care in the world. That's when he opened the door to his mother's room, and found her, half off the bed, soaked in blood. It was clear that the life was gone from her, but to make sure, to make absolutely sure, he touched his hand to her face, and, as Wendi said, she was cold.

But now a thought struck Tim like a bolt: Where was his other niece? Where was Toni?

He ran into the back bedroom—but he didn't see her. All you could see between the bed and the wall in the spare bedroom was a pillow. Frantic, he ran around the house, a thousand thoughts running through his mind—whoever had done this, had he kidnapped Toni? Where could she be? Who could do such a thing?

Back at Tim and Nicky's, Wendi, still calm, was asking to have the pillowcase removed from around her neck. Nicky managed to work it off.

"Eddie did this," she said. "He made me watch and everything."

Nicky was dumbfounded. "You have to tell your uncle Tim that," she said.

Nicky had already called 911; Tim had already run next door to his friend Frank's, and the two men returned and searched the house for Toni. Minutes later, two officers from the Casselberry police department, Eddie Robinson and Valerie Mundo, arrived. It was Eddie who noticed the pillow against the wall in the spare bedroom, and moved it aside. Nothing could prepare him for the sight. A beautiful little girl, her body bloody and twisted, in the position she was in when she died: her dead arms pointing straight down, her dead hands clutching her genitals, her last act in her short life on this earth being one of self-preservation, trying to stop the pain that, thank the Lord, she no longer could feel.

■ ■ ■

So there I am, leaving the gas station, headed to the hotel room in Orlando. I'm thinking, Why didn't I call Lance? I gotta call Lance. I gotta call Lance.

Lance Heflin, our executive producer, started out in the business as a shooter—a cameraman—and has always retained the shooter's eye for detail and the shooter's ability to focus instantly and totally on what's in front of him. This drives his staff crazy sometimes: It's not always useful for the big boss to get so focused on a single story that he forgets, say, to come to a show meeting. But it's also why he's as good as he is—because he has that ability to laser-beam in an important case.

Like this one.

Lance knows exactly how I feel about child-killers. They are the lowest form of human life. In that moment, I know—we have to catch this guy.

And I know that we can catch this guy. This is what we're good at. This is what we do. I'm thinking, Eddie James has crossed the line, Eddie James has nothing to lose, Eddie James is nothing but a desperate, extremely dangerous scumbag who will do anything to survive.

Here's what happens with fugitives: It becomes a game. A survival game. A game of beating everybody and everything—beating the cops, beating the boredom, beating the odds, managing to stay out there.

After they're caught, they shed rivers of crocodile tears, but while they're on the run, there is no remorse. There is only the focus: Stay low. Stay clear. Do whatever it takes.

And that's why I know we have to go after him, and fast.

As soon as I hit the hotel, I make the call.

I tell Lance as much of the story as I know. We talk for a brief minute about how impossible it is to believe—who could rape and kill an eight-year-old girl? What lowest form of life in the most barbaric of societies could even conceive of such an act against a child, any child, let alone one you consider your adopted niece, a child who believed in you, trusted you?

Lance stops me, as he always does. Lance is all business. He wants names. I give him names. He wants a police department. I tell him to call the Casselberry police department. I give him the area code. He says, as he always says: "All right. Lemme get on it. Talk to you later." He doesn't say goodbye. He hangs up. He is already working.

And that's all it takes. And the process begins. The mercurial, improbable, unique process of catching a killer by using a television show.

I try to gather my thoughts. In a few moments, I will go make a speech to law enforcement officials, and after that I will meet my wife and kids. We will have a nice dinner, and we will not mention this terrible crime. The kids will not have watched the news, and it's my job to make sure that they don't have to live every day in the nightmare of crime. And so we will go out to eat, and I'll stay calm, and we'll just have a nice fun family dinner.

And then I'll go out and nail the son of a bitch.

■　　■　　■

Back in Casselberry, Lisa Neuner had returned from the beach late, and had gone home to sleep. She'd thought about picking up the kids at her mom's, but she knew they'd already be sleeping, so she figured she'd get them in the morning.

Instead, she stood watching the ambulances and police cars surrounding the house where her four beautiful children had gone to sleep the night before, and no one knew what to tell her. They told her that her mother was dead, and that Wendi was down at the police station, and that the two little boys were fine.

But how do you tell a mother that one of her daughters is dead? At first, she was told—someone told her—that Toni had been kidnapped. But on her way to the police station, she stopped at her boyfriend's house. "Bobby," she said, "Toni is dead. I can feel it."

By then the sky was beginning to show the first signs of light.

Detective Mike Toole, a tall, good-natured man in his mid-forties, got the call around 5:30 A.M. at home about the murder of a fifty-eight-year-old woman in Casselberry; halfway through the twenty-five-minute drive, he heard that a second body had been discovered. About two hours later, Detective Lynn Cambre, who looks a bit shorter, a bit balder, and a bit older than his partner, was called as well: It was his day off, but this was not a usual case. He joined Toole at the scene.

Both men have children of their own. Both had been to many homicides and death scenes before.

Both said then—and say to this day—that they have never seen anything so horrific in their lives.

"Lynn processed about ninety-five percent of the crime scene," said Mike. "Both of us can do it, but I have no desire to process a crime scene like that."

A day like this drags on endlessly; hours and hours of taking statements, collecting tiny bits of evidence; long, mundane hours of doing what cops are trained to do—be thorough, remain detached, gather the facts. And intertwined with it all is the horror, the pain, the suffering, the torture of all these good people around you, holding each other, breaking down and crying. As the sun climbed in the sky, onlookers gathered on the street outside the yellow crime-scene tape, first one or two, then groups of five and six, trying to make sense of what happened, the day growing warm and beautiful, a good Florida "beach day," a good day for a grandma to take the kids to the beach.

Everyone tried to make sense of it in his or her own way; one of the relatives decided he had to go in and see the crime scene, to see Betty, to see for himself. By now the crime scene had been sealed, and the officers literally had to tackle him to keep him from going inside.

Mike Toole had left his partner the tougher part of the crime-scene detail, but he would have the toughest task of all.

He headed down to the station, to take a statement from little nine-year-old Wendi Neuner.

It was a videotape of this statement that would be the first tape to reach the offices of *America's Most Wanted*. It was a tape to break your heart.

■   ■   ■

The *America's Most Wanted* offices are located in a nondescript building in Washington, D.C. We've always tried to keep the location fairly quiet; there are just too many people out there with too big a grudge against us. There's nothing on the outside of the building that announces our presence.

Our studio, the Crime Center, is downstairs. A few flights up, in a little warren of offices that could pass for an insurance office—except for the mountains of papers and open boxes of videotape strewn everywhere, the writing on the walls, the gaggle of young producers running around discussing murders and rapes and dismemberments and kidnappings, and the metal carts on wheels bearing Zenith TV monitors and Sony Betacam viewing machines—are the production offices of *America's Most Wanted*.

It's a little disconcerting for first-time visitors, for a couple of reasons. One, as you walk through the office, you pass edit rooms and viewing stations from which the sounds of reenactments emanate—so almost every conversation is punctuated with the sounds of screams, car crashes, and gunfire. We are so used to it we don't hear it anymore—like people who live by the airport not noticing the roar of the jets—but newcomers are usually startled to come into what sounds like John Walsh's House of Horrors.

The other thing that strikes people as odd is the laughter. There's lots of it. A lot of gallows humor.

"How'm I going to put this story on the air?" Lance was saying at a story meeting the other day. "It's all filled with dismemberment and body parts."

"Yeah," came the reply. "But they're all attractive people, so they're attractive body parts."

I think the gallows humor is a defense mechanism. You have to understand that producing a show like *America's Most Wanted* is a very, very stressful activity. For one thing, producing *any* reality TV show is tougher than you'd think. There's just so much involved. Let me give you one example: Let's say you're a reporter for a newspaper, and I'm a producer for *America's Most Wanted*. We both need to get a quote from a guy in, say, a small town in Florida. We both call him on the phone. You get the quote, thank him for his time, and go to lunch.

I call him on the phone, get the same quote, and decide I'd like to get it on tape. If he agrees, I have to fly a producer down to Florida, or find a freelance producer who already lives there. Then I have to find a camera crew to work with the producer. Get them to the guy's house. They've got to haul lights and gear into his house, attach a microphone to his lapel, and the producer—we hope—will ask him questions that elicit the same response that he gave spontaneously on the telephone.

Then, after breaking down all that gear and loading up their trucks, they have to find a facility that can uplink to a "bird"—that is, feed the tape to us via satellite. Satellite time can go for up to four hundred dollars for a fifteen-minute window, so you don't want to screw up this part.

If I'm lucky, and all has gone well, I've just made thirteen seconds of television.

This process, in various forms, is repeated hundreds of times a week to produce the forty-seven minutes and seventeen seconds of television that comprise an episode of *America's Most Wanted*. Add to that the actual reporting of the story itself—getting the facts perfectly accurate, describing the story in an understandable and interesting way, finding pictures to go with your words. So far, no different from any other TV producer's job.

But now add to *that* the fact that our producers aren't dealing with any happy stories, or fluff pieces, or human interest features. They're dealing with the worst of the worst, under the incredible pressure of knowing that if they don't do their jobs well, and fast, a maniac will remain on the loose and could kill again. Think of how odd it seems to you, the reader, right now, to be pondering these minute details of television production, when just a minute ago you were reading about the most heinous crime imaginable—doesn't it seem odd? Doesn't it seem strange?

Well, that's the schizophrenia that goes on behind the scenes at *America's Most Wanted.*

Which is why the people who've lasted are the ones who have a sense of humor. The ones who take their jobs very seriously, but don't take themselves too seriously. Laughter is a defense, a protection against letting your mind get overwhelmed by the sheer sadness of the stories you hear day after day after day.

But on that day, there was no laughter.

On that afternoon, you could hear a pin drop.

Lance, the executive producer, walked into the office after lunch to see his entire staff huddled around a cubicle in the back of the room. Sitting in the cubicle was Amy Green, a freelance producer with a little daughter not much younger than Wendi Neuner, screening a tape on one of the metal roll-around carts. One by one, staff members had gathered around to watch the tape with her. Keep in mind that these are seasoned professionals who deal with murder every day. It takes a lot to get their attention.

On the videotape, recorded by the Casselberry police, a tired little Wendi Neuner, her head leaning against her fist, her voice oddly matter-of-fact in comparison to the content of her discourse, was telling detective Mike Toole what she saw the night before. It is a conversation you never want to have with anyone, let alone a nine-year-old child.

■　■　■

"So, somewhere around eleven-thirty, somewhere around there, shortly after that you fell back to sleep?"

"We fell, everybody fell asleep again and then, he [Eddie] fell asleep for about an hour, until it was like one o'clock. And then, I guess he went and got a knife or something and started stabbing my grandmother."

"You didn't see him go get a knife or anything, right?"

"No, I seen it in his hand."

"Okay, when you wake up, what wakes you up?"

"My grandmother screaming."

"And when you wake up what do you do?"

"I went in there and he has her like that and his hands are right there"—she indicates the position of holding someone by the throat—"and he grabbed me by my neck and threw me. And I smelled beer on him, on his, um, on his breath. I smelled beer."

"Okay, and what's your grandmother doing while he's doing all this? I mean, what do you see when you go in the room?"

"She, she grabbed, um, he kept on choking her and stuff and he goes, if you're not dead by the count of three, I'm going to start stabbing some more. So, she wasn't, and he started stabbing her some more."

■ ■ ■

I am, by my profession, a hunter of men. I can look back at the police file on Eddie James, and I can read the interviews, and I can see that he was turning into an animal long before he met the Dick family; that by the time he knew them he had already become a sick, twisted monster, waiting to strike out. After the crime, people were starting to ask me, John, wasn't this family at least partly to blame? Shouldn't they have seen what a cruel, heartless individual he had become?

This is the burden of being a crime victim. Outwardly, everyone wants to comfort you; but inwardly, they want the little details of the crime, they want somehow to figure out how you were to blame, how you were at fault. I know that my wife, Revé, and I have asked ourselves a thousand times what we could have done differently that day that our beautiful son Adam was abducted and murdered. You can torture yourself with these questions until you can't function anymore, and I've seen so many crime victims' families torture themselves this way.

The reason people want to blame the victim is simple: They want some reassurance that these terrible, terrible things won't happen to them.

Think of yourself: If you are a person just like the crime victim, if there's no difference between you and these tragic individuals, then there's nothing to say that you, or your own family, won't meet the same fate that they did.

But if you can find something this victim did wrong, then somehow you feel protected. You think, all I have to do is *not* make that same mistake, *not* walk that same erroneous path, and it won't happen to me.

But the truth is, you can't protect yourself, ultimately. You can take precautions, you can make all the right moves, but you can never be perfectly safe. Crime victims are no different from everyone else. They *are* everyone else, until that one fateful night.

Betty Dick and Lisa Neuner did nothing wrong. You can't blame the victims. They're not in our profession. They're not trained to spot animals like Eddie James.

We're trained to spot them.

And, should they flee, to catch them.

■ ■ ■

By Thursday morning, we had our team in place, and a producer on the ground. Because of the nature of what we do, the typical *America's Most Wanted* producer is a little different from the people who produce other shows. Many of the producers who stay with us have been victims of crime; all have a particular softness, a concern, for the crime victims we deal with. The one thing I insisted on when I agreed to do the show, way back when, was that we would not re-victimize the victims of crime. That what was done to me after my son's death—the screamed questions, the horrible, unsubstantiated accusations, the rumors presented as news for the sake of selling papers, the terrible, callous way producers tried to get my wife to cry for their cameras—would not be done to others. I felt, either that had no place in our operation or I had no place in our operation. Those were the rules we started with, and those were the rules we stayed with. The public might perceive us as a fugitive-chasing show, but we perceive ourselves as a victim-advocate show. Our producers are on the side of the victims.

And Susan Baumel is no exception.

Susan is a freelance producer working in Washington, D.C., a single mother of a sixteen-year-old boy. She is a scrappy, skinny woman with a wide smile and a startling mop of big, frizzy black hair that makes her look like a refugee from the sixties; but her strong spiritual bent comes not from sit-ins and be-ins but from someplace deeper. Her parents were both Brethren ministers; she was raised with a sense of peace and spirituality that would be sorely tested in the days that followed.

She got her marching orders from the Washington team. She would be the field producer, our person on the ground in Cassel-berry. She landed in Orlando, where the weather had turned steamy and hot, and met her camera crew, a team of two young men—a cameraman and sound man—and they drove her to the Casselberry police department.

Detectives Toole and Cambre were happy to see her: The cops knew that we were their best chance at catching Eddie James. They drove her to the crime scene, 111 Cloisters Cove, and led her under the yellow crime-scene tape and into the house, her crew in tow. Other than the two detectives and their fellow officers, she would be the first one allowed in.

"There was a feeling of horror in the air," Susan remembers. "It was hot, and disgusting, and there was this feeling, as if something had gone horribly wrong."

The feeling was strongest as she walked into Grandma Betty's room. "In my mind's eye, Grandma was still in that bed," Susan would say later.

The crew got the shots they needed: The officers walking the crime scene explained in calm, measured tones the outrage that had taken place. It was now three days after the murders, but it was as if it had all happened just moments ago, as if it was happening again as the officers were telling the story, as though Betty was again gasping, as though drowning, and crying out, "Why, Eddie, why?"

It was a question that would echo throughout the day. Because the next stop was to visit the relatives left behind: Tim, who first discovered the body; Nicky, who untied the bloody pillowcase from around Wendi's neck; and finally Lisa Neuner, who had lost both her mother and her daughter.

Now, a lot of people ask, why is this necessary? Why, if you are so sensitive to crime victims, do you make them go on camera like that? Why not just put the guy's picture on the air and have people catch him and be done with it?

I think it's a fair question. Believe me, if we could do it like that, nothing would make me happier. But there's a dynamic at work here, and it's as simple as this.

We have to do two things to make *America's Most Wanted* work.

One, we have to get people to watch.

And two, we have to get them to care.

It's sad but true: The American public is inundated with crime stories. Most of their local newscasts, more often than not, begin with a crime story. We have to cut through all that noise. Somehow, we have to get viewers all over the country to pay attention to one single case, and to believe that they—personally—can become involved and make a difference. The process of watching television is a passive one; to turn that into an active one, to get people to exert the energy it takes to get up out of that chair and do something in response to what they've seen—that takes a unique kind of passion.

It is the passion that only a crime victim, only one who has stared into that great dark void, can possess and pass along. And so we ask the victims to come on the air, in the hope of engendering that passion.

But we have several rules that govern our behavior in these situations.

One, we never, ever try to get a sound bite from a crime victim who has decided, for whatever reason, not to be interviewed. We never, ever stick a camera or a microphone into the face of an unwilling crime victim or family member.

Two, we do not try to elicit tears. We've learned, over the years, something that I wish all news organizations would learn: that viewers don't like to see people crying hysterically. They find it terribly intrusive. Tears are inevitable when you're recounting the life and death of a loved one, but we tell our producers: Be kind. Be sensitive. Don't push.

Three, we give victims the option of backing out. I remember that this started with a teenage girl who wanted to come on camera and talk about being raped. She felt that she had done nothing wrong, and that she wanted other young teens in the same situation to come forward. After much discussion, Lance and I agreed to have her tell her story on camera, but only if her mother and her psychologist both told us they felt that the girl was ready, and understood the ramifications of her actions—and then, only if our producers agreed to call the girl the day after the interview, and see if she'd changed her mind about airing it. The agreement was, if she wanted to back out, then we'd burn the tape.

That girl did decide to go on air, with her mother's and therapist's approval. As we expected, we got dozens of calls from other teenagers saying, I was raped, or I was molested, and I've never told anyone before. It was an amazing moment for us—and we've kept those rules ever since. As a result, we've thrown away better footage than a lot of programs have ever aired; but also as a result, we've gained the trust of crime victims, who know we are sincere when we tell them that we are on their side, and that we need their help in catching their attackers or the killers of their loved ones.

It was that trust that greeted Susan Baumel when she entered the home where Lisa Neuner and her relatives were waiting. It had already been agreed that we would not put little Wendi through the trauma of talking about the case anymore. When Susan arrived, she found that the mother, Lisa, was also too upset to talk.

She also sensed something else.

She realized there was a terrible fear, an awful anxiety, among the people gathered in the yard that day; among Betty's son, Tim, his girlfriend, Nicky, and their friends, and among the children.

And then she realized what that fear was.

They feared that Eddie James hadn't taken off.

That he was still around.

And that he would come back for them.

Actually, I've learned that that rarely happens. As I mentioned earlier, after a crazy, irrational, heinous act like the one Eddie James perpetrated, the survival instinct kicks in for a period of time. He was unlikely to return to this block, where he'd be spotted instantly. It's not true, despite what you see in old black-and-white detective movies, that the criminal always returns to the scene of the crime; in fact, it's quite rare.

But in this particular case, there was an extenuating factor: Eddie had left a witness behind. For whatever reason, he'd allowed little Wendi to see what happened, and to live. That altered the equation. Because now there was no way to guarantee he wouldn't change his mind—no way to guarantee he wouldn't come back to kill the witness, or to take out anyone who stood in his way.

In the days that followed, the fear grew worse. Wendi stopped sleeping: Family members would try to sit up with her all night, but they would doze off, and when they did, she would shake them, and say, Did you hear that? Did you hear that? I think it's him! I think he's back! It was terrible, seeing this little child go through such torture. Her mom, or her uncle Tim, or his pretty girlfriend, would put their arms around her, and try to tell her, don't worry, child, Eddie isn't going to come back, but a little voice inside them was saying, how can you be sure?

Susan recorded the interviews she needed as quickly as she could. They were heartbreaking. Lisa's sister Brenda talked about one of Lisa's sons, who had slept through the entire ordeal: "It's sad when her little boy comes up to her and says to her, 'Mommy, can you please turn me into Captain Planet so I can go up and bring my grandmother and Toni home?' And we don't know how to explain to him that they can't come back," she said.

The most articulate was Tim, who managed to hold it together for much of the interview, until Susan asked about Betty's relationship with her grandchildren. "They loved their grandma, and their grandma loved them," he said. And then the tears came, and he walked away, and the interview was over.

His girlfriend consoled him, and he told her: "She asked me a question that hurts. But I don't mind answering," he said through the tears. "It's hard. But we gotta do this. We gotta let people know. It's the only way they're going to get him."

■ ■ ■

Susan relayed what she had learned back to the folks in Washington, who briefed me that evening.

And when I talked with Lance, we made each other a promise.

This was a case like none other that came before it, and we would do something we had never done before.

We would commit all the resources of the show to catching Eddie James, come what may. We would air Eddie James's story every week, for as long as it took, until the bastard was caught.

■ ■ ■

Emotionally torn up, Susan Baumel nevertheless made it through that weekend. Hour after hour, she and Amy Green screened the tapes, the two women crying as they listened to Wendi's interview. Susan told Amy what it felt like, being down in Casselberry.

"It was a feeling of evil," Susan would recall later. "You could feel it when you were in there. When you're in that place, you are fighting the devil, and I didn't feel prepared for that." It was almost as though the bad karma of Eddie James was a tangible thing, a physical presence, that threatened to suck her in. "I don't believe that anyone is Satan—just that Satan can prevail over them—or us, if we're not careful.

"Spiritually speaking, it was the end of the line for me."

This would be the last *America's Most Wanted* story Susan would work on for a long time.

Anthony Batson, the news chief, had also been working long, long hours, coordinating the hundreds of little details that comprise a breaking news story. At night, he would go home to his wife, Annette, and their baby boy, Alex, just five months old. He would ask Annette how her day was, and she would fill him in on the details of life with a toddler. But he would not tell her how his day went. He couldn't bring himself to relive all the terrible details, all the horrible facts, that had cascaded down on him all day, couldn't relive the moment when he saw little Toni Neuner on the tape, and realized that this was the very same girl who had been raped and killed.

"You're wearing three hats," Batson would say later. "Crime fighter, producer, and dad. So when you see that tape, it's like, 'Oh, my God, how could this be?' It was very different, after Alex was born. It was a lot harder."

So Anthony didn't talk to Annette about his day—"to protect myself from reliving all those details, and to protect my family as well." And then he went back in the morning, and it all started again.

They worked through the weekend: Amy, plowing through hours of tape; Anthony, trying not to think of his newborn son as he watched home movies of a girl who was no longer alive; and Susan, knowing this would be her last story, but trying to put the thought aside and get the job done. They slogged on, through the long hours it would take to put together the trap that they hoped—that we all hoped—would catch a killer.

■ ■ ■

We aired the case on Tuesday, September 28, 1993. It was our first show since we'd heard about the case, but a full eight days since Eddie James had taken flight, so we knew we had our work cut out for us.

From time to time, we take the show on the road, to focus on a particular city's crimes. That week's show was scheduled to be taped in San Francisco. It would be easy to work in Eddie James, because we had a San Francisco connection in his case—he'd been arrested there once, when he was drifting around the country.

Lance was already in his hotel room in San Francisco when I landed there. The way we worked a remote like this was, Lance and I would handle the San Francisco end, and the show production team—a mix of good, solid TV producers and former print journalists—would handle things back in D.C. The first thing I did when I landed was call Lance, with one question. Did they catch Eddie James yet?

There were other stories in the show, of course, other cases to worry about. But I didn't care. For me, this was the only case.

I was thinking, this guy shouldn't be so hard to spot. But I also knew, both from my experience searching for my son Adam, and from the years of chasing fugitives at *America's Most Wanted*, that a small police department doesn't really stand a chance. The Casselberry cops were hard-working, and well-intentioned, but what kind of resources did they have? What kind of sway? If Eddie James was spotted in Los Angeles, would the L.A. cops or the FBI there even know about the case, even care about it?

And I knew that if he stayed out, he was going to hurt people. This was not some mobster with big connections to give him money and passports; this is a lowlife, a bottom feeder who was going to kill again. I could feel it.

When I called Lance, I was hoping that he would tell me they'd already arrested Eddie James. And, in the best of all possible worlds, that he tried to shoot it out with the cops, and they shot him dead like the rabid dog that he is.

I know that sounds harsh. But I've seen it too many times. These are brutal beasts; you can study them forever, you can take pieces of their brains, you can study their genetics, their backgrounds, you can find out about the father who abandoned them or turned them on to drugs—but once they've crossed that line, there's no coming back. I wanted to see the Dick family and the Neuner family spared the horrors of a trial, the horrors of the description of the rape, the dehumanizing, devastating experience of living this hell all over again. I wanted to spare the rest of us the very real possibility that Eddie James, even if convicted, would get out of jail at some point, as so many violent offenders do, and kill again.

There was no question who committed this crime. No question. So I was just hoping that Eddie James had the balls to try not to be taken alive, or that he would be found somewhere with a gun in his hand and a bullet in his head, having done the right thing—tried himself and found himself guilty and given himself the death penalty right there in a cheap motel room. Go on to the next life and try again, and maybe that time you'll get it right.

But once I got to San Francisco, and checked in with Lance, it turned out, of course, that none of that had taken place.

So the hunt was still on. It was time to get busy.

■   ■   ■

I went up to Lance's room. He had received a VHS tape of the rough cut of the piece, and he popped it in the VCR.

I must say, I was so proud of what our staff had put together. It showed how dangerous Eddie James was, how horrible this act was, without being graphic, without being exploitative. It included a good, strong "call to action"—good photos of James, and a good description of the car he stole from Betty Dick that night: a 1984 four-door Chevy Cavalier station wagon, with a license plate bearing the slogan "You've got a friend in Pennsylvania." That was damn ironic, I thought.

We reminded people that James had stolen a lot of Betty's jewelry and might be trying to pawn it.

There was one surprise I hadn't heard about: The team had tracked down Eddie's mother. She had agreed to come on camera and plead for him to turn himself in, then stunned the producers when she said: "If I'd thought, ever, that he would hurt a child, I would have ended his life myself. That might sound cruel, and cold, but if anyone ever hurt my daughters, I know what I would do."

The story was solid. We phoned in a couple of minor changes back to the staff in Washington, then headed out to shoot the introduction, in front of the Golden Gate Bridge.

America's Most Wanted was a different show back then. In the last couple of years, Fox has given me the leeway to say what I want to say; but back then, I was still supposed to be acting like an "objective" journalist, just sticking to the facts. So we opened the story this way:

"A few years ago a drifter from Florida named Eddie James passed through San Francisco. He stayed just long enough to get arrested for grand theft, and then moved on. Police say he recently returned to his hometown of Casselberry, Florida, just outside Orlando. He rented a room from Betty Dick, the mother of a friend.

Betty was matriarch of a large family. Nine days ago, her grandaughter Wendi was sleeping over. Police say what happened next is one of the worst crimes they've ever seen.''

Here's what I wanted to say—and if we were doing this story now, here's what I would say:

''This is the number one guy on my list. This is the kind of guy who goes out and kills innocent people for no reason. This is a coward, a scumbag, a despicable human being who really does not deserve to walk on the planet.''

■   ■   ■

The show aired at 9:00 P.M. on the East Coast, and almost immediately, the hotline started ringing. Detective Cambre was in our studio, helping to field the calls. We were still back in our original studio then, a small room decked out to look like a fifties police station, with mug shots and blown-up photos of fingerprints on the walls, and big ugly filing cabinets everywhere.

It is, by the way, just a set—but when you watch the show, the phones you see behind me are the real thing. Our real hotline.

And at nine-thirty on this particular Tuesday evening, it was overwhelming: Hundreds of calls were pouring in. This is partly a reflection of how moving the story was: People *wanted* to help. They *wanted* to have seen Eddie James. If you think that people don't care about each other anymore, you only have to listen in on calls like these.

They came from New Jersey, from Mississippi, from Florida; from a bail bondsman who travels all over the U.S., calling to ask if he could help pass out posters of Eddie James, free of charge; from jewelers and pawn shop owners offering to send in jewelry that had recently been pawned, to see if it matched what James had stolen from Betty Dick. Dozens of callers told us of Chevy station wagons they'd spotted all around the country.

The calls continued to flood in, from all over the East Coast. We must have heard about every blond man missing a front tooth from Bangor to Key West.

At about 10:30 P.M., the calls subsided. They picked up as the evening wore on and the show aired again, first in the mountain time zone, then on the West Coast.

Those airings would be the key.

■ ■ ■

Aaron Nelson, a young man with waves of curly dark hair and a Bruce Springsteen goatee, was in his kitchen, making dinner, when *America's Most Wanted* came on in the next room. He heard the terrible story about the family that had rented a room to a man who turned on them. As he walked into the room where the television was, he saw the picture of the man accused of the crime.

He couldn't believe his eyes.

Two days earlier, on Sunday, September 26, Aaron had been working behind the counter in the pawn shop he owned in Glenwood Springs, Colorado, about two hours west of Denver.

At about 1:00 P.M. that afternoon, a guy he thought appeared "pretty scary looking" walked in. Snarly, broken teeth, nasty scar on the right side of his face, dressed in blue jeans and a sleeveless T-shirt. Kind of dirty-looking, like he'd been on the road. He wandered around the shop, pausing to look at the guns behind a glass case.

"He was a pretty cool character," says Aaron. "He came in and acted just like he was a normal Joe. Wanted to know if we'd buy some pearls from him and we talked about it and it was no big deal."

The law required that Aaron ask the customer for ID. When Aaron noticed it was a Florida driver's license, they made some small talk; by coincidence, Aaron was also from Florida, not one hundred miles from where the customer lived.

They couldn't agree on the price for the big string of pearls, so the man left, and came back a short time later with about eight smaller strings of pearls, along with two nice watches and a crucifix.

"He wanted three hundred dollars for them," says Aaron. "I talked him down to taking a hundred dollars for them, which is a pretty good deal. I mean, he must have been pretty desperate, to settle for a hundred dollars for this stuff."

Two days later, as he carried his dinner into the living room, he saw the same face, staring up at him from his TV screen. It was the same photo I had seen in that Orlando paper the week before.

"I just about got sick to my stomach. I just couldn't believe it," Aaron said. "It was a shock. I knew it right from the second I saw him. I knew it was him. I mean, he's a pretty scary looking guy. He's not somebody you'd forget real easy."

Aaron picked up the phone, and dialed 1-800-CRIME-93.

And the line was busy.

■   ■   ■

Back at the hotline, Detective Cambre was having a field day. The hotline supervisor had the twenty-four hotline operators furiously taking down information on tip sheets, which they piled up on the desk next to Cambre. The operators were pointing out the ones they thought were on the money. Cambre was fielding some of the calls himself. Before long, all of the lines were lit up, and the twenty-four standby lines were also filled with people waiting to get through. It was a total informational traffic jam.

The first trick of working the hotline is triage—prioritization. Any calls that (a) contain information making you certain that the caller has identified the fugitive, and (b) indicate that the fugitive's location is known at that very moment—"He just told me his name is Eddie James, and he's missing his left front tooth, and he's sitting next to me at the bar and about to pay his check," let's say—those are the ones you move on fastest. You call the FBI or the local police in the town the call is coming from and you ask them, politely, to get their asses in gear and nail the guy.

We didn't get any of those calls. But we did get the next tier: calls that could be verified as definite sightings of James.

By midnight, James's trail had begun to become clear. A pawn shop in Indianapolis faxed a pawn ticket showing that he was there on Tuesday the twenty-first, one day after the crime. He'd used his own name. Some states require pawn shops to fingerprint out-of-staters; this pawn ticket indeed bore an inky thumbprint that matched Eddie James's. So it was a confirmed sighting of James in

Indianapolis—which would be a crucial factor in sorting out the calls for the rest of the evening.

A few hours later, the next bit of solid information came from clear across the country in Pueblo, Colorado, about two hours south of Denver. Another fax: James had once again used his Florida ID.

Now we were on Eddie's trail. But we couldn't figure out exactly where he was. Disappointed, our tired crew headed home, and a tired Detective Cambre headed back to his hotel. He'd catch a few winks, then pick up the chase in the morning.

■   ■   ■

Back in Colorado, Aaron Nelson had had a fitful night. He kept thinking, this killer was right here in Glenwood Springs just a couple of days ago! It was too scary to think about. He tried the call again; still busy. He slept in fits and starts. In the morning he called *America's Most Wanted* again. This time, his call went through.

When we'd gone to sleep, the last known sighting of Eddie James was two hours south of Denver, apparently heading west. Now, here was Aaron, calling from a pawn shop two hours west of Denver. The hotline operator knew right away we had a live one. Eddie had clearly headed north on I-25 to Denver, then west to Glenwood Springs. Another piece of the puzzle fell into place.

After he got off the phone, Aaron headed down to the pawn shop. He knew no one there would believe him—that one of *America's Most Wanted* had been in the shop just three days before!

When Aaron arrived at the pawn shop, Justin Glasenapp, one of the salespeople, was helping some customers.

Aaron told Justin his frightening tale. About realizing he'd had a murderer for a customer, that the killer had been right there in the store.

As he listened to Aaron's description, Justin's eyes grew wide.

Not ten minutes earlier—*not ten minutes!*—a man fitting the same description, blond hair, scary looking, scraggly teeth, scar on his cheek, had come in to pawn some jewelry for fifteen bucks. He was better dressed than Aaron's man, but otherwise he sounded the same.

Aaron told Justin the name of the man on the television program. Eddie James.

Justin looked down at the pile of pawn tickets for the morning. He picked up the top one, the one he'd just made out, the one for the blond guy with the scraggly teeth.

He handed it to Aaron.

Aaron read the name on the ticket.

Edward T. James.

James had been so nonchalant, so cool, that the morning after he had appeared on *America's Most Wanted,* he had walked back into the same pawn shop to pick up a few more bucks before hitting the road.

Within hours, we'd relayed word up and down the line. Cambre was faxing BOLOs—"be on the lookout" sheets—to every agency west of Denver. Our staff sent photos of James to all the law enforcement agencies around Glenwood Springs—the county sheriff, the Carbondale police department, the Newcastle police department (two neighboring towns)—and they were scouring the streets for James. No sign.

But the next morning—Thursday morning—the cops got a call from a pawn shop in nearby Carbondale. James had tried to pawn another item, and had produced the Florida ID. Sirens blazed on the streets of Carbondale. But at the end of the day, Eddie James was still on the loose.

We knew what car he was driving.

We knew what towns he'd been in.

We'd done everything we could.

The cops had done everything they could.

And it wasn't enough.

Back in Washington, we were going crazy. How could this have happened? How did we miss him? How could he get away? How could we be this close? How could someone so stupid still be out there?

To be honest, I was worried. About twenty-five percent of our captures happen within twenty-four hours of broadcast. A good number take place in the twenty-four hours after that. Once two days have passed, the calls start to diminish, and the chance of capture starts to diminish. In this case, we had an advantage—we knew a lot about the fugitive, where he'd been, which way he was headed.

But I couldn't help wondering. Where was Eddie James? What was he thinking right now?

■ ■ ■

James was cruising along in Betty Dick's car, trying not to think too much about what he had done. Every once in a while he'd pull into a rest stop, and some state troopers would pull in, and he'd think, well, this is it. But somehow they never caught up to him. In his heart he knew he couldn't run forever; but he figured he had at least six months before anyone caught up to him.

He had not seen the *America's Most Wanted* broadcast.

Although he'd later say he was filled with remorse, he clearly wasn't so upset that he was going to turn himself in. No, Eddie James—pothead, cokehead, crackhead, boozehead—was stone cold sober and enjoying the drive, planning to see some old friends for perhaps the last time. Pawning Betty's most precious possessions, the jewelry her husband had given her over the course of a lifetime, pearls and rings and a crucifix, in exchange for a few more hours out in the bright sunlight.

The hunted man will always seek out a place he has some familiarity with, someplace that he at least has a sense of, so that he can operate with at least a modicum of comfort. He won't go someplace obvious— like back to his mother's house. But he usually won't go to a place he has no knowledge of at all. He'd feel too exposed.

Ironically, Eddie James was headed to the very place where we knew he had once hung around, the very place we'd started this story, the very place we'd been just three days before.

San Francisco.

■ ■ ■

Back in Washington, we turned our attention to the next airing of *America's Most Wanted,* on Tuesday, October 5. There was no question as to whether we would air the case again. The only question was what information we would divulge.

That's probably the biggest way we differ from "straight" news operations. Any straight newspaper, or TV broadcast, would love to have the information we had. It would be a big exclusive, a big scoop. But for us, there was a more important question. Would focusing the public's attention on the Colorado sightings help, or hurt, the hunt for Eddie James? Sometimes, clues like those are vital: They can give viewers exactly what they need to focus in on the fugitive. Or it could have a negative effect: The people outside Colorado might let down their guard. And that can cost you a crucial clue.

Sometimes, you want the fugitive to know that you're on to his trail—it spooks him into making a mistake, or scares him into turning himself in. Sometimes you decide just the opposite—let's not let him know we're on to him. Let's not tip our hand.

In this case, we agreed that alerting the viewers on the West Coast that Eddie was headed their way was the wise move. We decided to go with the sightings.

In the studio, the tape was rolling, playing the one-minute-forty-second update that Anthony Batson had put together about the Colorado leads.

The director keeps my microphone open while the tape is rolling, so I can talk to the control room. I told them to stay with me after the piece—that I wanted to ad-lib a little something.

At the end of the piece, I pleaded as hard as I could, asking our viewers to help this family find justice. I wanted so much for this to work.

I thought, this one's for you, Toni.

And for you, Adam.

I took this job because I was so angry, so filled with rage, after my son's death, and I needed a place to channel that anger. A case like this brought it all back. It felt like I was trying to *will* our viewers into spotting Eddie James.

That night, the hotline lit up again.

And again, the night came, and the night went, and Eddie James was still on the loose.

I thought, how could we have failed again?

How could this lowlife have avoided fourteen million pairs of eyes?

How could he be so lucky?

And what if he hurts someone else?

I went to sleep that night praying for a miracle.

And God sent us a saint.

■ ■ ■

Priscilla Valdez is a young, proper woman of impeccable taste, with an air of quiet strength about her. She is the kind of woman you can never imagine losing her temper; she fixes your eyes as she speaks, fixes you with the tranquil, peaceful gaze of a person who has decided what she believes about life.

At the time, Priscilla lived with her husband in Bakersfield, California. She'd met him in 1986, when she was working as a dental assistant. One afternoon, across town, a young man working on a construction job was hit in the face with a two-by-four, and fell off a bridge. Somehow he'd survived fairly intact, except for two loose front teeth. He walked into the office where Priscilla was working and, as she later joked, it was love at first bite.

They married and had three children. Priscilla raised them as she had been raised, in a deeply religious Catholic tradition; in her words, "believing in God, and believing that there is evil out there." It was her job "to teach the children who the good guys are and who the bad guys are."

Their youngest, Michael, was just eight weeks old, and Priscilla was suffering from a normal case of postpartum blues. She wondered, what is my lot in life now? What is my purpose? How will I make a difference? She prayed to God for a sign.

That evening, the family gathered for dinner. Normally, on a Tuesday night, Priscilla would watch *America's Most Wanted;* but on this night, as her family was finishing dinner, she was planning to skip it. Her husband had some early business in the morning, and she liked to be up with him for breakfast, so she put the kids to bed early. Her husband headed off to the bedroom, and she locked up the house. It was a little after 9:00 P.M., and as she crossed through the living room she thought, well, I'll just see what they have on tonight. And she watched the update on Eddie James, and saw that virulent face, and heard the details of that despicable crime.

"I was just playing it over and over in my mind. I went to bed thinking about it, and I woke up thinking about it, my mind was just going all the time, and I'm thinking, why can't I get this person out of my mind? It must have been the hideous crime he committed. And the number, 1-800-CRIME-93, kept playing over and over in my mind, too, like an old song."

With her dental-technician background, Priscilla took particular notice of James's teeth. "They're a dead giveaway," she thought. "He can alter his features, except the teeth."

Priscilla had just returned to work part-time after her maternity leave, so the next morning, after getting her husband out of the house, Priscilla had to head to work herself. She couldn't stop chattering on about the *America's Most Wanted* case she had seen the night before. It had affected her so deeply, so heinous was the crime. "They're gonna catch this guy," she told her co-workers. "It's going to be his teeth."

At lunch hour, Priscilla had to head to the state unemployment office to drop off some paperwork for her boss. It was a huge office, a hundred yards long, with a long glass window, and a partition about halfway along the building.

She had her five-year-old son with her, and was third in line from the window, when she felt it. A presence, moving behind her. "I just had an eerie, uncomfortable feeling, about anyone moving so close, I guess."

So she looked over her left shoulder at the man who had passed behind her. And he turned to look at her as well. And she saw the eyes.

"First, I thought to myself, it can't be this person. Not in Bakersfield. Nothing ever happens here in Bakersfield." She took one more glance, memorizing what he was wearing: black shirt, baggy pants, tennis shoes. He looked disheveled, like he hadn't slept.

She kept an eye on him by watching his reflection in the glass. She saw him walk toward the wall, sit down in a chair, put his hands behind his head and lean back, stretching his legs out, like he had nowhere to go, nothing to do, not a care in the world.

Her son, meanwhile, was about as antsy as kids can get waiting in long boring lines in big boring offices. He kept wandering into the area where Eddie James was sitting. As calmly as she could, she called him to come back and stand next to her, and each time she did, she took the opportunity to take one more peek at Eddie James.

And then she saw the teeth. And she knew.

After what seemed like an eternity, Priscilla made it to the counter.

"I need to use the phone," she told the woman behind the counter. "The gentleman sitting against the wall was featured last night on *America's Most Wanted*."

"I don't watch that program," said the teller.

"Believe me," said Priscilla. "I need to use the phone."

"You can't use this phone. You have to use the public phone," came the reply.

The public phone was three stalls down.

Right next to where Eddie James had parked himself.

Priscilla pleaded. "I can't use that phone!" she cried in a hoarse whisper.

She was directed to another pay phone, across the room. She made the slow, painful walk, grasping her son's hand, all the time repeating, like a mantra: "1-800-CRIME-93. 1-800-CRIME-93." She was afraid—what if he gets away? What if he sees what I'm doing, and comes after me? But bravely, she took a deep breath and picked up the phone.

Her son began acting up. Why do we have to stay here so long, Mommy? What's going on? Who are you calling?

She listened to the phone ringing, her heart pounding, and finally she heard the words *"America's Most Wanted."* It all came flowing out at once; the explanation of why she was calling, where she was, where Eddie was sitting. She described Eddie James perfectly, right down to which teeth were missing.

The hotline operator recognized this as a Level One call—he's here, I'm sure it's him, and he's paying the check.

The operator promised Priscilla that someone would be dispatched immediately.

In our office, the news spread like a bolt of lightning. There is a gray partition, about six feet high, separating one series of cubicles from the main section of the room. During the week, hotline chief Sharon Greene sits on one side of this partition; Anthony Batson, the news chief, sits at an open area in the center of the main newsroom, on the other side. When there was big news, Sharon, rather than running all the way around the partition, would get up on her desk and poke her head above the partition.

Anthony saw a short shock of jet-black hair popping up, and a hand clutching the pink carbon copy of a tip sheet. Sharon got up on her desk and waved the sheet at Anthony.

"Woo-hoo! Anthony, we got a good tip on James! He's in an unemployment office in Bakersfield right now!"

Everyone knew Sharon had the best radar for these things; when she said it was a good tip, you knew it was solid.

In the next moment the two spoke at the same time.

Anthony: Did you call the cops? Are they on the way?

Sharon: I called the cops. They're on the way!

But while Sharon and Anthony were anticipating a capture, Priscilla Valdez was terrified that no one would get there in time. She walked out of the unemployment office, her mind racing.

This guy has no business here in Bakersfield, she thought. He's just going to leave. Someone's got to stop him.

What she didn't know was that a plainclothes deputy had already been dispatched, and was already in the building.

■   ■   ■

The detective, Vernon "Dusty" Kline, was pretty close when the call went out for a patrol car, so he arrived first, entering from the north side of the building. Eddie was sitting on the south side. By the time

Deputy Norman Stone and his partner pulled up in their cruiser and were walking into the building, Kline had already approached the suspect.

Problem was, he approached the wrong suspect.

He had heard what little information had come through the call, and the man he approached did seem to match the description.

Except that he was black. And Eddie James was white.

Kline quickly figured out the mistake. Fortunately, James hadn't spotted the commotion.

The two uniformed deputies approached him from the north door.

The plainclothesman approached him from the south sector.

Finally, finally, Eddie James had nowhere to run.

■ ■ ■

Eddie James had still not seen *America's Most Wanted*. On his meandering route to San Francisco, he had run out of gas in Bakersfield. He spent the night at a homeless shelter, and that morning had left the car and walked the mile to the unemployment office. He hoped to get some food stamps, or score some work, possibly get some emergency cash and move on.

When the deputies approached him, he looked exhausted.

"He looked at me," said Deputy Stone, "like, hey, this is the end of the road. He didn't offer any resistance."

And there it was: the chase was over. The handcuffs were on. The bad guy didn't get away.

Finally, finally, Eddie James was captured.

They put him in the back of the patrol car, and drove him to the sheriff's office. They had about half an hour alone with him. They gave him his Miranda rights; then Dusty began asking some questions.

You never know with fugitives. You want to get them to talk as soon as possible. By the time they've gathered their thoughts, they may decide to clam up. So this is a key moment. Eddie James didn't disappoint them. He began to tell them his story.

Later that day, he would tell it to us.

Priscilla Valdez had walked inside the unemployment office, to see the arrest happen. To see the answer to the prayer she had sent heavenward: God, what is my purpose? How can I make a difference?

She watched them walk Eddie James out to the squad car, and thought of the people she had seen on television the night before.

"Honestly, the first thing I thought of was the family," she said. "I thought, they can finally rest, now that he's been caught. They can lay their people to rest as well."

■　■　■

By that time, it was approaching 4:00 P.M. on the East Coast. The shadows were getting long on that cool afternoon in Casselberry, Florida, when Nicky Angel, girlfriend of Tim Neuner, came running around the corner from their house onto Cloisters Cove. "They caught him! They got him! They got Eddie!" she was screaming.

Tim was following on her heels. One by one, friends and relatives came running out, hugging each other, crying.

It was over.

It was really over.

Lisa Neuner had gone to stay with her sister Brenda in Erie, Pennsylvania. When the call came in from the police, "I was stunned," said Lisa. "And then we all started crying and laughing. We didn't know what to do."

"I laughed at first," said Brenda. "And then I cried, because it won't bring my mother and my niece back. But at least it's a start, and he didn't get away with it."

And with that, Brenda realized what we all must realize, all of us who have become victims of crime.

That it's never really over.

The wound closes, but the wound does not heal. You find closure, but you do not forget. In the two weeks since the crime, we had all had a purpose: to find Eddie James. It gave us all something to do, something to think about. You could wake up in the morning, and get an update.

Now, there are no more pressing issues. Not until the trial, anyway. There are no updates. There was nothing to take your focus away.

And for the first time, you truly look back at what happened, at the hole that has been left in your life, at the empty place in your heart, you hear the wind swirling through you, and you know now what the rest of your life will be like.

You had hoped for peace. You did not find it. You found closure. It is not enough, not nearly. It will never be enough. But, as Brenda said, it's a start.

"I'm glad they got him," said Lisa, "because now my mom and Toni can rest in peace. . . ." and her voice trailed off in tears, and she held her sister, for a long time, and their thoughts turned to Lisa's daughter, Wendi. The Survivor.

"We've all got a long hard journey ahead, but Wendi's got the longest journey of us all," Brenda said. "But she's not going to be alone in this. She was alone when that happened, but she's not going to be alone anymore."

About six-thirty that evening, Lisa called Wendi, who was staying at her father's house. She laughed, and went "Yippee!" and said a few words in relation to Eddie James that she's not supposed to say.

And that night, for the first time in what seemed to everyone like a million years, Wendi lay down in her father's bed, and went to sleep, and slept, and slept, all through the night. And sometimes, when you are looking for proof that there is a God, you look at a child, asleep in her father's arms, and it is all the proof you need.

■　　■　　■

Back in Washington, Anthony Batson saw the shock of jet-black hair popping up above the gray partition. "It's him!" he heard. "Eddie James is in custody! Direct result!"

"There's about two seconds of jubilation," he remembered. "And then you realize, there's a lot of work to be done, and you get to it."

Batson got on the phone with Priscilla Valdez, but could hardly hear her over the yelling and screaming in our office. He was busy setting up interviews, for the report on the capture we would air on the next show. The rest of the staff was busy high-fiving.

We have a wall, in our conference room, where we started writing the names of everyone who was captured. In a high-tech world, it's a nice low-tech way of keeping track. Like that board you see on *Homicide*. The latest capture had been number 266, Mark Adams, a murderer who had escaped from San Quentin. Someone grabbed a marker pen, and wrote above it: "267—Eddie James!"

■　　■　　■

They called me at home that afternoon, to tell me that Eddie James was in custody, direct result—meaning the capture was a direct result of a viewer tip to our hotline.

I remember being ecstatic. And I remember thinking about Adam.

This capture brought back a flood of memories. The days and nights of searching for Adam, the smell and feel of the parking lot outside the Sears where he was taken, the phone call when I found out that he had been murdered in a horrible, horrible manner, that the killer was still out there, capable of doing anything; I thought of all the years and years that Revé and I waited for some arrest, some word, some closure, and how years and years went by without that closure coming; and now, it felt that almost by dint of sheer will, we, *America's Most Wanted,* had helped capture Eddie James. My chest just welled up with pride for what we had done. And now Eddie James couldn't hurt anybody else. There would be no more Adams, no more Tonis. Not because of this guy, anyway. And that was something. That was something.

Then I started to wonder. Wait a second. What else has he done? Has he hurt anyone else? Are we gonna find a string of bodies he left behind? What is the next call gonna be?

In time, those answers would come: Thank God, there had been no more victims. We had found Eddie James in time. I thought about the family of Toni Neuner and Betty Dick. I knew that they would be torn, in this moment, as I was, feeling elation, but also feeling that nothing would bring back their loved ones. Still, I knew that this moment would bring them some peace, some closure, and—depending on an interview that was about to take place—some answers.

■ ■ ■

"Thank God it's finally over."

That's what Eddie James had to say to our reporter when they sat down in the jailhouse that afternoon. The reporter's job: to see if James would verify, or correct, what we had pieced together about the story so far. And to see if James would talk about the crime.

He was successful on both counts.

Some of our producers, when they watched the tape later, said it helped them understand why Eddie James was able to sucker people in so easily. There is something charismatic about him, they said, something fascinating, some way his eyes make him appear powerful and focused, something perfectly real and sincere, that draws people in.

I don't see it.

I look at the tape and I see a sniveling coward, with no sense of the boundaries of human existence, speaking matter-of-factly about the most heinous moment imaginable, as though he were as shocked and concerned as his listener, and trying to understand how someone could do such a thing. The reporter began by collecting the details about Eddie's flight from justice, his background, and his relationship with the Neuners, all of which basically jibed with what we'd put together so far. Then he moved on.

"Let's talk about the incident. . . . Was Betty in bed?"

"She was in bed sleeping. And all the kids were sleeping, I remember that. I'm, why I chose to do the way I did, I don't know, what prompted that. That's a blank, still."

"And what did you do?"

"I strangled Toni and stabbed Betty a bunch of times."

"You, um, you stabbed somebody you were so close to. Seems like you must have gone off for some reason. You have no idea."

"None, none. I wish I did know."

"Can you recall Betty that evening, did you wake her up and kill her or kill her in her sleep?"

"Nah, she was awake when I—when it started out. I hit her with a candlestick or something, and that woke her up, and then I killed her. Stabbed her."

"What is going through your mind at that point?"

"Just pure anger, pure rage. Anger. I remember, I remember when I was strangling Toni, I was like, 'Just die, you little bitch.' You know, just pure freakin' anger. Raw anger."

"And at Betty, were you screaming things? Was it pointed to her, or just anger?"

"I don't think it was any direction in it at all. Really don't. I'm still, right now, I don't understand, like I said, why I did what I did. . . . It's just like a blank wall. It's like standing at a blank blackboard and trying to figure out what used to be writ on there. . . . That's not making, I'm not trying to excuse anything I did. What I did, I did, and it wasn't right. It wasn't right at all. It was rather sick."

"What about Toni?"

"That's a hard one to talk about."

"Let's talk about it. Let's try to get that out. You left Wendi. Did you go to Toni . . . ?"

"No, I killed Toni first."

"So she was the first one you killed."

"She was in on the couch, I don't know why I chose, I don't know why I picked and chose, if I did, or if it was just the first one I reach for. And I just strangled her. And I remember, she was like, right there. I was holding her up in the air, and you can hear her bones cracking and stuff. I was squeezing so hard, telling her, 'Die, you little bitch.' And, uh, they say I raped her, and I remember when we was talking and it was, she was dead, and I figured, what the hell, why not. You know, and I did what I did, and then I went and killed Betty. . . ."

"You said you did what you did. What did you do?"

"I raped her."

"You remember that now?"

"Yeah, I remember it. I remember doing it. Yes, and it's not an easy thing for me to live with. For me. And I'm sure it's not easy for anybody in the family or nothing. I can't believe I did something like that."

"What was going through your mind?"

"I couldn't begin to tell you."

"Try."

"I try . . . I really wish I could. I just can't right now. It's, I remember, I can close my eyes and I see what I've done. But why I'm doing this and what I'm thinking, I guess, I'm scared to think, or bring back the memory of why I did it or what I was thinking."

"You crushed her with your hands."

"Yeah, I remember the blood coming out of her mouth, and her little facing turning all purple. [Turns his head like he's going to cry.] Damn."

"A lot of family members and friends out there lost two beautiful people. What do you want to say to them?"

"I would like to say that I'm sorry. I'm remorseful for what I did, but to say I'm sorry for doing something like that, to think it's going to make it better. It isn't. It's not going to make nothing better for them. You know, I pray to God He helps them out, makes them stronger, and you know, survive it. And like I said, I pray to God He makes it easier to live with. Maybe my death will make it easier for them to live with. I hope."

"If you were released today, would you think you could commit a crime like this again?"

"I'd be afraid I would. For the simple fact that I've done it once already, and that means I'm capable of doing it again. I don't think there's anything—that part of my mentality is always going to be there, I think. Which scares me. It goes for anybody. Once you done something like this, I don't think there's any way you can change to where you can actually guarantee anybody, even yourself, that you won't never do it again. Cause it's too deep. It's too deep a part of the psyche."

"So you accept the fact that you might be put to death for this crime."

"I look forward to it."

"Look forward to what?"

"To dying for this. Like I said, saying I'm sorry is so insignificant, my death would be a life for a life."

■ ■ ■

An officer in a green shirt and glasses was assigned to guard Eddie James during the interview. Afterward, he had a disgusted look on his face.

"You look like you don't believe what you just heard," the reporter said to him.

"In my opinion," said the officer, "that's the smartest thing that an attorney or anybody else would have told this guy to say, is what he said. 'I'm sorry, I did it, I'm ready to take my medicine.' I just don't buy this guy being so sincere right now. I mean, he's caught. He's red-handed, and I really don't think that when the time comes, and he's sitting in the electric chair, that he's really going to agree with everything he just said."

Man, you have no idea how smart that cop really was. We'd find that out a few months later, when the case of Eddie James reached the courtroom.

■ ■ ■

The day after the capture, detectives Cambre and Toole flew out to California to collect Eddie James.

They picked him up at the Bakersfield county jail, and were driving him back to the sheriff's office, when Cambre noticed one thing: James stank. Even for a prisoner, he was filthy.

A little later, Cambre found out why.

Earlier that morning, James had been on a bus with a group of other prisoners. There is a code: Even among the most violent of criminals, a man who molests or kills a child is considered the lowest of the low. Everyone looks down on you: They don't care if you have killed ten people, raped a goat, robbed an orphanage, or mugged the Pope. Child molesters are scum even to scum. So on that day, after everyone had heard what Eddie James had done, they made him sit in the front row of the bus, and then wait there while everyone else got off.

And as each prisoner passed by, he spit on Eddie James.

So there's Eddie James, in the back of the car, covered in dried drool and spit, smelling to high heaven, with Cambre thinking, "This is not going to be the most pleasant interview I have ever done." But James was polite, and willing to talk, which was all that mattered. They got to the sheriff's office, ordered some pizza and Pepsi, and started talking. "He talked about the murder like you and I would talk about a *Monday Night Football* game," Toole would say later. They talked about fishing, and hunting, and Louisiana, and hot sauce, and working offshore, and they talked about murder; James's handcuffs rattled as he raised the pizza to his mouth and gave up the details that would—we all hoped—seal his fate.

■ ■ ■

There was one more very important visit that needed to take place.

Most of the time, our victims never get to meet our tipsters. They live in different parts of the country, and don't get a chance to look into each other's eyes, even though they have had a profound effect on each other's lives—the tipster on the victim's life, mostly, of course, but it works the other way too; the tipsters, once they realize what they have done, also find themselves changed, forever. Empowered, as though they've learned a lesson that they want to share with everyone, a lesson we began closing every broadcast with shortly after this case was completed: one person can make a difference.

The emotions were so strong on both sides, that we thought it would be great to give Priscilla Valdez and Lisa Neuner a chance to meet each other. We decided to fly Priscilla east, to bring the women together.

I was going to join them.

I had wanted to visit with Lisa ever since this story began. I knew that family was hurting. I always call it a terrible club that we belong to, we parents of murdered children. And within that club, there are those who must live with the fact that their children not only were taken from them, but that they suffered terribly at the hands of a brutal madman in their last hours. That is an image that never, ever leaves you. I knew Lisa needed to share her pain with someone.

But I'll tell you, when I walked up to Lisa's house, I was terribly nervous. I fumbled with the gate. I slipped my hands in and out of my pockets. I struggled in vain to think of the words I would say.

I wanted to tell her so much. Mostly, I wanted to tell her, you will survive. You must survive. You must survive for those three beautiful children you still have, especially for little Wendi, that beautiful child who is probably damaged, horribly, forever, that fragile flower. I wanted to tell her, make sure everyone is strong, and rallies around her, and showers her with love, and she will survive too. The mother and daughter you lost, I wanted to tell her, are in a better place now. They're out of the pain and torture of this life, this imperfect planet that we live on with death and violence and sadness and all the horrors that we have to put up with. It's those of us left behind whom we have to help. And I wanted to tell Lisa that with love, and with patience, it will be okay, she will be okay, that I am living proof it will be okay.

But I was dreading the visit as well. I've seen so many crime victims, so many over the years, who have been torn apart, destroyed, devastated by what has happened to them, and I know that nothing I can say can help them, that they are beyond help, beyond words. Many who had succumbed to alcohol or drugs or just plain despair. Others who'd been divorced or lost their jobs. I remember one man I met in Rochester, New York, whose daughter was raped and murdered on spring break. He had been very successful, but afterward he lost his business, became an alcoholic, and got divorced. But then he went into rehab, became a big supporter of the Adam Walsh Center, and got his life back together. And just when I thought he was doing so great, he killed himself.

People think I'm a strong person, nerves of steel, Mister TV Guy, but in moments like these it's so hard. Not just to open the wounds of Adam's death, but to have to look into the eyes of the family members left behind, and see their pain, and wonder if they are gonna make it. I'm no guru. I'm no leader. I'm just a brokenhearted father who has tried to channel my anger and frustration into something positive. As I walk up the stairs, I'm thinking, I don't have any answers. They're going to want to know, how did you survive? How do we survive?

And what am I going to tell them? They're going to ask, are we going to descend into the darkness of hell, will this haunt us forever? And what will I say?

So Mister TV Guy, with a gut filled with self-doubt, walked up the stairs, and knocked on the door.

"Hi. I'm Lisa," said the woman who answered the door.

"Hi, I'm John," I said.

"Can I get a hug?" she asked.

And we put our arms around each other. And she began to sob, a little, but then she looked up, and she smiled. And I felt, in that moment, that maybe, just maybe, she would be all right. It would take a long time, but I felt strongly, in my heart, that she would be one of us. The survivors.

■ ■ ■

So we talked about what had happened, and about what was going to happen. I tried to prepare her for what could be the worst horror, aside from the murders themselves, which was the potential for a trial in which she would have to relive this terrible tragedy. And I told her that I knew, from the time right after Adam's death, that one of the hardest things for everyone around you is just knowing how to talk to you.

"I want to ask you something," I said, "because people ask it to me all the time. They ask, how are you dealing with it? And I'm not sure I'm the expert, or that I even know how I'm dealing with it. How are you dealing with it?"

"I don't know," said Lisa. "I guess God up above, and my mom and Toni up above, are just helping me get through life. The kids are there, the two little boys and Wendi, are there, and I have to take care of them. They still have a whole life to live. It's day by day. It's not easy, but life does go on."

I noticed that there were no pictures of Toni hanging anywhere.

"No, right now, we don't have any pictures of Toni on the wall," Lisa said. "Because we just can't handle it right now."

There was such a sadness, such resignation in her voice.

"There will come a time," I heard myself saying. "I always say it about Adam. The worst day of my life was the day he went missing. But I had the most wonderful six-and-a-half years. I was lucky to have him. I was lucky. And you were lucky to have that little girl."

And Lisa smiled. Through her tears, I saw the brightest, warmest smile, and her gaze was far away.

"Toni was something else," she said. "If you would have known her, you would have been proud of her. She was a good girl."

She returned her gaze to me, and told me something she hadn't told anyone before.

"Toni came to me," she said.

I asked her what she meant.

"After Eddie was caught, I felt her present, but she wasn't present. Her spirit, maybe. Before he was caught, I couldn't feel anything from her. But when he was caught I could feel her spirit. It's strange. Toni's got this funny laugh. You know you all have gotten this video, where she's doing like this"—Lisa wags her finger at me—"and laughing about it?

"When I woke up, I woke up to Toni laughing. I could see her laughing."

■   ■   ■

A few minutes later, Priscilla Valdez arrived. Lisa went out to greet her. If she had a smile when she was remembering Toni, that smile turned into a giant grin now.

"We thank you every day, in our dreams, for what you've done," Lisa said.

"I'm just glad I could help," Priscilla said. "How are you doing?" she asked.

"Better than we thought we would. We just thank God for what you've done. If it hadn't have been for you he might never have been caught."

"I'm just happy," said Priscilla, "that there's a family, and a little girl, who can sleep better at night."

Priscilla Valdez was just what we knew she would be, from having seen her on tape: an outgoing, effervescent person, with an aura about her, an aura of kindness, an aura of self-confidence; a self-assured person, but a calm and gentle person. And what I was so touched by was that she didn't think she had done anything all that special. She didn't think she should receive any accolades or acknowledgment. She felt it was one human being treating another in the right way, with some decency. I loved what she said to me, and I'll never forget it: "If it was me," she said, "if it had happened to my son, to my little boy, I would wish that somebody out there would spot the killer and have the courage to make the call to help me out. And that's all I did."

It's a meeting like this one that helps reaffirm your belief in humanity. As I left that place, I felt energized, proud of what we had done, inspired by the dignity of these two people. I thought, as much sadness as there was here, here are two women, sitting and talking with each other, two women who live three thousand miles apart, from different backgrounds, different lifestyles, talking about their lives, and how their lives had intertwined, and I thought how strong it made us all feel.

And I thought, this is how you go on.

Whether you're the father of a murdered child trying to hunt down miserable scum-of-the-earth fugitives, or you're a cop who's processing a crime scene like you've never seen before, whether you're a TV producer watching a tape of a little girl describing how she was tied up with a bloody shirt, or whether you're a woman trying to get out of bed and face the unfathomable loss of your mother and daughter at the hands of a madman—this is how you go on. Every once in a while, you meet someone who reaffirms your beliefs, people who really care about other people's pain, people who put their own safety at risk to ease the path of another. You meet them, and you see how calm they are, how centered, how simple it all seems to them; and you are touched by their grace, by the grace of their being, and in a way you are redeemed. And you can go on.

■　　■　　■

On May 31, 1995, a very polite-looking man walked into a courtroom, dressed in a nice suit, with a nice trim haircut, wearing neat, conservative glasses, sporting what was by that time a neat, professorial goatee. He had clearly been eating well, sleeping well, and appeared to have been working out. He had a quiet and reserved air about him, no glare in his eye, no swagger in his step. You could no more imagine this man committing murder than you could imagine him, say, gnawing on the bark of a tree, or breathing fire.

Eddie James had pleaded guilty to murder. But in a sort of mini-trial, the state would have to present evidence that this case was worthy of the death penalty, and Eddie could try to plead for his life.

I thought about what that cop had told us, right after we interviewed Eddie James, and it hit me.

You sly, devious, son of a bitch.

Eddie James, you're playing this perfectly.

After all that that false bravado about how giving your life would be the only proper price to pay to the family you destroyed—after all that, you're going to give yourself the best chance you have of saving your own, miserable skin.

He was redeemed now, Eddie James was; yes, that was the image he was trying to convey, and that would be the argument that would unfold. He was a righteous man now, here to deliver a message, a message of hope and redemption.

It was enough to make you sick.

Fortunately, the jury didn't buy it.

At the end of the mini-trial, their advisory sentence was read to the judge:

"In the case of the state of Florida against Edward Thomas James, case number 933237CFA, advisory sentence of the jury, as to count one: A majority of the jury, by a vote of eleven to one, advise and recommend to the court that it impose the death penalty upon Edward Thomas James for the murder of Toni Neuner.

"Advisory sentence of the jury for count two: A majority of the jury, by a vote of eleven to one, advise and recommend to the court that it impose the death penalty upon Edward Thomas James for the murder of Betty Dick."

There was no jubilation among the family members. It was decided that Brenda Dick would speak for the family.

"It brings some relief, but it will never be closed," she said. "There is no closing this matter. Eddie says he lives with this every morning. Well, I live with this every day. I'm the one who pays, my kids pay. He didn't just take a life, he took Toni's generation of children. He didn't just kill two people, he killed a whole generation. There's no getting over that in one day."

Two months later, on a steamy August 18, Judge Alan Dickey handed down the death sentence. "The defendant is hereby committed to the custody of the Department of Corrections of the state of Florida for execution of this sentence," he said. "May God have mercy on his soul."

■ ■ ■

Betty Dick would have been sixty-three this past spring. Wendi, who adopted Grandma's birthday, is fourteen. Her sister, Toni, never saw her ninth birthday, or her tenth; this past spring she would have been thirteen.

The spring before that, if he had he lived, I would have attended Adam Walsh's college graduation.

Life does go on.

The first of James's appeals has been denied; the entire appeals process, however, could take another eight years. The closure and the sense of justice that the sentence offered the family has grown stronger, but remains tempered by the long wait ahead.

And while Eddie James sits in his cell and contemplates his fate, a group of small plastic bags sits in an evidence locker at the police station.

It contains most of the jewelry that belonged to Betty Dick.

A few of the pieces were melted down by the pawn shop owners, but the rest has been recovered: several rings, a few solid bracelets, and several chain bracelets.

Until the appeals process is completed, these items remain as evidence. The family cannot get them back; they cannot even go sort through them to find out exactly what is there.

For the most part, Wendi Neuner does not talk about what happened on the morning of September 20, 1993.

But she does ask, once in a while, about the chain bracelet that Grandma Betty always promised her. There was supposed to be one for Wendi, one for Toni. Wendi cannot have her bracelet now. Someday perhaps, she will be allowed to wear it.

Wendi's doing very well now. She does great in school—she's made the honor roll—and her counselor has advised that, as long as she is not asking questions about the murders, she should not be forced to talk about them.

Someday, of course, she will begin to ask questions.

And her family will tell her the story, the story of her grandma Betty, and how she gave up her birthday for Wendi; they will help her remember all the fun she had with her little sister, Toni, who used to shadow her everywhere.

And, perhaps, Wendi will look down at a chain bracelet on her left wrist, and ask about the man who did this to her grandma, and to her sister.

And her family will be able to touch her cheek, look her in the eye, and say what so many victims' families will never be able to say, what so many of us ache to be able to tell our children:

He didn't get away with it.

That's not much, I know.

But it's a start.

CHAPTER TWO

Murder Most Unholy

I'm sure many will say, "How could anyone do such a horrible thing." My only answer is it isn't easy and was only done after much thought.

—JOHN LIST

It seems so long ago, now. I look at myself on that first *America's Most Wanted* show, and I think, was I really that guy? That tousled-haired, frightened, stiff-as-a-board guy on that ludicrous spaceship of a set, trying to figure out whether I had launched a new career that would help victims like myself—or whether I'd made the biggest mistake of my life.

There had to have been a hundred people on the set that day— lots of Fox executives with their arms folded across their chests, all the producers of the show biting the ends of their pens—and it was dead silent. I don't know why, but nobody was talking in between the takes. It was really unnerving. I felt like I was at somebody's funeral. I hoped it wasn't mine.

I was on shaky ground to begin with. I'd had some TV experience—on the movie *Adam,* about our son's death, I'd worked closely with the producers, Alan Landsberg, Linda Otto, and Joan Barnett; and later, I worked with the guy who played me in that movie, Daniel J. Travanti, on a special called *How to Raise a Street-Smart Child.* But I was still really a babe in the woods when it came to television. I didn't know what the hell I was doing. The *America's Most Wanted* producers said they just wanted me to "be John Walsh," so they wouldn't give me any direction or guidance. Meanwhile, I didn't know what a voice-over was, I didn't know I was supposed to look at the camera with the light on the top, nothing. All the other TV anchors sat down, back then; they decided I would stand up, and I couldn't figure out what to do with my hands. Finally they handed me a script, as a prop, and I held on to it for dear life.

They'd screen-tested real actors—guys like Treat Williams and Hal Holbrook—but somehow decided they wanted a real crime victim, someone who could speak from the heart.

I'd been pretty close to turning the whole thing down. I never saw myself as a TV guy. I was, by then, deeply into trying to get missing-child legislation passed, and I was afraid hosting a TV show would ruin any credibility I'd built up with legislators.

The one who turned me around was Michael Linder, the first executive producer of the show (Lance Heflin, our current e.p., would come on two years later).

I met Linder for the first time in the lobby of a Fort Lauderdale hotel. He was an imposing fellow: a big strong guy, with a deep voice and a shaved head. He had a portable TV monitor and battery-operated VCR out in his station wagon, and he asked me if I'd like to see the first case that *America's Most Wanted* was going to air.

It was the case of David James Roberts, an FBI top-ten fugitive.

I went out and watched it.

It was horrifying.

David Roberts had killed a young couple and their child by setting their house on fire. He kidnapped and raped another woman, then locked her in the trunk of her car, and left her baby by the side of the road to die. The child crawled more than one hundred yards before succumbing to the cold of the night, the mother still pounding on the car trunk.

As I stared at the video monitor, I was riveted, I was repelled, I was all sorts of things. Mostly I was thinking, here's a guy who killed two children. As the parent of a murdered child, wouldn't it be great if I could help catch this guy?

Later, I'd come to realize how much of Linder's passion and vision was reflected in that tape. I also realized that by viewing it, I'd been the victim of an emotional ambush: I hadn't expected to feel the depth of emotion that the case would bring forth; but, once confronted by it, I couldn't turn away.

I agreed to host the show.

That first show wasn't aired on the full network. You see, Fox wasn't any more sure about me or *America's Most Wanted* than I was, so they aired us only on small stations in seven cities.

So there weren't a whole lot of people watching that one night.

But there was one viewer who'd watch with an unusual amount of interest.

A year later, that viewer would turn the tables on Michael Linder—with an emotional ambush all his own.

And that ambush would change the world of *America's Most Wanted* forever.

■ ■ ■

The viewer that Sunday night was a New Jersey lawman named Frank Marranca. Frank, forty-two, was spending the evening with his fiancée, Margie. Normally, he'd be taking her out to their favorite Italian restaurant in Union called Bento's, where she loved the veal Parmesan and he loved whatever the special was. But on this night, she insisted on staying home and watching TV—a new cop show was premiering and she just had to see it.

Frank, a twenty-year veteran of the prosecutor's office in Union County, New Jersey (where he was known for his hobby—he loved to play the bagpipes), wasn't hot on cop shows. I see this stuff at work, he thought; why should I watch it at home? But Margie was sweet and easygoing, and Frank liked to do what pleased her. So the tough Italian cop who plays the bagpipes, and his sweet Irish bride-to-be who loved Italian food, cuddled together and turned on the tube.

As Frank watched that first episode, he realized he was seeing something very new, and very different.

And a bell went off in Frank's head.

This, possibly, was his chance.

His chance to solve The Case.

It was the case that stuck in the craw of everyone who worked for the Union County prosecutor's office. The case file was kept separate, in sealed Rubbermaid boxes, and every detective who came to work for the police in the Union County town of Westfield, New Jersey, was made to sit down and read it. It was one of the most famous cases in the state's history.

And it had gone unsolved for seventeen years.

The next morning, Marranca went to work and asked permission to pitch the case to this new TV show. He drafted a letter, and went back to the file to pull out all the old clips. As it turned out, one of the reporters at *AMW* happened to be from Union County— a former reporter at the *Elizabeth Daily Journal*—and was familiar with the case. The reporter made sure the pitch was made to Michael Linder and the other producers of the show.

And they turned it down.

It was too grisly. It was too old. We'd never tried to air a seventeen-year-old case before. What would we do for photos?

Marranca got the bad news, and that was that.

For a while.

Just after New Year's, Marranca heard that Michael Linder was going to be speaking at an armed robbery conference in Wilmington, Delaware. On January 26, he packed up his material and headed down the New Jersey Turnpike. He and a Union County sergeant got a room at the hotel where the conference was being held, laid out their files, and then waited in the lobby, outside the door to the conference room where Linder was speaking. "We waited until he came off the stage," said Marranca. "As soon as he came out into the hall, we grabbed him."

They told him of the bizarre case of John List, a milquetoast accountant from New Jersey, whom they'd been looking for for seventeen years. After about half an hour, they invited Linder upstairs to their room.

It was an emotional ambush to match the one Linder had pulled on me a year earlier. He couldn't turn away. Once Linder heard the tale, and saw the photos of the crime scene, there was no question about it. We would have to take the case.

He didn't agree right then and there, but it was inevitable. And so on into the night the three men talked, going over the details of the weird case, sitting next to a hotel bed strewn with eight-by-ten black-and-white photos, and in the middle, a larger photo, a big eighteen-by-twelve blowup of an aerial view of a house, a huge, hulking, two-story mansion surrounded by trees, a house so filled with evil that the neighborhood kids dared each other to enter; a house where the unexplainable had taken place, where a man had committed the most horrible sin possible, and done it in the name of God.

■ ■ ■

John List came about his devoutly religious nature quite naturally. His mother, Alma, had raised him in such a strict Lutheran atmosphere that even his childhood pastor commented that the mother of this "model Christian child" had been "a little too correct, if you know what I mean," according to Tim Benford and Jim Johnson, who would later write a book about this case.

His father was already sixty-one and his mother was thirty-eight when John was born, four years before the Great Depression. Benford speculated that maybe because John was her only child, born relatively late in her life, Alma became enormously overprotective. She was already a stiff, proper, and religious woman; after John's birth she became somewhat obsessive.

So, he noted, when other children ran barefoot, John would be overdressed; while the other kids played together at the firehouse up the block, John would sit home, reading the Bible, under the watchful eye of his mother; while the other kids loved to run to the railroad and watch the trains go by, John was not allowed—too sooty, too dangerous.

Dancing, too, was forbidden—because it brought one in contact with the wrong sorts of people. Although there were these and many other rules to follow, John was only spanked twice—once for being unruly in church—but the spankings had a profound effect on him, and he grew up rigid, trying to keep perfect order, trying to never make waves. "I've always been somewhat anxious," he said years later, "about pleasing and not disrupting. I was well-behaved and obedient in school, in the army, with my employers, with my wife, with my mother."

The timid boy grew to become a timid man, who turned to accounting—the perfect profession. He needed rules to follow, and here was a profession filled with rules, with order, with perfectly clear right and wrong answers.

One night, the accountant was out bowling with a friend when he spotted Helen Morris Taylor—"a knockout," according to Benford—and, although it took a while, the shy, awkward List began courting the beautiful blond Helen, a widow with one child who'd lost her husband in the Korean War.

Although they were quite mismatched—the earthy, worldly Helen and the pious, upright John—they fell for each other, and things progressed quickly. "I was always taught that I should not have intercourse before marriage, but I slipped into it." John believes that that first time, in October of 1951, was the night Helen got pregnant. "I debated in my mind, should I get married. I decided we should go ahead with it."

Of course, he must have felt like God was punishing him for the sin of intercourse. And of course, he must have figured that marriage was the proper penance. In any case, he knew it was the right thing to do, and John List always, always tried to do the right thing.

He proposed.

On November 30, 1951, the eve of the wedding, Helen told him she had learned that she was not really pregnant. "In later years," List said, "I thought, if I had had a few hours, a few days, I would have postponed it. I thought maybe I was getting married because I thought she was pregnant. I'm not sure to this day whether she was pregnant or not pregnant." Maybe she just made it all up, to find a father for her seven-year-old daughter.

But it all happened too quickly for the methodical, plodding John List to deal with sensibly. He didn't have time to think it through, clearly and logically. So he just kept moving forward. The next morning, he went through with the wedding.

One other odd thing surrounded the wedding plans: Although they were living in Virginia, Helen insisted on driving three hours north, to Baltimore, to get married.

The most likely reason: Maryland, back then, was one of the few states not requiring a blood test before a wedding.

So John would not find out that the woman he was marrying was suffering from syphilis.

■　■　■

Helen had evidently contracted the disease from her first husband, when he returned from World War II, although at first the disease did not make itself evident.

In those days, one treatment for syphilis was, barbaric as it sounds today, to give the patient malaria—in the belief that the malaria would kill the syphilis. Helen's long bout with untreated syphilis, and perhaps even the treatment itself, did leave her with certain problems: a lack of equilibrium, blindness in one eye, and some internal damage.

The deterioration of her brain would not be fully evident until later.

Despite her condition, Helen became pregnant in 1954, and gave birth to a healthy baby girl, Patricia Morris List, on January 8, 1955. John lost his job (although his accounting skills were good, something about his personality irked his superiors), but he got another before his next child, John Frederick List, was born in October of 1957. The youngest, Frederick, would come along the next year; he would turn out to be quiet and well-mannered, like his father. List also adopted Helen's daughter, Brenda.

They settled in Kalamazoo, Michigan, where, as always, John found solace in the church, although neither John nor anyone at Zion Lutheran could convince Helen to join him there. Helen was doing less and less housework, too; it bothered John, but rather than make a fuss, he just took over the cleaning. Cleaning was very important to him.

He was often described as the kind of guy who mowed the lawn in a jacket and tie; while no one directly remembers this, it is an image of List that stuck, and it is an apt, if not entirely accurate, one.

"I don't believe I've ever seen him in a short-sleeved shirt," Helen's sister, Jean, would say later. "That doesn't mean he didn't wear them, but I don't believe I've ever seen him in one."

List was drawn to war simulation games; the rigid discipline of thought they required gave him many hours of pleasure. And he later would come to love *America's Most Wanted*—with its clear delineation of good and evil, and the sense of finality that a capture gives to criminal cases.

John and Helen's sex life, by his accounting, was poor; it was Helen, of course, who tried to spice it up. "She suggested erotic movies, which helped our sex life," he said. But of course, he insisted on the tamest of porno: "It was just pretty much straight sex," he said, because he did not believe in "kinky sex."

His attempt at leading an orderly, linear existence was thwarted at every turn by the increasing forces of chaos leaking in from everywhere—most notably because of Helen. As the years went on, Helen's behavior became stranger and stranger. At first, she just left more and more of the housework and child-rearing to John and the oldest girl, Brenda, while she spent more and more time lying in bed. Then she began drinking heavily.

Soon things became worse.

Helen began calling John at work and leaving pitiful messages. According to Benford and Johnson, one day Helen left a message at the switchboard: "Your son messed in his pants. If you want them changed, come home and do it." List went home and changed his son's diapers.

Helen's mind was deteriorating. So was List's financial health.

John was now working for Xerox, where he experienced the same problem he'd had at his first job, the problem that came to define him: He could do the accounting work fine, but when he was moved up to supervisory positions he didn't have the person-to-person skills. He just couldn't relate to people, and while no one could quite put a finger on it, he just . . . bugged everybody. He couldn't look you in the eye, he couldn't delegate, and if something went wrong—just as he did at home—he ignored it rather than confront it. "He was too nice," Benford and Johnson quoted a co-worker as saying. "He'd take the heat himself [rather] than criticize someone." So problems in his department continued to mount—and all John would do was exhort everyone to be nice, then go sit nervously at his desk, where everyone noticed ugly red blotches rising all over his face.

He was eased out of Xerox in 1965. John then landed a job as a vice president at First National Bank of Jersey City—so the family moved to New Jersey. He located a community near the bank where his children could attend a good Lutheran school, instead of the public schools. And Helen found a house she liked: the big, eerie mansion on a hill in Westfield. He would have preferred something smaller, but Helen insisted. They bought the mansion, and, in exchange for ten thousand dollars to help with the purchase, it was agreed that John's mother—the straitlaced, overprotective Alma—would move in with them. They couldn't afford furniture, so except for beds and a few random pieces, the house was echoey and empty, filled only with the growing furies and frustrations of its occupants.

The tensions between John's strong-willed, domineering mother and his equally strong-willed and increasingly irrational wife were palpable. But no one knew how badly Helen's mind was deteriorating until her sister, Jean, along with her husband, came to visit in 1968.

■　■　■

Jean and her husband were disturbed as they walked through the empty, gigantic ballroom—"you could sit my home in it," she said—under the huge stained-glass ceiling, then up the stairs of the creaky and sparsely furnished old mansion. The house was clearly in severe need of repairs, with its peeling paint and leaky roof and dripping plumbing. When they reached the top of the stairs, they were confronted by the most disturbing sight of all.

Jean's sister, Helen, unbathed, lay in swaddled in filthy bed linens, in a messy room. On the night table were a number of bottles of medication—she'd evidently become addicted to prescription sleeping pills—and Helen's lunch: peanuts and a jar of peanut butter. As the visit went on, there were other oddities: like the time Helen, dressed in a yellow shirt and shorts, decided to come down the stairs, but was so weak she had to descend on her fanny. The time that Jean went to answer the phone, heard a thump, and turned to see her sister collapsed on the floor, unconscious. The fact that John had taken over all the household roles—mother, father, cook, dishwasher. He never complained, but in fact, it was eating away at him. He resented his wife, her drunkenness, her pill-popping, the ease with which she dismissed him. And he began to resent himself, his uncontrollable urge to accommodate.

There was no place for him to hide from the torments that left him feeling powerless and impotent. From a job that made him so nervous that his face broke out in blotches, he came home every day to not one but two domineering women. Even now, in his forties, he had to endure his mother telling him to wear his mittens and galoshes, and his wife taunting him about how he wasn't really a man, the way her virile first husband was. The two women detested each other, and their constant fighting and carping made him more and more anxious.

Helen had been admitted to the hospital for treatment four times, diagnosed with what John was told was "brain atrophy." Meanwhile, John, the accountant who couldn't manage his own finances, was continuing to find and lose jobs. This is how little he understood his shortcomings at work: Fed up with his failures in the accounting field, he took a job working for an insurance agency, believing he could make a go of it selling life insurance policies. But you can't sell someone an insurance policy if you can't look him in the eye, and soon, his commissions dried up.

By 1971, he was growing desperate.

"Everything seemed to be going wrong," List said. "I couldn't do well at a job. I was unemployed. I was borrowing from my mother. Helen was getting worse." The bills piled up. The utilities were about to be disconnected. The mortgage hadn't been paid in three months. Two bank loans were past due.

And then there were the children.

For someone who craved order and detested conflict, the psychedelic sixties were a horrible time for John to try to raise three children on his own. He especially feared for his daughter Patty, then sixteen. He was afraid that her love for theater and acting were drawing her into what John thought was the wrong crowd. He suspected she had tried marijuana, and that she was being lured away from the church. In fact, she had taken an interest in witchcraft, and reportedly believed herself to be a witch.

He feared for the soul of young John, then fifteen, an unruly boy he had to spank to keep in line. He feared for his youngest, Frederick, then thirteen: What effect would it have on him that his mother had stopped attending church?

He contemplated running away, but he feared what might happen to his mother if he decided to leave.

He began to think of the most horrible alternatives—again, in his orderly, logical way.

"If Helen was the problem and I shot her," he thought, "we would still have a problem with my mother and the children. I didn't want them to have to go to a home, to go into poverty. I was raised in the Depression. I knew that things were tough. I didn't want to put them in that position."

He contemplated suicide, but because the Lutheran church forbids it, he realized it would mean that he could never go to heaven.

John heard no voices, had no visions, was not visited by angel or demon; he took no alcoholic beverages or drugs. It was the logic of the situation that dictated his actions. Yes, there would be just one answer.

"I kept praying," he said later. "There was no other solution, so finally I just decided it was the only way."

■   ■   ■

I will tell you, I'm not one who dwells a lot on the motivations of criminals. I think it's useful sometimes, when you're hunting someone, to know what propels him, so that you can try to anticipate his next move; but I'm not one of those guys who has this morbid fascination with the criminal mind, who likes to delve into the psyche of psychos to find out what it was that triggered their heinous acts. I figure, once we've determined that they committed the crimes, let's lock them up, throw away the key, and soon enough God will have them back, and He can figure out what went wrong.

But I will admit, as I read the *AMW* case file our reporters had prepared on John List, I was drawn in. The more I dwelled on the events that took place that night, the more I found myself, almost against my own will, wondering: How could this happen? From where does this madness arise?

How could any man who had worked so hard to raise a family do what John List was about to do?

■   ■   ■

Having planned his strategy meticulously, John List slept soundly on the night of Monday, November 8, 1971, awakening the next day to get the children off to school. Mrs. Barbara Baeder, the friend from church who drove the List kids to school along with her own, picked them up at 8:30 A.M.

John had found the guns a month earlier, two keepsakes: a nine-millimeter Austrian weapon, a souvenir of World War II, and a .22-caliber revolver that his father had used many years ago as protection when he carried large sums of money around during the workday. He had gone to a rifle range to make sure that the guns were working properly. He obtained ammunition for both weapons at a gun shop.

Everything was in place.

At 9:00 A.M., Helen was having toast and coffee at the kitchen table. He went up behind her. In his memory, he shot her from behind, because he did not want her to know; but in fact she was shot in the side of the head, near the ear, so in fact John List could see the side of his wife's face just before the gun went off and she crumpled to the table.

He then walked upstairs to his mother's apartment on the third floor. "What was that noise?" she asked.

John List walked up to his mother, and shot her once. Again, he would later say that he believed he was shooting her from behind, but in reality the shot entered the side of her head. He tried to drag her body, but was unable to.

He then went downstairs, and dragged Helen into the ballroom.

He mopped up the mess he'd left behind, then spent the rest of the morning caring for small details: He stopped the mail and the milk. He went to the bank. He drew out what little money he had. Everyone who saw him at the bank said he appeared calm, collected, and pleasant. When he cashed the savings bonds that he and his mother owned jointly, he took the time to make sure the interest had been figured correctly.

I try to imagine anyone in that situation, having murdered his wife and his mother, and I think: Wouldn't you be a little nervous? Wouldn't your hands shake? Could you go to the bank and calculate the interest on your savings bonds? Here's a guy whose face went blotchy if he had to tell an employee she made a mistake. Why wasn't he throwing up or lying on the ground in a fetal position mumbling prayers for forgiveness?

And how, given the hours to contemplate your actions before the kids came home from school, could you continue on with your terrible plan?

Go back and look at his rigid upbringing, his overdeveloped superego, his work and home pressures, go back and look at all that if you want.

I look at one thing: This man was now moving coldly, dispassionately, with dispatch, through his horrible plan. And he was just getting started.

■   ■   ■

Sixteen-year-old Patricia had complained of menstrual cramps, and reported to the health office; at 11:30 A.M. she was signed out of school. At around noon, she was seen on the bleachers by the ball field, smoking a cigarette with a friend.

Usually she would go to work in the afternoon at an insurance agency—part of a work-study program—but on this day she called in sick, and called her dad to come get her.

John List picked up his daughter, drove her home, and shot her in the jaw with the .22. The bullet went through her brain and ricocheted out her temple, lodging in the wall near the washer and dryer. He put her on a sleeping bag in the ballroom, at her mother's feet. Patricia, stone cold dead at sixteen, lying on her side, facing away from her mother, the two bodies placed at perfect right angles.

Orderliness, even in murder. Each killing taking place in isolation, one at a time, no one witnessing another's death, no one to look at him with accusing eyes.

After classes, John Frederick List reported to the school newspaper, where he wrote all the sports articles, and remained there until a little after 3:00 P.M. He promised the faculty adviser that he would have his article in by the next day. The family friend, Mrs. Baeder, picked him up and drove him home, dropping him off around 3:15 P.M.

John was different when he crumpled to the ground after being shot; his body continued to twitch, causing his father some discomfort. The senior John List pulled out the .22 and shot his son several more times, in the chest, so that the boy would not suffer. When he was done, he deposited the boy next to his sister in the ballroom, their bodies parallel, neatly spaced.

Frederick, in the eighth grade, worked in the same office as his sister on Tuesdays and Fridays; this day, when he arrived there, he found out that his sister Pat had called in sick. At the end of the day, he was overheard calling home. His father came and picked him up, and drove him back to the eerie mansion on the hill. And with a single gunshot, he completed his mission: All members of the family murdered, cleanly and methodically, one at a time. With the exception of his mother, all of them were lined up neatly in the ballroom, beneath a huge stained-glass ceiling, an appropriate place from which to begin their ascent to heaven.

Now it was time to tidy up.

■ ■ ■

With his house filled with dead people, List's mind filled up with details. He called the insurance agency he was working for, to tell them that there was an illness in Helen's family, and that he would have to go to North Carolina for a while. He called Patty's drama group with the same story, wrote notes to the boys' teachers, and a few other notes, taking care of little bits of business.

There was one other note he wrote.

It was to his minister, Pastor Eugene Rehwinkel.

John List had something to say.

Dear Pastor Rehwinkel

I am very sorry to add this additional burden to your work. I know that what has been done is wrong from all that I have been taught and that any reasons that I might give will not make it right. But you are the one person that I know that while not condoning this will at least possibly understand why I felt that I had to do this.

1. I wasn't earning anywhere near enough to support us. Everything I tried seemed to fall to pieces. True, we could have gone bankrupt & maybe gone on welfare.

2. But that brings me to my next point. Knowing the type of location that one would have to live in plus the environment for the children plus the effect of them knowing they were on welfare was just more than I thought they could and should endure. I know that they were willing to cut back but this involved a lot more than that.

3. With Pat being so determined to get into acting, I was

also fearful as to what this might do to her continuing
to be a Christian. I'm sure it wouldn't have helped.

4. Also, with Helen not going to church, I know that this
would harm the children eventually in their attendance.
I had continued to hope that she would begin to come
to church soon. but when I mentioned to her that Mr.
Jutzi wanted to pay her an Elders call, she just blew up
& stated that she wanted her name taken off the church
rolls. Again, this could only have given an adverse result for the children's continued attendance.

So that is the sum of it. If any one of those had been the
condition we might have pulled through, but this was just
too much; at least I'm certain that all have gone to heaven
now. If things had gone on, who knows if that would be the
case.

Of course, Mother got involved because doing what I did
to my family would have been a tremendous shock to her at
this age. Therefore, knowing that she is also a Christian, I
felt it best that she be relieved of the troubles of this world
that would have hit her.

After it was all over, I said some prayers for them all—
from the hymn book.

That was the least that I could do.

List went on, in the note, through his carefully thought out
funeral arrangements, and then continued:

Originally, I had planned this for Nov. 1—All Saints Day.
But travel arrangements were delayed. I thought it would be
an appropriate day for them to get to heaven.

As for me, please let me be dropped from the congrega-
tion rolls. I leave myself in the hands of Gods Justice &
Mercy. I don't doubt that He is able to help us, but apparently he saw fit not to answer my prayers the way I had hoped
they would be answered. This makes me think that perhaps it
was for the best as far as the childrens souls are concerned. I

know that many will only look at the additional years that
they could have lived, but if finally they were no longer
Christians, what would be gained?

Also, I'm sure many will say, "How could anyone do
· such a horrible thing"—My only answer is it isn't easy and
was only done after much thought. . . .

One other thing. It may seem cowardly to have always
shot from behind, but I didn't want any of them to know
even at the last second that I had to do this to them.

John got hurt more because he seemed to struggle longer. The rest were immediately out of pain. John didn't con-
sciously feel anything either.

Please remember me in your prayers. I will need them
whether or not the government does its duty as it sees it. I'm
only concerned with making my peace with God & of this I
am assured because of Christ dying even for me.

P.S. Mother is in the hallway in the attic—third floor.
She was too heavy to move.

John

This is the mentality of the killer. This is the mind and soul of the
scum of the earth. I know a lot of people have expressed great
sympathy for John List. Because he was a poor misguided soul, who
sincerely believed he was doing the right thing, saving his family
from a life of religious indifference, thereby assuring they would all
go to heaven. And because he could not kill himself, since his
chance of joining them there would be gone.

I know that some of you, reading this account, will feel
sympathetic to List. Or maybe you have felt that way about some
case you read about in your local paper. That the poor killer was just
confused, had lost contact with reality, and therefore, while he must
be punished, he should also be pitied.

Perhaps there are some cases like that.

Perhaps.

But I'll tell you this.

There are a lot more cases of simple, cold-blooded murder,

where after the fact—sometimes moments after the fact—the killer begins spinning a web of deceit designed to confuse—if not the legal issue, then at least the moral issue.

And John List is just such a case.

Look again at his letter. It starts with the classic convict dodge—"I know that what has been done is wrong." Already, he's talking about the event as though he's some disinterested third party. It's not "what I did was wrong" but "what has been done is wrong." He is already stripping the act of its reality, of its horror. He talks about how Mother "got involved," how his youngest son "got hurt more."

He then goes on—just like Eddie James—to separate himself from the person who committed the crime. When you read the letter, it's as though List isn't even the killer; it's like he's saying about the killer, "He, whoever he was, may have committed it; I, a much better person, know his actions to be wrong, although I understand what he did."

And then he goes on with the greatest blasphemy of all—it was God's fault. List is arguing, see, He didn't answer my prayers. That's why I had to kill my children, my wife, my mother. God could have prevented this, but didn't; if He isn't going to stop it from happening, how could I?

That's why I feel no sympathy for List. I look at how he commited these murders, and I look at what he did afterward, and I see the same cold-blooded logic, the same self-serving excuses, that I've seen in hundreds of cases. John List is no different from any common street killer. Just a little more articulate, maybe, and a little more organized. But morally, he's from the same cloth.

If List were truly repentant, he might have found some way to atone for his sin—by turning himself in, for example. If he were truly sorry, he might have shown some inkling of emotion. Some affect would appear in his words or deeds.

Instead, in the most emotionless, efficient, accurate series of steps a man in his position could take, John List arranged his own disappearance.

He sent his things west, by railway express. He turned down the heat in the house, so the oil would last and the pipes would not burst. He headed for New York, took his car to Kennedy Airport in Queens, and abandoned it there—but then took a bus back to Manhattan, mingled with the crowds at Grand Central Station, and vanished. All so calculating, all so cold-blooded.

And for seventeen years, that was all there was to the story of John Emil List.

■   ■   ■

The bodies were finally discovered nearly a month later. Neighbors wondered about the frugal Lists having left all the lights blazing, but it wasn't until Patty's drama coaches became concerned that someone entered the house and discovered the gruesome tableau.

Tim Benford, one of the authors of *Righteous Carnage,* the book about the List case, noted later that the bodies had been eerily preserved in the morgue-like temperatures, and a funeral dirge filled the air: List had left the radio playing over the intercom.

He and his co-author also uncovered one of the great ironies of the case. If part of John List's motive was the fear of what poverty would do to his family's existence, then he had another way out.

And it was right over his head.

The List house mysteriously burned down about a year after the murders. The man who bought the house told Benford that the enormous stained-glass ceiling in the ballroom was signed by Louis Comfort Tiffany. In 1971, it would have been valued at more than one hundred thousand dollars. Had List only turned his eyes to heaven before the murders, and seen what was actually in front of him instead of what he imagined, he could have solved all his problems.

"It's an absolute pity nobody realized what it was before the tragedy," the buyer told Benford. "A Tiffany masterpiece of this size would have said a lot about the people who lived in such a house. It was quite a statement. It would have brought recognition."

Benford mused: "Quite a statement indeed." And recognition, he noted, would come in a very different way.

Benford came across his curiosity about the case naturally: He'd lived in Union County since 1974; after a heart bypass, he had to walk every day as part of his recovery program, and used the List house as a milestone—it was exactly a mile from his home. So every day, he walked past that house, and wondered, and wondered, and wondered.

He wasn't alone. A lot of the guys at the station house in Westfield, New Jersey, wondered about the case, too. They certainly didn't feel any sympathy for John List: "He's the type," said Detective Bernard Tracy, "that could stick a guy in the oven and say, 'boy, it's hot in here.'" Tracy, a local guy, was assigned to the List case in 1980. He grew up on the other side of the tracks from where the beautiful mansion held its ugly secrets; he was nineteen when the murders occurred.

"When I came on the job, the only thing I knew was from playing sports here, and it was the place where that guy killed his family." Tracy would get to know the case intimately, and it would gnaw at him, like it gnawed at everyone else in the town.

How could he have done this? And how the hell did he get away with it? How could a guy who's so stupid be so smart?

Every year, on the anniversary of the murders, and on other key dates—the children's birthdays, certain holidays—Tracy and his compadres would stake out the graveyard, to see who stopped by, who sent flowers.

It yielded nothing.

And so the local obsession would grow.

James Moran, a detective on the scene when the bodies were first discovered, always carried the FBI most-wanted poster of List folded in his pocket. Moran would later become the chief of the department. His desire to catch List was so strong it became a running joke around the office, and he would get postcards from all over the world: "Having a great time, glad you're not here. Your friend, John List." At the prosecutor's office, they made up memo pads reading "From the desk of John List" and would send the chief taunting memos.

Frank Marranca, the investigator who brought us the case, told us, "Everyone would send postcards when they went on vacation, including myself. One time, we had a new secretary, and I called and asked for one of the detectives. She said, 'Who's calling?' I said, 'John List.' And she didn't know, so she put the call through.''

Moran retired in 1986, but didn't lose interest in the case, and was excited when our producers said they'd take the case on.

There was only one question.

How the hell were we going to do it?

We'd never before found a fugitive who'd been on the run for what was then eighteen years. We knew that to solve the case, we were going to have to try something very, very unusual. Something we'd never done before.

Fortunately, we knew just the guy for the job.

■   ■   ■

Frank Bender was a bored commercial photographer from Philadelphia with aspirations of becoming an artist. He'd been taking some night classes in sculpting at the Pennsylvania Academy of Fine Arts when a friend invited him to tour the morgue at the medical examiner's office. Not the kind of invitation you get every day, and not the kind you or I might accept—but Frank was trying to learn about form, about the human body, and so decided to give it a try.

The medical examiner, during the tour, came to a corpse with a decomposed face. It's almost impossible to solve a crime if you don't know your victim's identity, as was the case here. "We don't know who she is, or what she looks like,'' the examiner said.

"I can tell you,'' Frank said.

The examiner, intrigued, invited Frank back that Saturday. He looked at the decomposed face, and began sculpting. The resulting bust had an uncanny quality to it—like a sad woman, frozen in time, not quite alive, not quite dead; the face seemed to change features as you walked around it, just as a person's face does. She stared ahead, dully, as though she were patiently waiting for something.

She got what she was waiting for: Photos of the bust were circulated, and the victim was identified six months later.

It was the beginning of a new career for Bender—one that suited his offbeat personality, and one that made use of an almost unearthly skill—the ability to see humanity, in all its ever-living and ever-changing forms, where others see only death; the ability to take a black-and-white photo and use it as a crystal ball to see into the future, where others see only a moment frozen in a time long past. "I draw and paint people wherever I go," said Frank. "I look at people and I store the information, get tips from how one form relates to another. It's like music. If you change one note, another note goes sour. There is harmony in nature and I follow it."

Bender set up his studio in a converted meat market in Philadelphia—his office is in the freezer. It's an odd, Daliesque sort of environment; here a cowboy hat hanging on the edge of a ladder, there a nude female mannequin with her hand posed gaily on her hip, sporting a bright blue hat and red scarf; and everywhere, heads, partial heads, completed heads, big ones, small ones, some still looking like an unformed mass of lifeless mud rising from the earth, others with that eerie Benderian quality of almost-life, staring and waiting.

Bender himself is a leprechaun of a man, with an elfin smile and pixieish goatee, and I always remember being struck by how light and humorous his demeanor is, even when we were dealing with the most morbid of subjects.

Frank was a real gentleman. I'd met him, and come to have an enormous respect for him, through his volunteer work for the National Center for Missing and Exploited Children and the Adam Walsh Center. Frank, in his spare time, would reconstruct faces from the skulls of children who'd been found murdered—gruesome work, but it's the only way we can identify these kids, and Frank did it for free. He knew that, for a parent, the worst is the not knowing. A good, good person, helping in cases that so many others would turn away from.

He was in the walk-in freezer when Linder, the executive producer, called him and invited him to Washington to look at what we had on an eighteen-year-old case.

"Linder showed me flyers he had that only had front views," Frank recalled. "There was no psychological profile, very little information from the FBI. He said, 'We're totally relying on you. If you can convince me that through your work he will be caught, then we will air it.' "

Frank was excited by the challenge. "I was very confident. I told him, 'Yeah, I can do it.' He said, 'If you feel confident, do the bust.' "

Linder gave Bender a month. Armed with the two-dimensional frontal photo of John List taken just before the crimes, and some background information, Frank went back to Philadelphia to start work.

First, he blew up the photos to life size, and used them to show where the highlights and shadows live on List's face, so that he could create an accurate image. He created an acetate overlay from one of the photos, then used that to create a wooden template, which he cut with an electric jigsaw.

"You have to stay within the confines, the parameters of the skull. I also think about the heredity factors—look at pictures of the mother and father."

And, like all the rest of us, he wondered about the man and the murders. Alone in his studio, with the head of John List forming before him, he considered the popular theory about the crime. And he rejected it.

"I never felt like he killed his family because he wanted them to go to heaven. He liked to play war games, and be on the side of the Germans, and his mother always made him clean up. The murder was just a board game in real life." And then, these thoughts brought him back to the bust before him: "He was self-centered, so he would have a fear of being caught, so I turned down the ends of his mouth."

Little by little, the bust took on life. Bender loosened List's jowls, receded his hairline, and thickened his neck. List had a mastoid scar that would change the placement of his right ear as the years went by, so he pulled the ear slightly tighter in toward the head.

He cut creases into the face, and, when it came time to paint the bust, he gave List the pallor of a man who works indoors. He knew from the New Jersey police report that the real John List was the kind of guy who always dressed formally—even when mowing the lawn, the story went—so he put his John List in a suit and tie.

When it came to putting glasses on the bust, Bender picked thick-rimmed glasses because List "wanted to give the impression he was more intelligent than he really was, so people wouldn't ask questions." He walked down the street to an antiques shop he frequented. "Hey Bill, do you have any old glasses?" he asked the proprietor. "I don't sell them, but I've got a basket here of my own," was the reply.

"I was rooting through them," Frank recalled later, "and I came to these thicker-rim glasses and said, 'Can I have these? This is exactly the pair I'm looking for.' He said, 'They're on me. I hope you catch the guy.'"

■ ■ ■

The FBI, frankly, didn't think we could catch the guy.

I was giving a speech that week at Quantico, the FBI's training center in Virginia. I'd gotten to be pretty close friends with some of the guys down there, and they were ribbing me pretty hard about the List case. To be honest, some of that legendary FBI ego was showing through, too: If we, the FBI, could not catch this man, how could you, a lowly television show, catch him?

"If we never got a clue in eighteen years," one agent told me, "then he's dead."

"You're wasting your time," another said. "You are never going to catch John List. He's evaporated, like D. B. Cooper." Cooper, of course, is the man who jumped out of an airplane over southwest Washington State carrying a briefcase full of stolen money, in the same year John List killed his family. The question of whatever happened to Cooper—like the question of whether John List would ever be found—haunted lawmen and crime buffs everywhere.

As skeptical as the FBI was, the executives at Fox were more so. They really weren't crazy about our doing the case. We need captures, they said. That's how we can promote the show. You'll never catch this guy. You were doing great showing up-to-date photos of fugitives who haven't been on the run so long. Why are you suddenly becoming Mystery Theater?

I do remember one supporter—Dick Ruffino, a sheriff's deputy in Bergen County, New Jersey, who helped us out a lot when we were searching for Adam. Ruffino's one of the great cops I've met; his sheriff had given him tremendous leeway to work with the parents of missing children. As a result, Dick would travel from state to state, crossing jurisdictional lines to solve cases, something a lot of cops can't (or won't) do. So he understood what it meant to bend the rules, to think outside the box. "I heard you're doing the John List case," he called and said. "Go for it. It's great that you guys had the balls to do it."

So we pressed on, and while Frank Bender was doing his job, we were doing ours. Our crew was out shooting the footage we needed to reenact the story of John List.

The reenactment did have its moments: It was a trick, on our little budget, to recreate a 1960s street scene—we couldn't afford all the old cars and other amenities you see in big-budget TV shows when they're doing 1960s scenes. But we did our best with a few old cars (which all showed up more than once; we were hoping no one noticed), and with a bunch of kids dressed as hippies, standing in front of a VW microbus while the actors portraying the List family walked into a church.

We minimized the exterior shots, and used period clothing for the interiors. It worked, and accomplished our two purposes. One, it gave our viewers a sense of how far back we were going in time on this case; and two, by showing daughter Patty's fascination with the hippie culture, it helped set up the conflict between John List's hopes for his family's religious upbringing and his fears about the temptations of the time.

Detective Tracy, the guy who'd played ball near the List house as kid, then grew up to find himself assigned to the murders, worked hard to help us put together the reenactment. Usually we film the reenactment at the scene of the crime; sometimes that's a little spooky for the actors, but we've found it helps us get all the little details as accurate as possible. But since the List house had mysteriously burned down a year after the murders, Tracy talked a friend into letting us film at his home. For our purposes, it could pass for the List place. He also helped us populate a scene with John List going to church to teach Sunday school: "I had everyone in there," Tracy remembers. "I had my kids in there. All my friends are in the church; the Sunday school class is my son's class."

For the scene of List teaching that class, the writer and director needed to find a Bible passage for the List character to be reading. They chose: "I know that you love God, because you are willing to give him your only son. And Abraham looked up, and saw a ram caught in the bushes. And Abraham took the ram, and sacrificed it instead of his son."

■　■　■

Detective Tracy was in the *AMW* studio the night of the broadcast. So was Frank Marranca, along with the FBI agent on the case. More than fourteen million people were watching that night, May 23, 1989. The hotline was flooded with tips—340 calls in all—but nothing substantial. The leads placed List from sea to shining sea: He was seen taking the A train in Brooklyn. He owned a restaurant called The Tavern in Northfield, Minnesota. He was a research librarian at Cal State Pomona. He had had a small apartment in Denver.

We all wondered.

Could one of those tipsters actually be talking about the real John List?

Actually, one of them could.

■　■　■

Robert Wetmore, by his own admission to a newspaper reporter, had spent most of his life "on skid row and in cow camps." When he landed a job as a janitor at the Holiday Inn West in Golden, Colorado, in 1971, things started straightening out. He made the acquaintance of the short-order cook, a tall man with a black mustache named Bob Clark, who'd started working there around

Thanksgiving. Clark said he'd moved to Denver from Michigan. They spoke often, but weren't exactly what you'd call friends.

Clark was too strange for that.

"He had no zip to him in any conversation," Wetmore said. "Kind of monotone-like. You couldn't really strike up a conversation with him on any subject, because it seemed as though his mind would wander. It was like he was always preoccupied with something."

Clark was living in a small trailer in a seedy trailer park, just passing time day to day. He had taken up with the local Lutheran church, and sneered when he found out Wetmore had left the Lutherans to become a Buddhist.

There was one time that Wetmore saw Clark get excited. The two men were sharing a cup of coffee at the old Roosevelt Grill when Clark told Wetmore: "If something should happen to me, you go to the American National Bank. What I got is in your name. You go get it."

Wetmore was flabbergasted. "But what about your family?" he asked. "Don't you have family back in Michigan?"

Inexplicably, Clark's shoulders snapped back, his head jerked back, and his response was harsh, abrupt, and explosive. "There's no family!" he hissed through clenched teeth. "There's nobody!"

■   ■   ■

Just before Christmas in 1971, Bob Clark had been in his little trailer, waiting for the world to fall in on him. A story had appeared in the Denver papers about a gruesome murder in New Jersey, and it carried a picture of John List.

He recognized the picture.

He remembered when he had posed for it.

Clark knew that his mustache was no great disguise, and that it was only a matter of time before someone spotted him.

But as it turned out, Clark had nothing but time.

He kept going to work, every day, just plodding along, and though there were one or two more articles in the paper, no one ever made the connection. So he laid low, living a quiet life, reading the Bible, listening to religious broadcasts. After a while, he began to think about the murders less and less frequently; pleas for forgiveness left his daily prayers, and would come up only on the anniversary of the killings. By 1975, four years after the murders, he felt comfortable enough to move into town, and started attending Saint Paul's Lutheran Church, downtown parish. He told the pastor, Robert West, that he chose the church because it was on the bus line and he didn't have a car; but a more likely reason is that a church in a downtown setting like Saint Paul's has a lot of people beginning their lives again—from divorces, breakdowns, whatever—and they find that in a downtown church their anonymity is respected. No one asks too many questions.

Clark never unburdened himself to the minister: He was actually enjoying his life, and didn't want to do anything to disrupt it.

He started playing war games again, finding others who shared his interest in their meticulous rules and strategies. In 1976, he answered a newspaper ad placed by H & R Block, and learned to become an income tax preparer. He and a man he met started a business preparing taxes, but couldn't make a go of it, so Clark took a job as an accountant for a small distributor. He moved to a nicer apartment, and, as he had done years before, took solace in a little gardening.

In short, the man known as Bob Clark was rebuilding John List's life. Attending the Lutheran church, playing board games, gardening, working as an accountant (excelling at the mechanical, rote parts of the task, but failing once again at those business duties that require human interaction).

Clark met an attractive blonde named Delores Miller at a church singles program in 1977. She was divorced; he told her he was also divorced, that his first wife had been sickly. Their relationship blossomed; Clark even showed a little emotion. "When Bob mentioned to me he had met this woman, the first time he actually seemed a little elated," Wetmore said. "And after a period of time he said he thought quite a [bit] of her—but he wondered if he wanted to get more involved."

Things proceeded steadily but slowly. There would be no

surprise pregnancies, no hurry-up marriages. They finally got married in 1985. Delores insisted, of course, that since her family all lived in Baltimore, they had to go back east to get married.

So Bob Clark, so comfortable in his new surroundings, now found himself back in Maryland. The same state where he had gotten married thirty-four years earlier, way back when he was John Emil List.

■ ■ ■

Safely back in Colorado after the wedding, Clark's new life hit the same bumps his old one had. He couldn't seem to keep a job, not one that paid well, anyway. "She was always hollering about finances," recalled Wanda Flanery, a neighbor who became a close friend of Delores's. "She did well until she got married. She had some savings, but they used that all up while he was looking for a job."

Still, despite the financial burdens, which List was well used to, they appeared to have a relatively happy and contented life. Delores taught Sunday school; Bob again developed a reputation as the guy you never saw without a suit on.

In 1986, he slumped through a series of jobs; finally, an employment agency found him an accounting job for $24,000 a year—in Richmond, Virginia.

Bold enough to move back east, Bob went ahead and took the job on February 2, 1988—coincidentally, the same week that a new fugitive-catching show would premiere on the fledgling Fox network.

Two months later, Delores joined him. They moved into a small house in the suburb of Midlothian, which they purchased for a reported $76,000—in Delores's name. It was a pleasant light-blue house on a cul-de-sac in a planned community.

The people he worked with at Maddrea, Joyner, Kirkham & Woody in Richmond thought of him as an ultra-nice guy—"almost too nice to be true," said co-worker Les Wingfield. He got to work fifteen to twenty minutes early every day; he answered the phones before the secretaries could; he informed his supervisor when he was going to the bathroom. He spent his lunch hour alone, in his car, listening to classical music. You could talk to him about the weather, about what was on TV, about gardening—but nothing more substantial. He had one odd habit: If you asked him about his past, he would stare out the window, as though you hadn't said a word, as though you weren't even there.

The only emotion he showed was on the telephone: It was a small, cramped office, so Wingfield could overhear him on the phone, talking to Delores. "He talked to his wife on the phone every day," he said. "He'd always tell her, 'I love you.' " Clark reportedly brought Dolores flowers every day.

There was one other oddity no one noticed. Clark had listed his age as fifty-seven (actually, he was sixty-three); either way, assuming he'd worked his whole life, his first job would have dated back to sometime around the early 1950s. But his resume only went back eighteen years. It started, for some reason, in 1972.

■   ■   ■

Even though we'd already caught nearly a hundred fugitives—most of them FBI cases—the FBI still kept a wary distance from *America's Most Wanted* back then. Today, it's not unusual to get a call from an agent telling us that tips from the show seem to be strong; that the bureau is following up a certain tip in a certain city, asking us to be on the alert for more information from that city, and giving us the heads-up that a capture might be imminent.

But that wasn't the case back in 1989. So we had absolutely no idea that the FBI, after sorting through the tips from the night of the List broadcast, was taking one of the calls very, very seriously.

It was from Clark's neighbor back in Colorado, Wanda Flanery.

When Wanda saw the bust, and the story, she had no doubt. The big ears were Bob's ears, the sullen expression was Bob's expression, the facial features were Bob's features. She had her son-in-law call our hotline. Delores had given Wanda her forwarding address, and Wanda's son-in-law gave it to us: 13919 Sagewood Terrace, Midlothian, Virginia. Wanda felt bad about doing this to Delores, but she knew she had no choice.

"I didn't do this to hurt her," Wanda said. "I hope I saved her from anything he would have done to her. Since he had done this before, I figured he might do that—he might kill her. There always comes a breaking point."

On Thursday morning, June 1, 1989, eleven days after we broadcast the story, FBI special agent Terry T. O'Connor walked up to the blue house on Sagewood Terrace. Dolores came to the door. He showed her pictures of John List.

"Yes, that looks like my husband," she said. "But it couldn't be him. He wouldn't do anything like that."

At 11:10 A.M., FBI agents went to the second floor of the office building at 1506 Willow Lane, past the blue bulletin board with the white removable letters listing the offices of Maddrea, Joyner, Kirkham & Woody, and found Bob Clark. They compared the man before them with the picture in their hands. They noticed the mastoid scar behind his right ear.

He was handcuffed, taken downtown, and fingerprinted.

He pretended not to know anything.

He insisted he was Bob Clark, and always had been.

But fingerprints don't lie.

In one moment, an eighteen-year-old lie came crashing down.

We had reached back through time, and found a phantom.

■　　■　　■

Margaret Roberts was one of the founding forces of *America's Most Wanted,* and its first news director. She was squirreled away in her office, preparing for the taping of the next show. We've always had a hybrid staff—half newspaper people, half television people—because we always knew we'd need to supplement people who knew about fast-paced television production with people who knew about solid, old-fashioned journalism. And that's where Margaret had come in.

She'd been a print journalist, first in Chicago and then in Washington, D.C. By 1987, Michael Linder was in Washington too, getting a staff together to start up the show; and I was there, fighting to get some missing-child legislation passed. Margaret was preparing to write a book about lobbyists. But then fate took a turn that brought us all together. "I was struck by lightning when TV came to town in the form of Michael Linder producing this television pilot," she remembers. "Never in my life had I had any thought of being involved in television."

Just like me.

So there she was at *America's Most Wanted*, at her desk, buried under a pile of paper, when the call came in: You did it. You caught John List.

Within seconds, there was hysteria throughout the office. Everyone knew this was a huge case.

We just didn't know how huge.

As always in television, delirium quickly gave way to panic. How in hell are we going to get this story on the show?

It was an all-hands-on-deck call, as producers were dispatched to Richmond, to Colorado, to New Jersey. Our tiny team of producers madly worked the phones, looking for some station in Richmond that might grab footage of List entering or leaving the courthouse for his arraignment that afternoon.

As luck would have it, one of them was already staking out the courthouse. List, at his arraignment that afternoon—ever mindful of finances—asked for a court-appointed attorney; but the judge, noting his $2,000 monthly salary and the $1,200 he had in a bank account, refused.

The TV station got the footage of List leaving the courtroom, and the production assistants worked frantically to have the footage fed via satellite into the tape room in our building, which was right down the hall from Margaret's office.

Everyone was nervously anticipating the tape. What would John List look like after all these years? Was Bender's bust on the money, or were we going to look like fools? Had Wanda recognized List because of our work, or in spite of it?

While she was waiting for the tape, Margaret's phone rang again. It was an old friend, Brent Staples. Brent had been a jazz and blues writer for a feisty neighborhood paper, the *Chicago Journal*, which Margaret had helped start. Now he was at *The New York Times,* and he called to ask Margaret about this story that was buzzing around his newsroom. Word was around that some TV show had helped nab one of New Jersey's most notorious fugitives, and since one of his old friends worked on the show, he was calling to find out what was up. Maybe find an angle for the story.

Their phone call was interrupted, however, by a clamor from down the hall. "He looks just like the bust!" Someone was screaming. "He looks just like the bust!"

"I'm sitting there at my desk," said Margaret, "with the shrieks of these young producers, a lot of them pretty new to journalism—but their eyes weren't lying to them. It was a dead ringer, and they knew it."

The producers burst into Margaret's office, and popped the tape into a viewing machine.

It was uncanny.

It was remarkable.

It was almost a little spooky.

And it was, certainly, an angle worthy of *The New York Times.*

■　■　■

The next morning, an obscure television show was obscure no more. On the front page of *The New York Times* ran the three-column, two-deck headline:

SUSPECT IN 5 KILLINGS IN 1971
CAUGHT WITH AID OF TV SHOW

Under the headline were three pictures: John List in 1971, a photo of the bust by Frank Bender, and a shot of List as he looked after his capture.

The story spread fast. By that evening, we'd made the network news. We'd made every newspaper in the country. And suddenly, after more than a year of toiling away and getting bashed by the critics, we had something we'd never had before.

Respect.

"That one moment is what propelled the success of the show," Margaret said later. "The human face is as indelible as a fingerprint, and this is the living proof of that.

"To this day—and this is ten years later—when I say I was one of the producers who helped start *America's Most Wanted,* people instantly make the connection—'Ooh, yeah, that's the show that captured John List.' It's incredible how people connected to that story. And even as it was happening, everyone on the staff knew— this was a huge and defining moment for the show."

■   ■   ▫

After List was convicted, the judge asked him if he had anything to say. For the first time since his arrest, the world heard his voice.

List said: "I wish to inform the court that I remain truly sorry for the tragedy that occurred in 1971. I feel that due to my mental state at the time, I was unaccountable for what happened. I ask all who were affected by this for their forgiveness, understanding, and their prayers."

I was furious when I heard List's statement. Once again, it was the criminal trying to distance himself from the crime. Again, it wasn't "I'm sorry for what I did," but it was "I'm sorry for what happened," as though what happened was some tragic, random act that John List stood by and witnessed.

This is a man who killed his own mother. This is a man who killed his wife. This is a man who killed his daughter, then sat patiently contemplating these acts for hours before killing his sons.

I was so moved by what the judge said that day. He showed none of the forgiveness List was hoping for, saying of List that "his acts stand as a permanent, pathetic, and profane example of the potential of man's inhumanity to man."

When I'm asked about the case, I often talk about what the judge said next, because it shows the compassion for victims that I wish all judges possessed: "After eighteen years, five months, and twenty-two days, it is now time for the voices of Helen, Alma, Patricia, Frederick, and John F. List to rise from the grave, for it is the criminal justice system, through its trial courts, that speaks for all victims of crime. It is easy to lose focus, in criminal trials, of the victims, particularly when faced with what appears to be a frail, quiet, benign, and elderly defendant. However, this court cannot be allowed to lose sight of the bloody carnage of the victims, what was taken from them.''

Amen to that.

And as John List showed no mercy for his victims, so the judge showed no mercy for John List. He handed down five life sentences for John Emil List, one for each life he had taken.

■　■　■

And so one of the strangest and saddest cases in the annals of New Jersey history came to a close. And with it, an era dawned for *America's Most Wanted.* I really believe that we would not still be on the air were it not for the John List case—that we would not have been given the opportunity to capture another four-hundred-odd fugitives had we not gained the nation's respect by taking on its most difficult case.

Believe me, I'm a pretty down-to-earth guy, when it comes to these things. In the end, John List was just another smug, cowardly killer who thought he could get away with murder, and thanks to our viewers, he didn't.

But I know that the forces that guide our hands, sometimes, are larger and greater than we can know. The sheer sadness of this case propelled us to try something we'd never tried before, and perhaps the spirit of the victims guided our hand as well. We were rewarded for our efforts, and I'm eternally grateful for that.

Soon, the letters started pouring in. In Westfield, New Jersey, it was like the Kennedy assassination—everyone seemed to know where they were when they first heard about the murder. Friends of the family, people whose taxes had been done by John List—they'd all had some connection to the case, they all felt it weighing on them all these years.

The letter that touched me the most came from a man who said he had been the best friend of Frederick List, the youngest of the List children. He was now married, with children of his own, but said he'd never gotten over the death of his best childhood friend. "I've visited my friend's grave every year for the last eighteen years," he wrote me. "I always prayed for justice for him. Now, he has that justice. You have found justice for all the List family, from beyond the grave. The heartache I have carried all these years, I can now put to rest."

And to all those who'd said to me, why are you bothering with this case? Who cares about an eighteen-year-old murder?—to them I could say, I have my answer.

■   ■   ■

And as for List himself?

He will be in jail until he dies, which is exactly where he belongs.

I don't believe that John List murdered his family for any sort of righteous reason.

I do believe that his children, his wife, his mother are in heaven, looking down.

Knowing that he was finally brought to justice.

Perhaps we have allowed them, in some sense, to rest in peace.

That would be the greatest reward of all.

CHAPTER THREE

The Strange Case of the Green Parrot

When you think of the probability of what happened, you probably have a better chance of winning the Utah lottery—and we don't have a lottery.

—CHRIS HALE, DISPATCHER,

SALT LAKE CITY POLICE DEPARTMENT

A lot of the time, manhunting is mostly a matter of paying attention to details. For example, we would never have caught William Joseph Moore, wanted for an attempted murder in Naperville, Illinois, if someone on our hotline hadn't done his homework that night.

Moore, we knew from our research, was a darts freak. The night we aired his case, we got a couple of calls from a bar in Aberdeen, Maryland, saying they thought one of their regulars was the guy they saw on our program. Not a particularly specific call, and not one that we'd pull out of the pile of two hundred tips and be rushing to call the FBI at eleven o'clock on a Friday night about—until the caller mentioned, "Oh, yeah, he's in here all the time; this is a darts bar, and he's the local darts champion." At that, we had the local authorities on the move and, before William Moore hit his next bull's-eye, we hit ours.

So as I say, most of the time, manhunting is a matter of doing your homework, paying attention to the little details, and being patient.

Then again, sometimes it's just a case of getting lucky.

In what the folks in our office came to know as The Case of the Green Parrot (they liked that, because it sounded so much like the title of a Sherlock Holmes novel), we got as lucky as we've ever gotten in our lives. The resolution of this case was so outlandish, so preposterous, so filled with coincidences, and ultimately so utterly unbelievable, that to this day people are still asking me, did it really happen the way we said it did?

And I tell them, yes, it did.

With one exception:

We left out a lot of stuff.

Because we figured, if we told this whole story on air, nobody would believe it.

The *America's Most Wanted* episode of March 19, 1993, had two new stories in it; the rest of the show consisted of updates of previous cases. These were not reruns per se, but cases in which the fugitive hadn't been caught, and the police had asked us to air them again and include all the new information we'd gathered since the first airing. Often we've caught someone on the fourth or fifth showing.

The two new cases were both ones I cared a lot about. I'll be honest: There are some cases we air that I don't really get overly excited about. Bank robbers are bad people who need to be caught, and there's always a danger that they're going to hurt someone— but they're not on the top of my list. The U.S. Marshals get upset with us all the time because a lot of their fugitives are drug dealers who've offed other drug dealers; we don't do a lot of those stories, because we just don't think our audience is going to have a lot of sympathy for the victim.

But there are two kinds of cases that hit me in the gut. As I've mentioned before, I care most about the cases in which young children are the victims. These are the ones I get most intimately involved in. I also find myself very moved by the cases in which a young adult is killed as the result of some senseless act. I always feel for the parents in these cases, especially when I hear them speak about the potential their child showed, the life he or she could have lived.

Both of those kinds of cases were represented in the new material for that night's show, so I was pretty pumped up when we went to taping. I remember arguing with Lance Heflin, the executive producer, about why we weren't leading with those cases. Lance liked to put the new stuff down near the end of the program, with lots of "teases" before the commercial breaks to let viewers know they were coming—the idea being to entice the viewers to stick around longer. I always want to see the new cases right up at the top of the show—get on the air and get down to business. But those are Lance's decisions, and he kept the order of the show the way it was.

So it was about nine-thirty that night when the two new cases aired: the case of Adam Blue Galli, out of Salt Lake City, and the case of Kenneth Lovci, out of Austin, Texas. The cases had nothing whatsoever to do with each other.

Not yet, anyway.

■　■　■

The main case, the one with the big reenactment, was the one involving the fugitive Adam Blue Galli. Galli was an unusual character for us: With the gaunt, haunted good looks of a generation-X rock star, his Andy Warhol mop of light blond hair, and his high level of education and intelligence, he was something of a heartthrob around Salt Lake City, Utah. But it was apparently neither music nor women that drove Galli's train. His passion was for what he saw as the great noble professions of old: The highwaymen, the rounders, the robber barons of great literature all created for him an irresistible image. It was a fantasy he was intelligent enough to conceive of and embroider upon—and dumb enough to try to live out.

And so he became a thief.

Adam, twenty-four, was joined in his endeavors by his brother Aaron, older by a couple of years; their cousin Christopher, just seventeen; and Christopher's brother Nathan, about to turn twenty. According to police reports, they liked to hang out in, and occasionally rob, bookstores and coffee shops. They usually left one person outside—usually Christopher, the youngest—to misdirect the police, should they arrive.

Adam's hero was Jesse James; and just as Jesse had his gang, so, at the ripe old age of twenty-four, did Adam Blue Galli.

"Adam would have done a lot better in the Middle Ages or in the Old West than he does right now," Ray Dalling, the lead investigator on the case for the Salt Lake City police department, told us. "His view of himself is that he is a highwayman and a robber baron and a rogue and a scoundrel who should be taking from the rich and giving to the poor—only in this case, the poor is himself."

As you can imagine, I didn't have a lot of patience with a bunch of preppie bums who had the intelligence and the resources to do something with their lives, but not the moral compass to steer them away from the childish notion of playing cops and robbers with real cops. They were dubbed The Preppie Bandits, and in their wigs and hats were responsible for more than two dozen robberies in just a few months. They thought of themselves as the elite of the criminal world, the kind of worthy opponent that Sherlock Holmes would match wits with.

"They were smart kids," said Chuck Oliver, also with the Salt Lake P.D. "They were pretty creative, outgoing, but still, you could feel that kind of sinister arrogance, almost like they thought they were better than you."

While the Preppie Bandits were doing their thing, another young man in Salt Lake City, Merritt Riordian, was doing his. Merritt loved the outdoors, and had a mountain bike that took him everywhere around the area's stunning, rugged landscape. The family comedian, he was also the family conscience: His mother spoke to us with pride about how, as an aspiring actor, he still took time to teach dance to the handicapped.

But you gotta make ends meet—so Merritt took a job as the chef at a nice fern bar downtown filled with dark woodwork, green lamps, and pool tables, a yuppie hangout called the Green Parrot. It was a friendly, *Cheers*-like neighborhood tavern.

But on May 17, 1992, the Green Parrot became the focus of someone else's career plans.

That day, Adam and Aaron targeted it for their next hit.

About an hour before closing, Adam and Aaron slipped into the Green Parrot, and made their way down to the basement. Their plan was to wait until the manager came down to deposit the evening's take in the safe. Instead, they were surprised by the chef, Merritt Riordian, coming off his shift, walking in to get his mountain bike from the basement. A struggle ensued.

Merritt Riordian was shot.

The brothers fled.

"He was the son that said to me, 'Mom, I'll take care of you when you're old,'" his mother, Ann Riordian, told us. "I remember seeing him in the hospital, and touching him, and telling him good-bye. I was so sorry, because he was so curious about life. I think he would have liked to have seen what the end of his story would be, you know, as an older man.

"But that won't happen for him."

■   ■   ■

The gang continued its robbing ways. Eventually, the Salt Lake cops, Dalling, the lead investigator, and Oliver, the homicide cop, caught up with them. Christopher turned state's evidence, and Aaron was convicted of the murder—but Christopher later recanted, and the state decided not to retry Aaron on the murder charge. He served his time for the burglary. Christopher and Nathan also spent a couple of years in the stir on robbery charges; all three were model prisoners, and all three were paroled.

Adam Galli—who would also be charged with robbery, not with murder—managed to flee. He made it all the way to Seattle before he was arrested outside a local coffeehouse. Police found a notebook he'd been using as a journal. It contained this passage, reflecting on the Preppie Bandit gang:

> We made ourselves in the images of old legends and glories of daring rogues and brigands, and asked for a short life and a merry one. And we came to be a terror in the land. Many fair kinsmen I had in that coven, robber barons and highwaymen we called ourselves. And now the battle has swept over and my life is not ended in glory, but rather it is poisoned and broken.

Oh, gimme a break. You want to know how poisoned and broken this poor lost soul was? Galli's family put up their cars and houses to get him out on bail, and to repay their kindness, he disappeared, skipping off into his fantasyland again.

An FBI bulletin went out—and landed in the offices of *America's Most Wanted.*

■ ■ ■

So the first big case we were airing on the night of March 19, 1993, was the case of Adam Blue Galli. The folks at the Green Parrot had helped us do the reenactment; we filmed it right at the bar, using many of their employees and regulars as extras. The restaurant was extremely helpful and enthusiastic—everyone wanted to see Galli brought back to Salt Lake City.

The second big new case—which would air right after the Galli case—was one that I'd been pushing to get on the air. The case of accused child molester Ken Lovci.

We rarely aired child-molestation cases in the early days of the show—we weren't sure how the public would react to such a touchy subject—but once we opened that door, and aired a few particularly moving cases, it was like a landslide. People despise men who hurt children; every cop wanted to get one of his molester cases on the show, and viewers wanted to see them caught. A torrent of cases came flooding down on us, and we were accepting as many as possible. Paul Sparrow, one of the producers of the show at the time, came up with the idea of doing a package of three quick forty-five-second blurbs on these guys each week, as a way of getting their faces on the air and clearing out the backlog. "Great—it's like a roll call of rodents," somebody said in a meeting, and the name stuck: Each week, on the show format, we'd include a Rodent Roundup (I always thought we should use that name on the air, but I got outvoted). By the time the experiment had run its course, we had taken twenty-one accused molesters off the streets—one of my proudest accomplishments at *America's Most Wanted.*

The case of Kenneth Lovci was one of those very moving cases that started the landslide. Lovci was a man who liked to project a tough-guy, Marlboro Man image. He was the manager of a country-and-western bar in Austin called the Back 40, which was frequented by the law enforcement community. That meant a lot to Lovci, because, just like Adam Galli, he had images of himself in a grand cops-and-robbers game—but in Lovci's case, he didn't want to be a robber. He wanted to be a cop. He became a reserve officer in Rollingwood, Texas, then later managed to snare a police job in Rockdale, seventy miles away.

Though married, Lovci befriended a woman with a ten-year-old boy, and would go to their house frequently. While the mother was in the kitchen, Lovci would be with her son, Michael, in the next room, not eight feet away.

Playing Nintendo.

And putting his hands down the boy's pants.

Michael kept his secret until he saw a film at school with an important message: It's okay to tell if someone is touching you improperly. He connected with the little boy in the film, went home, and told his mother about Officer Lovci. She immediately called the police, who issued a warrant on the charge of indecency to a child.

Lovci bolted, leaving behind a young boy haunted by the memory of him. "I see his eyes," little Michael would say later. "And sometimes in grocery stores I see his eyes a whole lot. Like, I just look, sometimes I look in the comics aisle, the toy aisle. And like, at the end of the aisle, I think I see his eyes. He just stares at me, like, 'I'm gonna get you.' And then I run to my mom."

By coincidence, the same night Michael had seen the film at school, he had also watched *America's Most Wanted* with his mom, and seen a case of three girls who had come forward to catch their molester.

"While we were watching it Michael turned to me and he indicated that they were just like he was, that they had been molested too," his mother said. When Lovci disappeared, Michael told her he "would like very much to be able to tell *Most Wanted* what had happened to him, so that Ken could be caught, because nobody knew where Ken was either. It was just real important to him, because he felt their pain."

The family and the cops on the case contacted us, and we put together the story. On the night of March 19, 1993, the case of Ken Lovci was set to go on the air.

Right after the case of Adam Blue Galli.

■　■　■

Show time.

At the Green Parrot, a large crowd of employees and regulars gathered to watch *America's Most Wanted*. The new night chef, the one working the shift that Merritt Riordian had worked the night he was killed, was busy in the kitchen trying to keep up with the orders.

Everyone else was crowded around the TV. It was the middle of the NCAA finals, and on a normal night, there's not a chance that they'd have the TV tuned to *America's Most Wanted*. But this night, a compromise was reached: One TV carried the game, the other carried our program.

Back at our studios in Washington, D.C., Detective Ray Dalling was ready to take calls on the Galli case, along with Special Agent Todd Carlile of the Salt Lake City FBI.

We had wanted Travis County to send Detective Mark Sawa, the lead investigator on the Lovci case, as well—but he was sick as a dog with the stomach flu. He was pissed off that he'd missed out on his trip to Washington—and even more upset that he wasn't going to get to work the phones on Lovci.

But Sharon Greene, the hotline chief, called him at home, and told him she'd keep him up on everything that was going on—and that she'd personally keep an eye on the Lovci tips for him.

Sharon had a bunch of new staffers on duty that night—all moonlighting from their day jobs at the Department of Justice. They looked like a Dockers commercial: young, good-looking, and extremely enthusiastic.

The mood at the Green Parrot was mixed: The excitement of everyone seeing themselves on television was tempered greatly by the sad events that had led them there. They watched the Adam Galli piece, then flipped the TV back to the NCAA tournament.

Bartender John Reseska answered the phone when it started ringing. It was Mindy Provstgard, an off-duty waitress.

Are you watching *America's Most Wanted?* she asked.

No, our piece is over, John said.

Turn it back on, said Mindy.

Turn it back on.

So he did.

And there, on the same show that had just profiled the death of the former chef of the Green Parrot, was the story of an accused child molester.

And they flashed the accused child molester's picture on the screen.

And it looked exactly like . . .

No. It couldn't be.

But . . . it was.

Ken Lovci, the accused child molester wanted out of Texas.

Now working as the *new* chef at the Green Parrot.

■ ■ ■

"I kind of looked behind me," said Reseska, "and sure enough, he was standing right back at our double doors. He must have had bad eyesight or something, because he didn't notice what was on the TV."

One by one, the patrons sitting around the bar got that look on their faces—that slack-jawed, I-can't-believe-it expression. Lovci, fortuitously, had walked back into the kitchen.

And John, along with another employee, and at least one patron, raced to various phones, to call *America's Most Wanted*.

What followed, Sharon Greene remembers, was like an Abbott and Costello routine:

"This is the Green Parrot. Our chef is the child molester out of Texas."

"No, the chef of the Green Parrot is the victim in the Adam Galli case. Ken Lovci is the child molester out of Texas."

"I'm telling you, Ken Lovci is in the Green Parrot."

"No, Adam Galli was in *The Green Parrot*. Ken Lovci was in the piece after that."

Sharon was sure that the callers were just confused. After all, they were calling from a bar; good chance they were drunk. (One of the cops on the case said later, "We didn't pay any attention. We just figured everyone was buttered.")

To make matters worse, the initial tips were mostly all taken by the new kids on the hotline—the moonlighters from the Department of Justice. They were jumping up and down about the calls, but Sharon shrugged it off as first-night enthusiasm.

Mindy Provstgard, the off-duty waitress who had called the bar, was one of the callers to the hotline. "Look, I know you're not going to believe me," she said. "But I work down at the Green Parrot, and the fugitive Ken Lovci works there as well."

She was right.

Nobody believed her.

The same kinds of calls were coming in to the Salt Lake City P.D., with the same result. "I thought that the people at the Green Parrot, because they had just watched the segment on Adam Galli, were maybe a little overzealous in wanting to have people arrested," said Chris Hale, dispatcher at Salt Lake P.D.

But in this midst of all the chaos, something began to dawn on Sharon Greene.

Oh my God, she thought.

What if they're right?

And in Salt Lake City, Chris Hale was getting the same feeling.

"As the call went on, I became aware that two of the people in the office with me were also on a phone call, talking to someone at the Green Parrot, reporting the same thing. I went ahead and entered that they had a Ken Norman Lovci at the Green Parrot. I asked the person on the phone if he happened to know his birthday, and apparently he was one of the employers, and he asked someone else in the room for the employment records. So he gave me the birth date. I ran a computer check—and came back with a $10,000 hit for this gentleman out of Texas."

So Chris decided that, discretion being the better part of valor, he had better scramble someone down to the Green Parrot to sort this all out.

When Sharon called Chris, they shared their disbelief—and their anticipation. "We've received the same calls you've received," Chris said. "We're dispatching cars at this time."

Scott Folsom, the public information officer at the Salt Lake City P.D., had helped get the Adam Galli case on the air. He was out on another call when he heard, over the radio, that cars were being dispatched to the Green Parrot on a wanted fugitive.

"I thought that there had been a terrible communication mistake. I thought they'd screwed it up," said Folsom. Or worse: He realized that this was exactly the kind of stunt Galli's cohorts would pull, to confuse the situation and help distract police from any legitimate Galli tips.

But back at the Green Parrot, they knew they hadn't made a mistake.

They knew they had Ken Lovci.

The question was, how long could they keep him in the bar—and in the dark?

So far, he hadn't caught on to the fact that half the bar was trying to turn him in (and the other half of the bar had no idea what was going on). Everyone was afraid that someone was going to say something wrong. And at first, all the waiters and waitresses were afraid to walk back into the kitchen and take their food orders from one of America's most wanted.

"Come on! Come pick up your orders! I have two cheeseburgers here! Whose chicken fingers are these?" Lovci was shouting, and the waitresses were whispering to each other, "I'm not going back there. You go back there."

Somehow, everyone summoned the courage to try to act normally in the face of this incredible situation.

But then another problem arose.

Because the police had still not arrived.

And the chef, still blissfully unaware, was taking off his apron, and getting ready to go home for the night.

"I thought he was gonna skate right outta here," said Reseska. "We found lots of extra things for him to do. Every time someone ran back for food, they kept checking him out, that he was still there. Then we said we'd buy him a beer—just to keep him around even longer. After that, he walked into the kitchen—and the police were right behind him."

The cops—finally—had arrived. One of them, officer Lon Halterman, approached Lovci in the kitchen. Lovci turned around—and his eyes bugged out.

"You could see it—for a second he thought about running," said Halterman. Halterman patted him for weapons, and then asked him for ID.

Lovci had ID, all right.

He was still carrying his reserve officer's ID card from Rollingwood, Texas.

In Washington, the silence was driving Sharon Greene crazy. She'd phoned in her tips to Salt Lake City, she knew they had scrambled officers to the Green Parrot—then, nothing.

She spotted Ray Dalling across the room—separate from all the ruckus, Ray was quietly working tips on Adam Galli. But he was also the best source of info on the Salt Lake City P.D.

"Ray! Ray!" she barked, hitting his arm. "You gotta call your office! You gotta find out what's going on!"

Ray made the call—and told Sharon that, indeed, it was all true. The scene of the killing of the old Green Parrot chef had just become the scene of the arrest of the new Green Parrot chef, the direct result of two consecutive segments on *America's Most Wanted*.

There were high fives and whoops throughout the studio. "Oh

my God! Capture! Capture!" Sharon shouted. "Ken Lovci is in custody! He took the place of Adam Galli's victim! Unbelievable!"

At the back door of the Green Parrot, Ken Lovci's attitude was somewhat more subdued.

Having established his identity, the cops loaded Lovci into the car. He realized the enormous coincidence that had led to his arrest, and he wasn't happy about it.

"Oh, man," he said, over and over again. "Oh, man. What are the chances of that happening?"

"You're an unlucky guy," Halterman told him. "But you'll have fifteen to twenty years to figure it all out."

■   ■   ■

Actually, it would be considerably less.

Lovci was convicted on the charges, but when his case came up for sentencing, he begged for mercy—telling the jury that as an ex-cop, he would be killed in jail. They bought it, and gave him ten years probation.

The good news is that he has to check in as a sex offender wherever he goes, he has to get counseling—which he pays for himself—and, most important, as a condition of his parole, he may not be alone with any child. It was not as tough a sentence as I'd like to have seen, but at least he was caught, and, we can hope, he won't harm another child.

But as we sorted this all out, there was one thing missing.

Where the hell was Adam Blue Galli?

And the answer to that, quite fittingly, would hold one more coincidence, and one more great irony.

■   ■   ■

Special Agent Carlile of the FBI in Salt Lake City estimates that, over the years, the FBI has probably tracked down more than three hundred leads on Galli from *America's Most Wanted*—leads from all over the world. But the tip that sealed Galli's fate came not from a high-tech electronic manhunt, but an old-fashioned wanted poster, the kind that used to carry the visage of Galli's hero, Jesse James.

The anonymous tip led the FBI to the little Minnesota town of Northfield, where Galli was working at a cabinet shop. He put up a struggle—but was subdued and arrested.

Chuck Oliver went to pick up Galli, and brought him back to Salt Lake City to face robbery charges. He went alone, because a very disappointed Ray Dalling had to stay home and testify at a trial—even though he was dying to go pick up Galli himself.

"Number one, I've been chasing this guy for years," Dalling said.

"Number two, it's Northfield, Minnesota."

He couldn't get over the coincidence.

Because Northfield, Minnesota, was the town where the James gang had been captured.

Adam Galli was living a quiet life in Northfield as Joe Citizen— mild-mannered and polite if a bit effete and affected—in an apartment with a small, sunlit den fitted with high, open windows, looking out onto the square where his hero went down.

"Northfield, Minnesota," Dalling moaned later. "Where the Jameses and Youngers had their last shoot-out. And I didn't get to go. Chuck brought me a T-shirt, though."

It was one of two T-shirts that would commemorate this case.

The other came from the Green Parrot.

When the dust had settled, the folks at the restaurant printed up some T-shirts of their own.

On the front is the logo of the Green Parrot.

On the back is inscribed:

"America's Most Wanted—
Catch of the Day."

CHAPTER FOUR

Breaking Silence

And ye shall know the truth, and the truth shall make you free.
—JOHN 1:5

It takes two to speak the truth—one to speak and another to hear.
—HENRY DAVID THOREAU

Sharon Marlene Stone has a dream. She has it almost every night. In it, there is a field of daisies. She is wearing a pink dress, running through the daisies. Her father is there, running with her, and smiling. She is warm, she is not hungry. Her father loves her, the way a father should love a child, with warmth and caring and tenderness.

In this dream there is no sex.

■   ■   ■

Sharon Marlene Stone has a memory. It is her first memory. She is five years old. Her father has taken her little sister, just a baby, out of her crib, and thrown her across the room. The baby has landed in a corner, her head flopped down onto her chest. Sharon's older sister has picked up the baby and is cradling her. Her father has gone berserk. He is ripping his clothes off with a knife. He is stomping on a pile of laundry on the ground, stomping and stomping. From the pile of laundry comes a voice: "Stop, Gary, stop!" But he will not stop.

Sharon realizes that this is not a pile of laundry.

This is her mother.

■   ■   ■

Sometimes Garrett Stone would try to cajole his daughter into performing sexual acts on him. "I have traveled on another plane of life," he would tell the eleven-year-old. "I know all the secrets of life. I can't tell you about it, because it would be dangerous for you, and dangerous for me." He would relent, after a while, and say, if you will do this thing to me, I will tell you the secrets.

Sharon would say no, and Garrett Stone would revert to a more common method of persuasion. He would strip his daughter naked and bang her head against the wall until she relented.

■   ■   ■

How do you go on?

How do you deal with stories like these?

Why, after ten years, would anyone continue to work as a cop, or a counselor, or a social worker, or an FBI agent, or a producer on a crime TV show, when you have to deal with stories like these, day in, day out?

That's one of the questions I hear a lot.

The other one is more important, and more difficult.

That question is: How does anyone survive a childhood like this?

How do people come out anything but shattered and torn and bitter? How do they live their lives in anything but perpetual pain and anger?

I will tell you the answer to both questions.

The answer is in this story, the story of three girls: Eve Stone, who is now twenty-eight; her sister whom we will call Irene, who is now thirty; and especially their sister Sharon, who is now thirty-one.

This is their true story.

It is, I will warn you, a difficult story. I will not tell you anywhere near the worst of what they went through, and still, you will find it a difficult story.

It is also, for me, one of the most uplifting stories we have ever dealt with. It is uplifting because of one remarkable young woman.

She taught me more about survival, and about the healing power of the truth, than any other victim I have met.

■   ■   ■

In 1963, an interesting little feature story appeared on page twenty-nine of the *National Enquirer,* under the headline: Dad Wins Battle to Keep His Wife & 5 Kids in Their Home—a Freezing Motorboat."

It told the tale of a bearded artist and his wife and five little children, living the simple life on a motorboat on the frozen Grand River in Fairport Harbor, Ohio. The artist told about how he used to be a used car salesman, but decided to drop out of the rat race and change to a simpler existence aboard the motorboat. He sold paintings to keep them in food; they had no heat or light bills because they had no heat or light. After a howling snowstorm, some neighbors, concerned for the children's welfare, alerted authorities, and welfare agents ordered the family to move out. But the artist refused, and townspeople rallied behind them, an early example of citizens railing against "big government." The case against the artist was dropped, and hailed as a victory for the little guy. "It's true that we don't have much money," the artist was quoted as saying, "but we don't want much. That would ruin our whole way of life. Everybody today is out after the almighty dollar. Can't they see how foolish that is? Sometimes, we spend the whole night singing songs—just the family together. Who could buy that?

"Besides," the artist said, "singing keeps us warm."

The head of this happy, warm family was Garrett Stone. He would later be named one of the Top 100 Artists in the United States.

■   ■   ■

The state of Ohio did not give up easily on Garrett Stone, but Garrett Stone gave up easily on Ohio. In 1967, probably spurred by ongoing tussles with the state, Garrett Stone, along with his wife, Elizabeth, and their children, took off on a cross-country meander. They would eventually spend time in all forty-eight contiguous states. There were six children when the trip started; three days later, child number seven was born, little Sharon. There would be two more girls in the next three years, Irene and Eve.

Anyone who's ever traveled with seven kids in a motor home can imagine how wild and noisy it can get—but not in this trailer. The children were so afraid of Garrett that sometimes they drove for hours in total silence, everyone, including Elizabeth, afraid of attracting his attention and his ire.

They were ridiculously well behaved; when the family stopped to do laundry, the kids would all help, or stand quietly, not talking to anyone. There was no giggling, no asking for a nickel for the gum-ball machine. Just silence and obedience.

Once, entering a gas station, the trailer tipped over; a fire started, and Irene, then a newborn, was burned severely; one of her brothers' heads was severely cut; the children were all screaming. But when Garrett screamed, "Shut up!" just once, loud, there was total silence, and eight children sat, burned and bleeding, quietly and politely, until the ambulances arrived.

In short, they lived in total fear of Garrett Stone.

And with good reason.

When they'd stop and settle in a town for a while, Elizabeth would go get a job, and Garrett would stay home with the children, while working on his paintings and sculpture. He was enormously controlling of his wife's every movement, every action, almost every thought. He was not a big man—five-feet-eight, 190 pounds—but he was extremely imposing, and in the eyes of his family he was a huge, hulking force. He was so imposing that once, when visiting one of the kids' teachers, he came up behind her unexpectedly; when she turned to see him, she was so cowed that she actually gasped and fell backward across her desk—such was the power of his presence.

Elizabeth was a few inches shorter, a bit chunky, with dull brown hair usually cut plainly and cropped tight against her head. She wore baggy Salvation Army clothes, no makeup or nail polish. When she came home from work, she would sit on a couch, wrapped in a blanket because Garrett insisted on keeping the house so cold. If he told her to get up, she would; if he told her to go to the bathroom, she did. She loved to sing, but was not allowed to; she enjoyed crocheting, but was not allowed to do this either; so she sat, staring into space.

Garrett kept the same control over his children, never allowing them out of his sight. They were not allowed to giggle, nor were they allowed to cry. Sharon, then a skinny preteen with a tentative smile and impossibly light hair, remembers that he had a thousand rules, and his enforcement of them was swift and severe.

"It wasn't a spanking," said Sharon. "It wasn't anything like that. He beat you. And he beat you senseless. And that's why we were so controlled."

The oldest girl, Ruth, tried to spur her mother to action—any action—but with little success. Elizabeth did actually leave Garrett once, taking the kids with her, but soon the unhappy family was back together. Ruth, disgusted, left home as soon as she could, followed in quick succession by the other older kids. By 1978, there were only four children at home; one older brother, who asked that we keep his name out of this story, along with Sharon, then eleven, Irene, ten, and Eve, eight.

They moved into some low-income housing near Pittsfield, Massachusetts. It seemed like Garrett's control was becoming even more fanatical. He had the children's daily life regimented down to the minute. He knew everything they were going to do, from the time they got up until the time they went to bed.

It started at five in the morning; he would go for a paper, and whoever's turn it was to make breakfast—one of the girls—had better get it done quickly. It would take twenty-five minutes for him to return with the paper, and breakfast was to be done when he came through the door. After breakfast they all had their chores, which had to be done before their specified times for leaving for the bus. He timed how long it would take to walk to the bus stop, and they all had to leave the house exactly that many minutes before the bus was due, so that they would have no time just hanging around the bus stop. After school—they all had to be home by a quarter to three, or suffer a beating—they would do homework until precisely five o'clock. Even if they had no homework, they would pretend they did, lest they be accused of lying.

And so it went, through the day, no laughing allowed, no friends allowed, only Garrett's rules, until their specified bedtimes.

The only breaks in the schedule were for Garrett's rages, and the inevitable beatings that followed. They could be set off by anything, they could be set off by nothing.

And Elizabeth, terrified into submission, would do nothing to protect her children.

"You always knew when the beatings were going to happen," Sharon remembers. "You felt like, 'Oh, God, what can I do? Where can I go? Where can I hide? He's going to come after me next.' Because usually when he hit somebody he went through the whole family. And you were like, 'Should I run? Should I stay? Where can I go?' You grab a sister, you grab somebody else, there's no mother to run to, she's not there for you, and she never was there for you."

"If he would get mad and start breaking things," her sister Irene remembers, "she would sometimes follow along and clean up, which made things worse. Then instead of breaking dishes he would hit her. So usually, she just sat there and did nothing."

There was rarely any affection or normal interaction between husband and wife. Occasionally, when he'd put on a little weight, she'd call him by a pet nickname—Budge—but it was rare that she showed any spunk at all. The control he had over his wife was remarkable. The girls believe he was beating and raping her regularly. "You could hear him raping her when you went to sleep," Sharon said. "You'd hear, 'Stop, Gary, stop!' She came to where we were sleeping and she was completely naked and bleeding from her vagina."

But as severe as the beatings were, as complete as Garrett Stone's psychological and physical control were over his family, as horridly as they lived—without friends, without laughter, without any of the things that make a child a child—Sharon and Irene had not experienced the worst of it.

The worst of it was still to come.

■　■　■

Sharon Marlene Stone has a memory. She is eleven years old, in the sixth grade. It is late at night, maybe it is two o'clock in the morning. It is dark, and cold, and she is awakened from a sound sleep by a pair of big, powerful hands, hands she has felt before, when they struck her with powerful blows, but now the hands are tugging her, taking her into another room. For some reason her mother is not in the house. Her father has his pants down. He asks Sharon to play with his dolly. She knows what he is referring to.

"He did things, and I knew it was wrong, and I was crying," she said. "I didn't know how things were supposed to be at home, nobody ever told me, but I know that your daddy doesn't touch you like that."

She remembers him pulling up her nightgown. She remembers him forcing her legs apart, and kneeling in front of her. The room is dark, but there is a little light coming from the hallway. She stares into the light, and lets her mind drift out of this room. She does not remember anything else about that night.

She would have clearer memories of the nights that followed.

■　■　■

Soon, the abuse became more regular, more pronounced, more obscene. "I remember him having me naked on his lap, and trying to rape me. I clenched my teeth when he tried to stick his tongue in my mouth. I just closed my eyes and went someplace else. That would make him angry, because I was in control. He would just throw me off his lap." When she denied him, he would beat her, or lock her in a closet. Eventually, the beatings were so severe that Sharon learned never to say no.

And so, at the tender age of eleven, Sharon Stone began to regularly submit to sexual acts with her father.

While the physical abuse was public, the sexual abuse was always quite private. He would send the other girls away on an errand, or out to the garage, and then would take Sharon into his private studio, or into another room.

The family moved several more times, finally landing in a small three-bedroom house at 745 Crystal Lake Park in the rural Bondsville section of Palmer, Massachusetts.

Garrett took two of the rooms, which were adjoining, for his studio; the third bedroom was his and Elizabeth's. He ordered the three girls to remove the insulation from the floor of the attic crawl space, to create an area where they could sleep in their sleeping bags. They still were allowed no friends, no laughing, no time out of Garrett Stone's control.

Sometimes, the sexual abuse would stop for a week or so, and then it would begin again. Sometimes, Garrett would just force Sharon into sex; sometimes he would bargain with her, telling her that if she submitted, he would leave her sisters alone.

She believed this.

She believed these terrible things were happening only to her.

She was wrong.

■　■　■

Sharon was the first one to leave for school in the mornings. Irene and Eve would be alone in the house with their father for a time after that.

"It was too easy for him then," Irene remembers. "He would take you into another room. Every day, when we lived in Bondsville, he would bring me into another room before school every day."

Nor was Eve, the baby, spared. She remembers being made to watch movies that made the girls uncomfortable—*Last House on the Left,* she remembers, is one in which a woman is raped: "Don't close your eyes, or he'll take you again," the older sisters explained. It was almost like the psychological torture used in wartime to break a soldier's resolve: "He would lock you in the basement with no lights on and tell you this killer dog was buried in the basement. He had an old fire engine down there and we couldn't come up until we banged on a specific part of it."

And then, when he had exerted the proper control over her, he began to sexually abuse Eve as well. In Eve's mind, the mantra formed: Save me! Save me! But it was a silent scream. She could not tell anyone of her pain.

Garrett would switch off, one girl one week, one girl the next. None was aware of the other's torture.

Until one night in the loft.

■   ■   ■

No one remembers who started the conversation. It was all in whispers, three girls, sharing the same terrible secret, finally letting it out, in hushed fits and starts: He did this to you? When? Where? He did what? He did this to me. And this. Why didn't you tell me? He warned me not to. He said he would kill me if I told. I'm your older sister, I should have protected you! What could you have done? I thought it was only me. So did I! Me too! What should we do? I hate it when he does this. I want him to stop. What can we do? Does Mother know? I don't think she knows. What can we do? What can we do?

■   ■   ■

Christmas was a particularly bad time. The girls made all their own Christmas presents, and so would sometimes go off in separate rooms, working for hours on their gifts, with no one else around.

This gave Garrett an opportunity to get each of them alone.

Merry Christmas.

■   ■   ■

The whispers continued, night after night in the cramped little loft, until they led to the inevitable conclusion.

We have to tell Mother.

Another Christmas was nearing, and Sharon and Irene were in the room set aside for craft work, watching their mother at the sewing machine. It took an enormous amount of courage to go against the man who had controlled their every action, to do the thing he told them never to do.

To speak.

It is a testament to the unyielding strength of the human spirit that they could speak at all.

But speak they did.

"I told her everything," Sharon remembers. "About the sex that was happening."

Eve was not there. But the words she said to herself, every day, floated silently above the room: Save me! Save me! Save me! But now the silence had been broken, and the girls poured out their hearts, hoping that the woman who had brought them onto this earth would save them from the horror they had found there.

Elizabeth sat quietly at the sewing machine, listening to her children tell her that her husband regularly forced each of them to have sex with him, and their baby sister too.

And this was her response:

"Don't tell Ruth."

Ruth, the oldest child, the first one to leave, would certainly break up the family if she knew, Elizabeth reasoned.

And under all conditions, we must keep the family together.

After a moment, Elizabeth continued. "He gets like that sometimes," she told them. "Try to stick together. Try to keep all three in the room together. Don't let yourself be alone in the room with him.

"It will take care of itself."

And she turned her back and went back to her sewing.

And then, in that moment, all hope was gone.

■　　■　　■

Listen to Irene: "My father used threats to make you not tell anybody what was going on, or to make us do things we didn't want to do. I used to tell him that I would run away and tell people. He told me he would kill me if I did that. After a while he didn't have to tell me much. He'd tied me up, and it wasn't pleasant, and I'd seen people get hit, so he just would have to say he would hurt me, and that would be enough, because I knew he could.

"When I was younger, I thought our family life was normal, that this was the way it was supposed to be. But as I got older, I knew something was wrong, that this just wasn't right. But there was nothing you could do."

■　■　■

Listen to Eve: "He'd use anything big—cast-iron pans, broom handles—and hit you until you passed out. I always urinated myself. At the end I urinated myself when he walked by.

"He would make us watch movies like *The Exorcist,* and come sit on his lap. Usually he would put a blanket over us and do sexual things, but this one time he didn't. I was humiliated—someone's watching!—but what can you do? He'll kill you."

■　■　■

Listen to Sharon: "We were so immature, we didn't even know what sex was, and it was happening to us. He would give you no warning. You didn't know what was happening to you, until he was taking off your clothes. He wouldn't give you any warning, he'd just do it."

■　■　■

Listen, because their mother did not.

■　■　■

A friend wrote Sharon a letter. She asked about a boy Sharon had liked back in Springfield (she was never allowed to play with him unless both families were around, so he had never become more than a friend); she also asked about an F that Sharon had received on a report card but hadn't told her dad about. She wrote in that run-on way teenage girls do, so in the letter, the two stories blended together, and it read, "How are things with Eddie? Have you told your dad about 'it' yet?"—the "it," of course, referring to the poor grade.

But of course, when Garrett read the letter—he always read everyone's mail, there was no question on this matter—he interpreted it differently.

It was Sharon's day to cook lunch. She was in the kitchen; Garrett came in from his studio. "I saw him come into the room and I thought, 'Oh, I'm in big trouble now.' He literally picked me up by the shoulders and swung me around to face him, and says, 'I want to know what's been going on with you and Eddie.' I said, 'Nothing.'

"He took his fist and punched me in the face. I gave the same answer. He punched me with the other hand. This happened four or five times. The only reason it stopped—my knees buckled, I saw stars. He held me up by my shirt."

■   ■   ■

Sharon went to school one day, not expecting anything unusual. But instead of one of her normal classes, there was an assembly for the entire ninth grade. The guidance counselor got up to speak to them. He was a gentle man with a relaxed way about him.

He said, if something is going wrong for you at home, come tell us. We are here for you. If you have problems, if anyone is hitting you, if you feel like running away, come tell us. You've done nothing wrong. We will help you. It's important that every child knows he or she has someone to turn to.

Sharon's eyes burned as she listened to this. Her heart ached to speak. She began to hyperventilate.

After the class, she walked past the guidance counselor's office, and saw him inside, through the glass partition, sitting and writing at his desk. He seemed so kind, so understanding. His hair was soft, he was so unthreatening. She stopped in her tracks. For five minutes she stood transfixed, staring at him. Inside, she was trying to will herself to go talk to him, imploring herself: Please go in! Please go in! Other students walked past, wondering what was wrong with that weird kid Sharon.

Finally, the counselor looked up from his desk, and saw Sharon.

And she began to walk.

And she just kept walking, quickly, away from his door.

And so the silence continued, and the abuse continued, and the beatings continued. It seemed that no one would ever break the deafening, overwhelming silence.

And then, a voice from the past, almost forgotten, finally spoke. And then, as if by magic, someone listened.

■ ■ ■

It was the morning of Friday, April 2, 1982. Sharon was in gym class. The teacher was called out, and talked to someone in the hall for a few minutes, then came back in and found Sharon.

"Your sister Ruth is on the phone for you," the teacher said, with a concerned look on her face. "She needs to speak to you."

The teacher put her arm around Sharon, reassuringly, and walked her down the hall. But Sharon didn't need reassurance; she wasn't worried. Ruth, the oldest, the strong, feisty one, must have given the teacher some indication of why she was calling, in order to get Sharon excused, but Sharon had no inkling of anything wrong, she was just happy for the distraction. She thought, "Wow, cool! Ruth is calling me at school!"

But when she got to the phone, she could not believe what Ruth had to say.

I have something important to tell you, Ruth said.

On Monday, a man named Mr. Lucie is going to come visit you at school.

He is coming to talk to you about Father.

Tell him everything.

Tell him how Father abuses you, how he rapes your sisters. Tell him everything.

Tell him, and you will never have to go home again.

Sharon put down the receiver.

Could this be true?

It did not surprise her that Ruth knew. Even though Sharon and Irene had lived by their mother's dictum—"Don't Tell Ruth"—all the girls had come to assume that each knew of the others' pain.

But what could have possibly brought Ruth to this action?

The previous weekend, Ruth, then twenty-six and living in Albany, New York, went to visit another one of the older kids, one who had also moved away. That sister, now serving in the army in Washington, D.C., was on leave, and the two traveled together back to Ruth's home. And for the first time, the sister began telling Ruth things she'd never told anyone before.

When the conversation was over, Ruth found herself infuriated—and worried. She feared for the welfare of sisters still living at home. In her heart, she realized that Sharon and Irene were lying to protect themselves from Garrett.

Well, not anymore, Ruth thought.

This stops now.

Ruth called the social services office in Massachusetts. She got the runaround; no one wanted to listen. No one wanted to get involved.

But finally, she found someone willing to pay attention.

"I'll tell you the details," she told the social service worker, "but I won't tell you who they are unless you promise to take them out of school."

A bargain was reached. A plan was formed.

And Ruth called her little sister, at school, and told her that liberation was at hand.

Mr. Lucie, an ex-priest and social worker, will come on Monday.

■　■　■

Sharon walked home from the bus stop in total, abject fear. What if he knows? She thought. She was walking alone, and for a minute thought that maybe they had left, all of them, that Garrett and Elizabeth had packed up the family and taken off, leaving her behind. But when she got home, there was Garrett, and her fear became even greater.

Miraculously, he seemed not to know anything. That night, when he was in the bathroom, she whispered the story of the secret phone call to Irene and Eve. All weekend, the girls whispered, and were alternately thrilled and excited and scared to death. Garrett sensed something was up, and tried to frighten the girls into telling him. But no one spoke.

For once, Sharon thought, they were in control!

The big day came—but Mr. Lucie, for some reason, did not. Sharon was heartsick. Maybe he will come tomorrow, she thought.

But the next day, a freak April snowstorm closed the schools. All the other kids were delighted, but Sharon was in torment. It was as though God Himself were keeping Mr. Lucie away.

But she knew it would have to stop snowing sometime. And Mr. Lucie would come. He had to. He just had to.

The next morning, she went to school.

And she was pulled out of class, and taken to a room, where a great big man with a great big belly introduced himself as Mr. Lucie.

And Sharon did what her sister Ruth had instructed her to do.

Sharon told him everything.

Everything.

At first, she was hesitant, but Mr. Lucie, in a kind, gentle way, got her to tell all the details, all the horrible, horrible stories that she had never told anyone before, except her mother, who turned away.

But thank God, Mr. Lucie did not.

He believed her. And he understood.

When it was over, Sharon was crying, and Mr. Lucie put his arms around the child to comfort her, and she rested her head on top of his big belly, and it felt so soft, and comforting, like a great big pillow, and Sharon thought, Oh, my God, it's going to be all right.

Mr. Lucie moved quickly. He got all the children out of school, down to the police station, contacted relatives in Pittsfield, and made arrangements for the children to go stay there. Meanwhile, the police were getting ready to serve notice on Garrett Stone. By coincidence, it happened to be his birthday.

You must understand that, with the exception of the dead-end conversation with their mother, that was the first time these children had ever, ever spoken about Garrett Stone to anyone other than each other—not a word to a friend, not a complaint to a relative, not a word. So their interactions with the police at first were a bit unusual. They spoke from their own perceptions: Be careful when you go to arrest him, they told the police. He's very powerful! He's armed and dangerous! He's got a lot of guns around the house!

Police approached the house cautiously. But they found a man there who was so different from the children's description that they must have thought they had the wrong house. The avuncular artist with the bushy beard who opened the door was friendly, calm, and cooperative.

I'm sure nothing I did was illegal, he told the police. Sure, I'm strict with the girls, but doesn't a parent have to be strict these days? Of course, they resent it a bit—what teenager wouldn't?—but these stories, no, they're not true. I'm happy to have a chance to get these matters resolved, officer.

His demeanor was so different from what the girls had told the police to expect that it threw their story into doubt. As a result, Garrett Stone was treated with much more respect than he deserved. An arraignment was set for the following month; in the meantime, he and his wife would be free on their own recognizance.

This always infuriates me. I've dealt with hundreds of these molesters, these pedophiles. And you always hear them say the same thing: "I want to get this matter resolved." As though having intercourse with a girl who has not yet reached puberty, as though forcing that child into all manner of sexual activities—as though these are matters for interpretation, gray areas, matters of debate that can be resolved among good men of robust minds. This psychopath, this pervert, after all he has done to his children— remember, as painful as the stories I have told you here may be, they are only the least offensive of the matters contained in the case against Garrett Stone—after all he has done, a friendly smile, a warm handshake, a conspiratorial wink with a cop, and suddenly it's the kids who are the suspects, the parents who start to get the sympathy, and if anyone wants to argue the point then tell me: Why on earth does someone accused of robbing a 7-Eleven routinely have to put up ten thousand dollars in bail, and someone accused of stealing the innocence and the purity and the very heart and soul of a child get released on his own recognizance?

But at least, on this day, the sun did shine, and the children escaped from Garrett Stone, never to live under the same roof with him again, never to feel his disgusting hands on their bodies again, in fury or otherwise. The police moved the children into their uncle's home. In time, Garrett Stone and his worthless wife finally stood before a judge. She faced three counts of failure to provide care and protection. He was charged with nine counts of incest and rape of a child.

Happy birthday, Garrett.

■　■　■

The liberation of the Stone children affected each of them differently. Irene, for example, sank into a dark place. "Life didn't really change for me," she said. "I couldn't accept what had happened. I realized that all those years of torment were unnecessary. I went into a very deep depression, and I would just sit in dark rooms—not talk to anybody. I didn't have friends until I was a junior in high school."

Eve, then thirteen, had an even harder time. She wouldn't talk in therapy, so she was allowed to stop going. "I became a very angry teenager. I used to attack my sister a lot, over nothing. Most of it was held in. I had an eating disorder and once you don't eat you don't think about other things, you're just focused on food. I wanted to take a knife and cut off everything, make it go away."

For Sharon, however, a change began to occur. She enjoyed her uncle's home; she enjoyed having meat and potatoes and vegetables for dinner, instead of the biscuits and honey she had become accustomed to. She took ballet lessons. Imagine—a child who was never allowed to laugh, now given the freedom to dance.

Like Irene, she had trouble interacting with other children because she'd grown up so sheltered; but for Sharon, the shell was beginning to show signs of cracking. "We went to counseling once a week—just telling someone is a tremendous relief, to release some of the pain."

And then came the trial.

■　■　■

Diane Dillon was thirty-seven at the time, and very involved in her work. Diane had been an assistant district attorney since 1976, sometimes juggling a load of one hundred cases—but from the time she agreed to take on the Stone case, she knew it would be different. The girls, from the beginning, moved her deeply. There was something about them that touched her heart; a single woman, she took them under her wing as though they were her own children.

"The girls were so vulnerable and so naive despite all they'd been through," Diane remembers of their first encounters. "They didn't know what was and what was not a sexual act. He was just an evil man."

Diane became the girls' guru, their mother confessor, their rock, as they entered the courtroom to state in public what they had barely whispered in private.

As she looked around the courtroom that first day, Diane noticed a kindred spirit, a woman she'd seen many times before. Ten years younger than Diane, the woman was nevertheless very much like Diane. They had already established a warm professional relationship. The woman, like Diane, became deeply moved by the innocence and pain she saw in the three young girls.

Her name was Helayne Lightstone. She was a twenty-seven-year-old reporter for the *Springfield Morning Union.* She'd been covering the courts for two years, having graduated there from covering local politics. She'd jumped at the court beat, and her work became her life. Right around this time, mandatory child-abuse reporting laws, passed a few years earlier, really started having an effect. "That triggered a lot of cases," she remembers. "I was astonished at the amount of abuse. It was the issue of the day." And yet, in spite of all she'd seen—like the man who asphyxiated his three-year-old step-daughter during a rape—she was not prepared for the Stone courtroom.

"I'd sat through a number of sexual abuse cases but none so horrifying as seeing these three girls get up and testify," Helayne said.

"To see three beautiful young women, so brave—because they had obviously been so afraid of their father for so long—it was horrible, because they were turning on their mother, and they were wrenched about it."

But testify they did.

The trial started on August 8, 1983, and one by one, they took the stand: Eve, the tall, stormy one; Irene, the quiet, introspective one; and Sharon, the shortest but the most forceful.

And Garrett Stone tried to intimidate them all he could. He made exaggerated, frowning faces at them: "Oh, you poor thing, no one's going to believe you, you know," was what Sharon read into them. He pointed at them, sneered, glared, tried to intimidate them; he even stood up and shouted "Liar!" at one point—causing the judge to consider moving him to a separate room to watch the proceedings on a TV monitor.

But the girls stood strong. "I refused to let him get me upset," said Irene. "He was trying to make me get upset, so I just looked at Diane Dillon."

"The power of one by one, three girls going up; each had their own pain," Helayne said. "Garrett Stone was very hostile and threatening. Their fear was palpable. You can't help but be affected by that."

Stone had pulled out every trick in the book to intimidate the girls. Nothing had worked.

But he had one trick left that no one anticipated.

■   ■   ■

On Thursday, August 11, the fourth day of the trial, Garrett and Elizabeth Stone, still coming and going on their own recognizance, were not present when it was time for court to begin. "We waited a good half-hour because initially everyone thought they were late," recalls Helayne. "Their attorneys tried to call and got no answer. The judge dismissed the jury and issued a warrant."

The police went to the Stones' home. They found a strange sight: All of the appliances in the house were in the bathtub, in a puddle of water.

Was this a message to the children that they would never have these paltry items?

Had Garrett Stone toyed with electrocuting his wife? Or himself?

No one knew.

Because there was no one around to ask.

Garrett and Elizabeth Stone had gotten into their rusty blue VW bus and disappeared.

Just like that.

■   ■   ■

Because the jury had heard testimony in the presence of the accused, the judge decided to ask for a verdict. The jury found the couple guilty on all counts.

For what it's worth.

Because there was no one around to sentence.

In fact, the judge would not even pass a sentence without Garrett and Elizabeth Stone in the courtroom. And so, even in his absence, Garrett was exerting control. After all the girls had gone through, the torture of sitting in that witness stand and spilling their hearts, they would not get the simple closure of hearing a sentence passed on the people who had ripped the fabric of their lives to shreds.

Not even that.

■   ■   ■

And so, in a story bereft of an ending, in a case without justice or closure, three teenage girls tried to move on. They struggled to comprehend that they could now live normal lives. They struggled to figure out what "normal" means.

Sharon, miraculously, began to blossom. She became less and less depressed, made some friends, did the things normal kids do, going to dances, to the movies.

She took an interest in drafting and design, and turned out to be pretty good at it; good enough so that after high school she made it into the Wentworth Institute of Technology in Boston, backed by grants from the drafting department at Pittsfield High School, and some help from local service organizations.

While most of Sharon's older brothers and sisters had moved on, one, her brother Frank, had not survived: He died in a motorcycle accident in Texas. "Shortly after we were removed from our parents it happened," Sharon said. "I believe he committed suicide. He was riding a motorcycle at two or three in the morning, no helmet, no shoes, going very fast. He smashed into the back of a Mack truck. He was going to be coming home for Christmas."

Now it was time for the three youngest—Sharon and her two younger sisters—to make their own lives. From her aunt's home, Sharon moved into a dorm at Wentworth. That first semester, in the fall of 1985, she met a good-looking young man named Shaun Sullivan in the computer lab. "I had no interest in him," she said. "He had a goatee and a Fu Manchu. Then one day I told him my father had a beard and I hate hair on men's faces. A week later it was down to just a mustache, and then after a while the mustache was gone. I remember thinking that that was a face I could live with, and saying to my roommate, 'I will have a date with Shaun Sullivan before February is out.'"

Sure enough, on Valentine's Day, Shaun took Sharon out to a movie and dinner. "He took me to a little Chinese restaurant and we spilled our guts," she said. "He was very supportive and didn't judge me. It was the most fantastic date."

They fell in love, and stayed that way. After college they moved into a small apartment in Framingham. He got a job designing roads for the state; she started drawing up designs at a small architecture firm for $250 a week. "We were young, happy—we spent all our money," Sharon said. Shaun proposed, and Sharon Stone became Sharon Stone Sullivan in February of 1988.

But try as she might, Sharon could not leave the past behind. Not fully. Not really.

Sharon would dream about her parents. She would imagine she saw them on the street. Once, on the highway with Shaun, she was sure she saw her mother in another car, and made Shaun follow it for miles.

When she found out she was pregnant, she cried. All children of abused parents know the grim truism: Most abusers started out as abused children themselves.

Whenever I meet children of abusive families, I always try to help them sort this out: It may be true that most abusers started out as abused children—but it doesn't work the other way. Abused children don't have to become abusers themselves. Especially if you're aware of the danger, and if you're getting counseling, you can break the cycle of abuse. Lots do.

And if anyone could do it, it was going to be Sharon. But she couldn't shake the fear. Then, when her daughter Cristen was born on June 29, 1988, a new fear arose; you might think it an irrational fear, but it was very real to Sharon, a paralyzing, gripping, cold-sweat, pit-of-your-stomach fear.

The fear that Garrett Stone would come back. To seek revenge.

"When I went to close the curtains I would always be scared I would see my father's face pressed on my baby's window. When she started going to school, I took pictures of my parents down there and told them, 'If they ever come here, call the police.'"

But Sharon and her sisters were not the only ones haunted by the memory of Garrett and Elizabeth Stone.

■   ■   ■

Helayne Lightstone, the reporter who'd covered the shocking trial, had moved on with her life, too. She'd moved to Connecticut, started a new career, had a child. She kept in touch with Diane Dillon, the prosecutor in the case. The two would trade a few phone calls a year.

One spring morning in 1989, the two women were talking, and Helayne asked Diane which case she would most have liked to have resolved. Diane's response was swift: the Stone case.

Diane was working with a new television program on helping her resolve another case—some missing bank robbers. "I remember Diane said, 'Too bad it's not the Stone case on *America's Most Wanted.*' I said, 'Why not?' The next day, I called the Fox network and got the numbers for the show."

Helayne, talking to one of our researchers, didn't just lay out the facts of the case. She managed to convey the pain, and the horror, that the victims had gone through. The researcher became infected with her passion for the case, and he asked her if she could get her hands on all the background information. The next thing Helayne knew, she found herself driving up Route 91, headed for Springfield, so she could get the copies of the articles she had written out of the archives of the *Morning Union*. Diane Dillon got involved, too, scouring her files for the documentation of this terrible case.

But there remained a huge question: Did the family want to go public with their story? To take their shame, their humiliation, their pain, and lay it out on national television? To take the secrets, once whispered between children in an attic, then excruciatingly brought forward in a courtroom, which, while public, still has the serene and sterile feeling of being in a doctor's office (you're still going by the book, excising a cancer in an appropriate and sanctioned fashion)— and now bring them forth on television, for all their neighbors to watch and listen to and cluck over?

This was a question none of us knew the answer to.

So Diane Dillon set out to find out.

■   ■   ■

Diane was determined not to push the family one way or the other—but to give them every opportunity to make the decision themselves. When she contacted the family, the emotions were mixed. Some of the older children flat-out didn't want to do it— they wanted to leave the past in the past. The boys still carried the Stone family name, so there was no protecting their privacy.

In the end, only Sharon and Irene said they'd consider it. The rest of the family flat-out decided against it. But even Sharon and Irene weren't sure.

Frankly, I wasn't sure, either, at first. Remember, we were still pretty new at this. We went in with the caveat that we would never re-victimize a victim. Now we had a family divided, and whatever decision we made, someone was going to feel deeply hurt. But this case was a little different, because it was a little older. Six years had passed since Garrett and Elizabeth Stone had disappeared. Everyone involved was a grown-up now. There were no twelve-year-old girls who had to go back and face their classmates anymore. Also, the whole story had already come out in trial, and even though the girls' names weren't used, the parents' names were, and so everybody back home pretty much knew everything that was going on.

And finally, there was a clear and present danger—I couldn't imagine a sicko like Garrett Stone going through life and never touching another child.

Everything, of course, still hinged on what the daughters wanted us to do. I decided that the only course of action was to set up a meeting with those family members who were thinking about doing the show, so we could talk it over.

We flew Sharon and Irene, along with Sharon's husband and child, to D.C. Diane Dillon came along as well.

"We flew down on a Friday morning and rented a car," Diane said. "We were staying at the Holiday Inn up the street. I had gone to Georgetown University, so I knew the town a little bit, and I took them around and tried to make them feel comfortable."

On Saturday, they met with the researcher. The meeting didn't go well. They found him abrasive, and intrusive—it's hard, after all, to know how to find that line between asking what you need to know, and asking too much. But still, he was passionate about the case, passionate about catching the Stones. It was his passion that had propelled the case forward; and after the meeting, the girls felt good about the prospect of finding their parents.

The meeting also had another positive effect: It opened up a conversation that no one had had in a long time. That night, as the group sat around in one of their rooms at the Holiday Inn, Irene and Sharon began to talk.

They talked about all they'd been through, all the years of pain and torture and humiliation, like Hansel and Gretel trying to find their way through the dark, frightening woods. They let loose details they had not spoken of since the trial. During it all, Shaun and Diane Dillon looked at each other. Finally Shaun turned to his wife, a catch in his throat, and said, "How can you even make love to me?"

Sharon, her face soft, her tone quiet, turned slowly toward her husband. "That's different," she said. "I love you."

The next day, Sunday, was our show-taping day back then. While the producers were getting the set ready, I walked up the block to the Holiday Inn to sit and talk with the Stone girls. It took us a long time to get ready for taping in those days, so I knew I was in no hurry as I walked out of the elevator and into the dining room.

My first impression of Sharon was how frail she seemed, how waiflike. I know, from my years of working with abused kids through the Adam Walsh Center, that it's not appropriate to hug someone who's been abused or make an overture to them, unless they want to, because many times men represent something fearful and reprehensible to them. No matter how much you want to put your arms around them and say, don't worry, it's going to be okay, you can't do that.

And Sharon seemed very shy, at first. Her sister Irene seemed stronger, more aggressive. Sharon seemed more vulnerable.

But it was Sharon who, once we got talking, was the more forceful of the two. Little by little, she opened up, and told me about her pain, her anger, her sorrow. I have been through hell, she was saying to me. And I deserve justice.

I assured them that, as a victim myself, I would make sure that they were treated with dignity. We've made mistakes; I remember a reenactment of a molestation case, early on, in which we showed the molester zipping up his pants after leaving a young boy's room. We got more angry calls about that than about showing a guy getting shot fifty times. But we've learned from our mistakes, and we've learned to treat molestation cases with the utmost seriousness and dignity. I told them, if there are things you don't want us to bring out, we don't have to bring them out.

But by then, there was little to hold back, they said. Look, Sharon told me. We went through all this. The humiliation of sitting on that witness stand in front of friends and people and strangers and the press, describing in horrible detail what our father did to us, our own father. What we did to get justice, and for him to be able to walk out with our mother and go on the run, everything we did, everything we went through, everything went for naught, for nothing. We feel like we've been totally violated for a second time.

How could the system let them walk out? Why weren't they in chains? Why does everybody treat child molesters like they're not real criminals, like they're not dangerous? What do we have to do? What more do we have to do?

And I sat there and listened to this remarkably eloquent young woman, giving voice to her pain in a way I'd rarely seen before, and I thought, you don't have to do a thing, anymore. You've done all you need to do.

We'll take it from here.

■ ■ ■

There was still a stumbling block. Sharon and Irene hoped to get the entire family united behind this effort. So we tried to get them all on board, for a while. There were a series of conference calls set up, but somehow someone would always back out at the last minute. So Sharon and I would wind up on the phone, and we would talk, for a long time. She would tell me more and more details about her life—and finally, I decided, it was time to move forward. I told Sharon, I have not walked in your brothers' shoes, I do not have any right to say anything negative about them, but if you want to go ahead without your family's blessings, then we're behind you. The question was, were she and Irene ready to participate with our researchers, make sure we had the story right—and, in addition to everything else, to do so at the risk of alienating the rest of the family, to add one more burden to their young and incredibly painful lives; as two girls who grew up without the love of a mother and father, are you willing to put the love of your brothers and sisters on the line?

And Sharon told me: This man's sex life is molesting young girls. He's going to do it to other children. And I'm afraid he's going to come back and do it to mine.

Enough's enough.

Let's go get them.

■ ■ ■

They taped the interview in a cottage in Orange, Massachusetts, which belongs to a friend of Sharon's. It was a place that the young women always felt comfortable in, and a setting where they could relax and bare their souls.

We sent Tom Shelly, a trusted producer who was going to do the reenactment, to conduct the interviews. Like the guidance counselor Sharon had wanted to talk to back in school, Tom was a quiet and kind soul, a gentle man with, as Sharon had put it, soft hair and an easy, unassuming smile. He came to the cottage with the usual *America's Most Wanted* brigade: lighting people, a cameraman, a sound man, all the accoutrements of television production. They all set up in the cottage.

A lot of times, people who've been through the trauma that Sharon and Irene have been through are—there's no nice way to put it—lousy interviews. There is so much they want to say, but their minds are so filled with trap doors and side alleys, and there is so much emotional weight attached to every sentence, that they're incapable of anything but one-word or two-word answers to questions. But not these two young women. Irene was powerful and clear in her interview; her anger was strong and pronounced. And Sharon—Sharon was remarkable. In simple, matter-of-fact terms, even allowing a little self-conscious giggle to escape now and then, she laid out the entire story, from beginning to end.

She wasn't expecting the effect this experience would have on her. "The day Tom came and interviewed me was a life-changing experience," she said. "Tom, this total stranger, sat across from me and asked me questions. I blabbed. I gave my secret away. I spilled my guts.

"It wasn't strange, it wasn't like he was a therapist. He emptied my trash. When he packed up his bags, I felt like he took it all away, and from that day, I didn't own it anymore. It wasn't my secret anymore—it was *AMW*'s secret. It lives in the archives at *America's Most Wanted*.

"When I stood up from that chair, I felt so light. I thought, 'I am happy, I am married to a great guy, and we have a beautiful child. Now I don't have a secret anymore. Now I don't have to lie about why I don't see my parents.'

"They gave me hope. Total strangers, doing something for me that even the police weren't doing. They made me feel like I was a special person. I felt like I was part of a team—here's this huge group of people working for a common goal. I would have loved for my family's experience to be like mine, but I had to realize I couldn't do that. But even though I had to give up my own family for a while, I gained another. You walk into *AMW* and feel like you're part of something special. It sounds corny, but it's true."

■   ■   ■

We aired the case on February 18, 1990. As I watched the tape of her interview, and Tom Shelly's sensitive reenactment—we showed the family's life, interspersed with the interviews from the girls, and my own voice-over—I thought, the audience will get this. They will hear her. They will understand her pain. They will come forward. I know they will.

We closed the piece with a quote from Sharon, something she had asked us to add: "To all the little girls or boys out there who are being violated," she said. "Do something. Tell somebody. I did. I got help. I'm happy, and you can be too."

And I thought, how incredible, that in this moment, this chance after all these years to get some justice, and for all the torture she was going through over the rift in her family, the one thing she wanted was to say something positive to children she'd never met. This, I thought, was a class act all the way.

And I was so sure we'd catch her parents for her, and for Irene, and for Eve.

And this was all going to turn out all right.

And I was all wrong.

■   ■   ■

The tips came from all over, but in the end, they were all false leads and dead ends. After a few weeks, it was pretty clear that nothing was going to come of the airing.

I spoke to Sharon afterward. She was pretty disappointed, but not downhearted. In a funny way, I felt like she was trying to cheer *me* up.

Somehow, she had gotten under my skin, in the way no victim ever had before. We talked every couple of weeks, just checking in. She got pretty savvy about the police end of things: She knew when there was a tip that the police hadn't followed up on properly, and she knew that a little pressure from *AMW* could help speed things along.

She also knew that we'd have to get the case on the air again.

I found myself energized by her: Her courage, her compassion for others, her belief that we could bring her justice, her strange blend of naive hope and savvy realism were infectious. And knowing how she could have become a warped, damaged, fearful adult after her incomprehensible, tortured childhood made you feel that much more amazed that she trusted you and believed in you. She was more grateful and thankful than any victim we'd ever had on the show—and we hadn't caught her parents yet!

For the second airing, about ten months later, Sharon came down for an interview, again with her husband and child, and this time with a new baby in tow. Between takes, I ran back to my dressing room, but one of the show's producers, Phil Lerman, was guarding the door.

"You can't go in there, John," he said.

"What do you mean? That's my dressing room."

"Sharon needed a place to nurse the baby."

And so we stood, willing to wait as long as it takes; because Phil, normally a pretty nervous, antsy, fast-moving guy on show days, had also been tamed by one of our most remarkable victims.

She'd gotten under his skin, too.

■　　■　　■

After the second airing had proven unsuccessful as well, the producers were pretty much giving up on running the story again. But now Lerman had picked up the ball. Sharon had started calling him, late at night, saying, Phil, when can we air it again? When can we air it again? And he knew that, without some fresh angle, he was going to have a tough time talking the story back on to the show anytime soon.

Then, one night, the two came up with an idea: Garrett Stone had been, among other things, a painter. He sometimes made money painting on the street. Maybe he's doing so now. Maybe, if they could get hold of some of his old paintings, we could show them to the viewers, and maybe—just maybe—someone would recognize his style.

In his heart, Lerman knew this was, at best, a long shot. But he also knew that he could use it as a wedge—to pitch the story not as a rerun, but as an "update with important new clues."

Lance Heflin, the executive producer, saw right through this ploy.

But like everyone else, he had developed a soft spot for this story. He wanted to catch the sons of bitches, too.

So he relented. We'd air the story a third time, and scheduled it for March 6, 1992.

It had been nearly nine years since the Stones had disappeared, more than two years since our first airing of the case. For two years, virtually alone, ostracized by much of her family, Sharon had kept up her lonely vigil, standing guard over the memory of what Garrett and Elizabeth Stone had done, a silent sentinel scouring the horizon for signs of the fugitive, a lone trumpeter reminding all of us that it was our job not to give up. I just kept thinking of how brave she really was.

When the paintings arrived at our offices, we were all taken aback. One, in particular, looked to me like a glimpse inside the mind of a crazed sex maniac. It was a dark, nightmarish picture, with a strange twisted tree growing out of a torn landscape; the tree trunk split into three parts, each of which grew into the figure of a nude woman, each woman with her hands outstretched in pain to the sky, each hand turning back into a tree branch. The show meeting that afternoon was bizarre: "I think we should say, in the show script, that this represents Garrett Stone's twisted image of his children," said Lerman.

"We don't know what the painting represents to him," said Rebecca Campany, the show's writer. "It could be his interpretation of *Charlie's Angels.*"

In the end, we showed the painting without interpretation.

As it turned out, the painting was of absolutely no use.

But at least the story had found its way back on the air.

The photos had been shown once again.

And once again, we waited.

■   ■   ■

The night we aired the case, Paddy and Harry Budge were over at a friend's house in the Marin County town of Corte Madera, California. Their friend Shirley Tiger, a sweet woman, motherly though childless, was recuperating from an illness, and Paddy and Harry were helping her out. Harry was changing the battery in her car, Paddy was cleaning the house. Just neighborly sorts of things to do. But then, Paddy and Harry were the neighborly type.

Shirley, a quiet and graceful woman of Native American heritage, had met the Budges about five years earlier. She was a home health care aide; never married, she supported her parents until their deaths, and took her pleasure in helping others. One day, while caring for a stroke victim, Shirley met Paddy, who was doing some painting and papering in the house.

"She was a lot of fun," Shirley said. "We worked well together. She was friendly and got along with her employers. But she would invariably break something. Once she blew up my boss's vacuum and he had to buy another." One other strange thing about Paddy Budge: She never liked to have her picture taken. Shirley wanted some before-and-after pictures of Paddy's work at the stroke patient's house, but Paddy refused to be in them.

Nevertheless, Shirley liked her new friend, and soon met Paddy's husband, Harry. The two were living together on a twenty-four-foot wooden cabin cruiser, *Duet,* in the San Rafael Marina in Marin County, and seemed very close. "Once I saw them going down the street on bikes with wood for the boat—he had one end, she had the other. They were a twosome, really in love. She'd talk about him every night, and how they made love every night. 'I bet you think I'm silly,' she'd say."

Shirley once ran into Harry on Valentine's Day at a local coffee shop. He sat down to share a cup of tea—and show Shirley the romantic little ad he put in the classifieds for Paddy.

The two always dressed the same; she in her plaid shirt, slacks, and jacket, he in slacks and a plain shirt. They both wore tan-and-blue hiking shoes, heavy dark-rimmed glasses, and hats pulled down over their eyes.

Still, something nagged at Shirley. Like the way Paddy always wanted to be paid in cash. Like the way Shirley had to cash checks for the couple, because they didn't have any ID. She figured, maybe they were in trouble with the IRS.

There was another strange thing: As lovey-dovey as the couple seemed to be, Harry seemed to keep Paddy on a very tight leash, and she seemed afraid of her own husband. "I know she was scared of him," Shirley said. "You should have seen the terror in her eyes if she was late for the five o'clock bus, because she knew he'd be there at the bus stop."

Once, while Shirley was away on a cruise, she allowed the couple to stay at her house. "It was like a second honeymoon for them," Shirley said. "They slept in a bed, and took baths, and did laundry.

"And when I came back, I couldn't believe it was the same house. It was so clean! And everything in the drawers were folded! I told her not to move anything, but when I came back, she had folded and cleaned everything. To this day, I still can't find things."

When Shirley returned from the cruise, her belly was killing her. At first, she thought it was food poisoning—but when she checked into Marin General Hospital, it turned out to be her liver. In October of 1991, they operated, but closed her back up immediately, saying she needed a liver transplant. In December, she was notified that, even though she'd served seven years in administration in the marine corps, the VA wouldn't pay for the transplant.

She was told she had six months to live.

So that's how it came to be that, when the liver problems would flare up and she was driven to her bed, the Budges would come over to help out. On that particular Friday night, though, their fastidiousness was driving her a little crazy. "I thought they'd never leave," she said.

Finally, they did take off, and Shirley plopped onto the couch to watch her favorite TV show.

America's Most Wanted.

"They started talking about this one man, and how he had mistreated his children," Shirley remembered. "Then at the end when they put the pictures on, I noticed he looked familiar, but he was full-bearded. Then they showed her, and said that she would be doing domestic work. Right then, I knew that was them."

Garrett and Elizabeth Stone.

Using the nickname she made up for him when he gained weight.

Budge.

Shocked and in tears, Shirley summoned up the courage to call *AMW.* The operator asked her why she was crying.

"They were my friends, and they were just here, they just left," she sobbed.

"That hurt for me to have to make that call," Shirley said later, "but knowing that they had lied to me, deceived me, and that they just left my home! Imagine what could have happened to me if I turned it on when they were there! They had been so good to me. They treated me like I was their own daughter—and then to hear what they did to their own daughter!

"I was so angry, I could have put my foot through the TV set."

The tip was passed on to the FBI. For a day, Shirley heard nothing, and was worried. I couldn't be wrong, she thought.

She wasn't.

The next morning, agents called Shirley at home. She gave them all the information she had on the Budges—the Stones—including all the coast guard information about the boat, which her friends had left with her.

Armed with all that information, FBI special agent Thomas R. Hopkins headed down to the marina, along with detectives Mike Fielding and Michael Vergara of the City of San Rafael Police Department.

They began by showing pictures of Garrett and Elizabeth Stone around the docks.

Everyone pointed to the same boat.

A small sloop called *Duet.*

You never want to enter an enclosed space to arrest someone, if you can help it. First of all, you don't want to take them on their turf—it gives them too much of an advantage. Second, you don't know if they're alone; if anyone else is around, and a fight breaks out, they could get seriously hurt (hell—so could you). Third, and most important, you don't know if there are any hidden weapons within reach.

So procedure calls for waiting. And that's what the agent and the cops did. They sat, and stared at that damn boat, for half an hour.

Finally, the hatch opened, and out came a skinny guy in glasses. The officers approached him. He stopped.

"Are you Garrett Stone?" they asked the man.

He said he was not.

"You know," said Hopkins, "we can get your fingerprints, and fingerprints don't lie."

The man paused, and looked at the officer.

"Do you have something to tell me?" Hopkins asked.

"Yes," the man replied. "I am Garrett Stone."

"I thought you were."

■　■　■

Shirley Tiger heard her landlord calling from the house next door. "Paddy is here, cleaning," he said. "Do you want to see her?"

Shirley panicked. She couldn't face this woman. She didn't know why Paddy hadn't been arrested. Why was she still here? And what if she knows that I called *America's Most Wanted*?

"No, I'm going out," she lied.

But when Paddy left, she walked right past Shirley's house. Shirley peeked from the window and saw Paddy go by.

It would be the last time she saw her.

When Paddy returned to the dock, Detective Fielding was waiting for her. He arrested her and took her down to the police station. "You've been on the run for nine years," he said. "Did you think you would be caught?" "No," she replied. "We live a law-abiding life, and don't attract too much attention."

Don't attract too much attention? What about that little matter of the television show you've been on three times?

"The case was on *America's Most Wanted*," he told her.

She was shocked. "We didn't know," she said. "We don't have a TV."

■ ■ ■

Sharon Sullivan had just gotten off the phone with the mother of a friend of little Cristen's, telling the mother that she was bringing Cristen over for a play date. She seat-belted Cristen into the car when she realized she'd left something she needed back in the house. Just as she walked in the door, she heard the phone ring. Oh, no, she thought, I hope it's not the friend's mother calling me back to cancel for some reason.

It wasn't.

It was Massachusetts state trooper Gerry Downs.

Word had reached his office, from California, that her parents had been apprehended.

The word, that cop-talk phrase, "apprehended," floated in silent air for a moment. Time froze, as Sharon's brain struggled to believe that what she had waited for for nine long years, since her parents disappeared—what she had waited for, in some deeper sense, ever since that first night, what now seemed like a thousand years ago, when her father woke her up and took her from her bed, ever since that night, she had waited for this moment, for this word, to float across her consciousness.

Apprehended.

And in the next instant, she was letting loose a torrent of words, coming from deep inside her—a proper woman, Sharon had never let loose such a barrage of curses in her life. She was just glad Cristen was in the car so she couldn't hear her—but the capture had unearthed something in her, something primal, something so powerful it was all she could do to control her body. Soon she was just screaming.

"Um, why don't you call me back later if you want the details?" offered the bewildered trooper.

"The emotion that was running through my body was elation," Sharon said. "Pure excitement. I just couldn't stand still. I was banging on the desk. I kicked the chair. I just couldn't believe it. And I sat down, and my body was shaking, my whole body, from my head to my toes. I was just shaking, and it was in that moment that it hit me—he'll never do it again! And that's what I was most happy about—that he'll never, ever be able to touch another kid."

In the hours that passed, as she took Cristen to her friend's house, and the two moms took the girls on a morning walk, she kept saying to herself, again and again; "It's over. We won." A million questions started up in her mind: "I wonder what they're doing. I wonder how they're reacting. I wonder what they look like! He must be such a scared little man right now. I was so happy to put him in his place where he belonged, because for so long, he tried to put us down, so far, and then finally, I was up, and I was in control."

In the days that followed, there would be mixed reactions from her other brothers and sisters. The rift in the family was still evident. But the one who was clearest about her feelings was the oldest, Ruth. She called Sharon to say that, for the first time in years, she was sleeping soundly through the night, without nightmares. That, for Sharon, was a special gift: to have brought peace to the woman who gave Sharon the avenue—and the courage—to come forward that very first time.

That night, when Sharon put her daughters to bed, she noticed that the big bay window in their room was open. It was the window

John Walsh on the set of *America's Most Wanted*.
[PHOTO BY EILEEN COLTON, COURTESY OF *AMERICA'S MOST WANTED*]

Executive Producer Lance Heflin leads a new story meeting—the beginning of the mercurial process of catching a fugitive by using a TV show.
[PHOTO BY EILEEN COLTON, COURTESY OF *AMERICA'S MOST WANTED*]

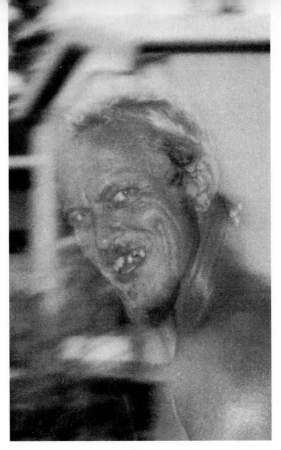

The famous photo of Eddie James: the violent, leering face was the most frightening our staffers had ever seen. Some viewers called in to say he seemed like the devil himself.
[COURTESY OF LINDA FIKE]

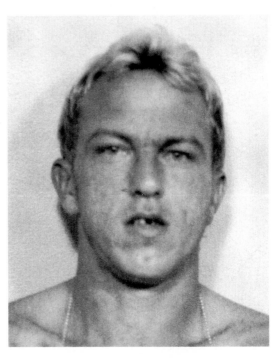

Eddie James, after an earlier arrest.
[COURTESY OF *AMERICA'S MOST WANTED*]

A studio portrait of
Wendi Lynn Neuner, the
survivor who saw it all.
[COURTESY OF LINDA FIKE]

The funeral card photos for the victims in the Eddie James case.
[COURTESY OF LINDA FIKE]

The moment of closure; Linda Neuner, whose daughter and mother had been brutally murdered, meets the tipster, Priscilla Valdez, who turned in the killer.
[COURTESY OF *AMERICA'S MOST WANTED*]

The List family.
[COURTESY OF TIMOTHY B. BENFORD, FROM THE BOOK *RIGHTEOUS CARNAGE*]

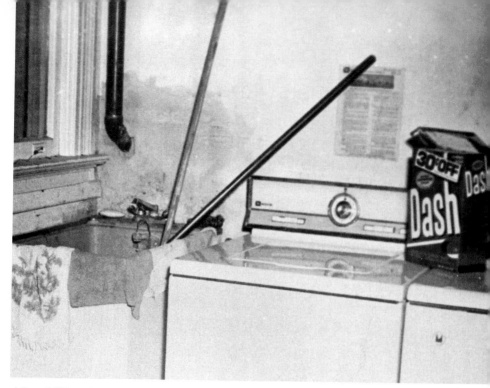

After killing his family, John List tidied up the scene—and even left the bloody mops soaking in the laundry room.
[COURTESY OF *AMERICA'S MOST WANTED*]

Frank Bender worked from photos of John List to create the bust that led to the capture.
[COURTESY OF FRANK BENDER]

Suspect in 5 Killings in 1971 Caught With Aid of TV Show

The capture of murderer John List put *America's Most Wanted* on the front page of *The New York Times*—and put the fledgling television show on the map. Their story featured the old John List, the new John List—and the *America's Most Wanted* bust that caught him.

Terry Hart,
displaying his telltale tattoo.
[COURTESY OF *AMERICA'S MOST WANTED*]

The Green Parrot Cafe. We started out looking for the leader of the
Preppie Bandits—and wound up finding a lot more than we
bargained for.
[COURTESY OF *AMERICA'S MOST WANTED*]

Every chance we could, we brought Sharon Stone Sullivan (left)
together with Shirley Tiger, the tipster who changed her life and
later became her surrogate mom.
[COURTESY OF *AMERICA'S MOST WANTED*]

Happy endings:
Sharon Sullivan
today, with her
family.
[COURTESY OF
SHARON SULLIVAN]

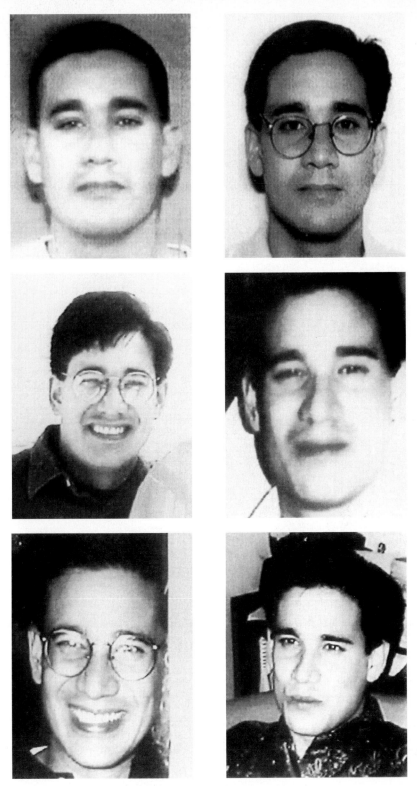

The many faces of spree-killer Andrew Cunanan.

KIDNAPPED
AT KNIFE POINT
Polly Hannah Klass
D.O.B. 1/3/81
Brown Hair • Brown Eyes
4'10" – 80 lbs.

SUSPECT
White Male Adult 30-40 yrs.
Approx. 6'3" Dark/Dark Gray Hair
Full Beard, Wearing Dark Clothing
With Yellow Bandana Around Head

LAST SEEN OCTOBER 1, 1993 in PETALUMA, CALIF
If you have any information on this child
CALL THE PETALUMA POLICE: 707-778-4481
or THE KEVIN COLLINS FOUNDATION: 800-272-0012

The original missing poster in the Polly Klaas case included early rough sketches of her abductor (above). A later sketch (opposite), done by forensic expert Jeanne Boylan, was much more accurate and helped break the case wide open.

[COURTESY OF *AMERICA'S MOST WANTED*]

REWARD
$200,000

KIDNAPPED

POLLY HANNAH KLAAS

Date of Birth: 1/3/81

Brown Hair & Brown Eyes

HT: 4' 10" WT: 80 Lbs

SUSPECT

White Male, 32-45 yrs, 5' 10" to 6' 3"
Thick, Wavy, Salt & Pepper Hair
Full Beard and Full Face
Slight Age Lines on
      Forehead & Around Eyes

POLLY WAS LAST SEEN OCTOBER 1, 1993 IN PETALUMA, CALIFORNIA

IF YOU HAVE ANY INFORMATION, PLEASE CALL:
The Petaluma Police at 707-778-4481 or the F.B.I. at 415-553-7400
Or the Polly Klaas Search Center at 1-800-587-4357 • PO Box 800 • Petaluma, CA 94953

Polly Klaas with her father, Marc.
[COURTESY OF MARC KLAAS]

The face of
a cold-hearted,
cold-blooded killer—
and a dead ringer for
the Jeanne Boylan
sketch: Richard Allen
Davis in court.
[COURTESY OF *AMERICA'S MOST WANTED*]

Christopher Abercrombie and his grandmother, Carol. They went to
visit her mom, but the visit made them victims of a terrible crime
that crossed three generations.
[COURTESY OF ABERCROMBIE AND MELANDER FAMILIES]

Delores McKim,
matriarch of the family—
and the eldest of the victims.
[COURTESY OF ABERCROMBIE AND MELANDER FAMILIES]

Kathy Melander (left) visits her sister Carol Abercrombie on the lake
in Tennessee where Carol was planning to retire with her husband.
Later, Kathy would be the one to find Carol's body.
[COURTESY OF ABERCROMBIE AND MELANDER FAMILIES]

These fugitives are still on the loose.

You could be the one to bring them in. If you know where they are,
call 1-800-CRIME-TV. You can remain anonymous.

Vernon Henry.

Jaime "Six-Fingers" Edwards.

These fugitives are still on the loose.

You could be the one to bring them in. If you know where they are,
call 1-800-CRIME-TV. You can remain anonymous.

[COURTESY OF *AMERICA'S MOST WANTED*]

Dennis Howe.

Margaret Rudin.

she was always afraid of, where she was always imagining her father's face peering in.

But on this night, she strode up to the window, with a smile on her face, and wound the crank to close the window, and looked out into the night, the night that held no more terrors for her, and she looked down at her daughters, and she smiled, and thought, I have always worried that he would come back and take you, my darlings, and I would be powerless to stop him, I would once again be that powerless child. But he will never do that now; you are safe, and I will never be that scared little girl, not ever, not ever, not ever again.

■　■　■

That summer, *America's Most Wanted* was getting ready to cover the extradition hearing of Garrett and Elizabeth Stone, where it would be decided if they could be sent back to Massachusetts for sentencing. We decided this would be a nice time to update the whole story, catch up on how the victims were doing.

Our correspondent on the story, Lena Nozizwe, had spoken with Shirley and Sharon, and thought, wouldn't it be great if we could bring them together?

After all, here was a woman dying of liver disease, who a year earlier had been given less than a year to live—a woman who, with tears in her eyes, turned in her two best friends, because a stranger on television had asked her to; a woman who was able to feel that stranger's pain and commit the one most selfless, honorable act she could commit; and for that, she had asked nothing, but had secretly hoped to meet this brave young woman.

And also, here was a young woman who wanted to go to California and see her parents in custody—and who Lena knew would so love the chance to look in the eye of the woman who had made it possible, who had changed her life, and say, thank you.

Don't these people deserve a chance to meet face to face?

And so we sent Sharon Stone Sullivan on a journey.

A journey to see her parents, one more time—but this time, to see them face justice.

And a journey to meet Shirley Tiger.

Her first stop, in California, was the boat where her parents had been living. She walked around the marina, and met some of the people who had known her parents. They all had kind words for her, and each one got a hug.

From the marina, Sharon was driven to Shirley's house. She was nervous, almost breathless, as she walked up the flight of wooden stairs to Shirley's front door. "Bless your heart," Shirley said, her arms extending to Sharon, the two women beaming at each other. They had seen each other on our show, and heard each other's kind words, and the moment felt more like a reunion than a first meeting. They were strangers no more, they were more than friends already.

The petite young woman threw her arms around the savior with the soft kind face, her dark hair now framed in gray, and she hugged her as hard as she could, and the tears began to flow, and she sobbed, deep, heaving sobs, a cleansing, purging cry. "Oh, my God," she whispered in Shirley's ear. "Thank you." Shirley's eyes too were filled with tears; the women leaned back, and held each other's faces in their hands for a moment, and could do nothing but let loose the little laugh that comes in the middle of a good cry, and throw their faces to each other's shoulders again, and laugh, and cry, and laugh again.

"Oh, you're so pretty," Shirley said. "You come on in."

Inside Shirley's neat, well-appointed house, near the healing Native American medicine shield that Shirley had made for her own mother, Sharon tried to put her feelings into words. "We thank you so much," she said. "You're a special lady. There should be more people like you."

"You're strong, having to go through all you went through," Shirley replied. "You sure are strong." And then she threw her arms around Sharon again. "Oh, I've been wanting to do this ever since I saw that on *America's Most Wanted*," she said. And then, in the next instant: "Have you called your husband yet to let him know you're here? Safe and sound?"

Lena Nozizwe, our correspondent, who was along for the

reunion, along with a camera crew, began to notice something strange.

"You're talking like you're her mom," Lena said.

The two women laughed. They were holding hands.

"Well, I got me a daughter, now," Shirley said. It was a puzzling statement, and Lena let it go by.

"I tried to be strong," she said, turning to Sharon, "for you, and your sisters and brothers, so you could go on with your lives."

And the tears came again. "We just waited so long, it's been so hard," Sharon said through the tears. Shirley held her again. "When this is all over, you just look forward, don't ever look back," Shirley said. "And you've got me—you've got me now."

"I do?" Sharon said.

"You do," Shirley said.

And Sharon lay her head on Shirley's shoulder.

And Lena realized, now, what had happened. These women had bonded, had become family, in the instant that they met.

"In addition to catching fugitives, that's my proudest achievement," Lena said later. "Getting them together."

Even though it was July, Shirley fixed a Thanksgiving dinner— because there was so much to be thankful for—and after dinner, Sharon and Shirley sat on the couch for a long talk.

"I'm so glad to have you here," Shirley said. "I just wanted to hold you. I don't know if I could ever make that pain go away. But I know you missed out on a lot, mother's love and everything. And I never had a chance to have any children, I just took care of my mom and dad, and Dad died in '85, and Mom just died in '90. So I'm free, and I'm all alone."

"Not anymore," said Sharon.

Shirley responded, "Not anymore."

■ ■ ■

The next day, Sharon went to her parents' extradition hearing. Outside of the courtroom, she paced in circles, as an *AMW* cameraman taped. She was wearing Shirley's ring on her middle finger, and was twisting it around and around.

This was such a different Sharon from the one *AMW* taped three years ago. That frail girl in a poodle cut and pink sweatshirt had blossomed into a beautiful young woman with cascading light brown curls, her features more defined with age, framing her infectious wide smile with a look of sophistication and knowledge; she exudes strength, spunk, and self-confidence, and she shares her true feelings openly and gracefully.

In that moment, however, she was anything but graceful, peering through the small round window in the courtroom door. "We've got them!" she squealed. "There they are! Freak me out."

Finally, she decided to go into the courtroom, and stood looking at her parents. They looked old, and remarkably alike, he in a gold-colored short-sleeved uniform shirt, she in a pink one, both wearing identical shoes and glasses.

Their attorney asked for Elizabeth Stone's release, on her own recognizance, to return to Massachusetts. Sharon, involuntarily, shook her head no. The judge did not grant the request.

As they were being led from the room, Elizabeth Stone turned to see her daughter. She spoke, the first time Sharon had heard her voice in nine years.

"Sharon, I love you," she said.

Some love. About ten years late, and said while in handcuffs. Right.

Later, outside the courtroom, Sharon muttered, "She wouldn't be in that courtroom if she loved me."

■   ■   ■

The sentencing hearing was held back in Massachusetts on July 20, 1992. Sharon, Eve, and Ruth were the only children who attended. They all were allowed to speak—and one by one, they asked the judge to uphold Diane Dillon's sentencing recommendations, and prosecute their parents to the fullest extent of the law.

The lawyer for the defense tried to throw the blame back on *AMW:* "Outside of the fact that they left, and the case was on *America's Most Wanted,* it's really just another case." Yeah. Just another case of child abuse, brutality, and lifelong incest.

In the end, the judge gave Garrett Stone a sentence of thirty-six to fifty-four years, with a twenty-four-year minimum. He will be eligible for parole in the year 2016, when he is eighty-five years old—although, with his list of crimes, it's unlikely he'll get out even then, if he lives that long, and you can bet that Sharon will fight it all the way. He's serving his term at the Massachusetts Correctional Institute in Walpole.

Elizabeth Stone got two years at Framingham—where her daughter Sharon happened to be living at the time.

Sharon went to see her mother once. She happened to be driving by—she hadn't even known where the prison was—and her husband said, "You know, she's in there." Some time later, Sharon returned, and went in, and her mother was brought to a large sitting area. She moved to hug Sharon—but Sharon waved her off.

"I wanted to know, was there a possibility of a relationship? Were my children going to have a grandmother? Was she getting therapy? So I put her on the spot. I wanted to know, 'How could you?' She said, 'We didn't do anything wrong.'

"I started talking about having a baby, about the responsibility of being a mother, of loving the baby that you carried for nine months, and I think I saw a glimmer of emotion. But through most of it, she stared at me with cold blue eyes. She was like a rock. No emotion, no glimmer of an apology, no nothing."

She has not seen her mother since that day, nor does she intend to.

Elizabeth Stone has now served her time. She's now working in home health care, living in a rooming house, and visiting her husband every day. He's tried to get her to cut down on her visits, but she remains totally devoted to him.

The family is doing well, although the rifts are still evident sometimes, especially in their feelings about their mother; some family members still believe she was a victim, too. But the brothers and sisters always manage to have Christmas Eve together, joining a party at one of the sisters' homes. Some of them remain angry at me, for some of the decisions we made along the way, and for that, I am truly, truly sorry. It makes me very sad. But I do know we did the right thing by this family. We treated the story with dignity, and we found justice for those who sought it.

People who commit crimes, especially trusted authority figures like fathers, should pay for their actions, and Garrett Stone is paying for his.

The family did have one more tragedy to live through. Ruth, the oldest sister, the one who finally set the wheels in motion for the family's secret to be revealed, did not make it. The day before the Stones' sentencing appeal was to be heard, Ruth drank herself into oblivion, went for a walk in the woods, and disappeared.

Her husband called Sharon and Shaun, and they searched through the night. In the morning, police dogs were called in, and they found her. She had fallen into a creek. She was found frozen to death. As with her brother Frank's death, Sharon considered this a suicide.

"She was a fantastic, beautiful person," Sharon said. "She was a guardian angel for all of us, and when she made sure all of us were basically okay, she cut out.

"That's what angels do."

■   ■   ■

The other guardian angel, Shirley Tiger, is hanging in there, seven years after she was given six months to live. She and Sharon talk once a week; Sharon calls her Mom now, and her kids call her Granny.

They don't get to visit too often, but we did fly Shirley out for a surprise visit for our two-hundredth-capture special. They were also reunited in May of 1996, when Oprah Winfrey did a special about *America's Most Wanted*. Sharon didn't know Shirley was going to be there. She called Shirley in California and left a message on her machine: "Hey, Mom, guess what, I'm in a hotel in Chicago, and I'm going to be on *Oprah!*"

"She didn't know," Shirley giggles, "that I was in the hotel next door!"

And we got them together again, one more time, for our five-hundredth-capture special, after Sharon had had her third child, so Shirley could meet baby Connor, born May 3, 1995.

Baby Connor, who, of course, will grow up to call her Grandma.

■   ■   ■

I was happy to hear that Eve, who had never spoken with us before, had agreed to talk to us for this book. Eve is twenty-eight now, living in New York City, where she's a freelance toy designer. She also started taking lessons at the Lee Strasberg Theater Institute this year, and loves it. "I have more passion than I need, but I've just started dealing with it"—her feelings about her past—"at Strasberg." Because the school focuses on childhood and inner feelings, it's bringing a lot of memories back. "They want you to feel. Even though I'm upset a lot, I actually feel a lot more alive than I ever have."

And there is a lot of joy in her life now. "I didn't know you could be this happy," Eve says. "I love the world, animals, and children. Babies adore me. I'll sit in the rain and smoke a cigarette until I'm drenched. I want to feel alive."

She also feels something her sisters haven't, yet: forgiveness, for her mother. "I never heard of a woman so abused," Eve said. "You're not thinking straight when you get your ass kicked every day. This is not a normal woman. She was blindsided. I don't want her in my life, but I love her—I don't know why. I don't want her to go to her deathbed feeling no one forgives her."

We were wondering why, after all these years, she'd decided to talk with us. She said it was because she was older, because she's learned to stand up for herself, because she's tired of hiding from the truth—and because "I have a lot of people to thank. Gerald Downs [the state trooper]; my fourth-grade art teacher, who still holds up my art in class; *America's Most Wanted*—every year, I think, I should thank people. I just needed time to think about it."

■   ■   ■

One day, Sharon Stone Sullivan bought herself a brand-new turquoise suit, and went down to the local high school. She was going to talk to the teenagers about her experiences.

A week earlier, the children had been shown Sharon's segment on *America's Most Wanted*. So they were a little scared. But Sharon, as she does for everyone she meets, made it easy. She talked lightly, she laughed a little, but she got her message across: Victims of abuse feel like they have a secret.

They don't.

Their abuser has a secret.

And once you tell, it's all over, she said: The moment I told was the moment my abuse ended, and that's a powerful thing.

The students sat and listened, transfixed. Later, teachers said they'd never seen the kids sit still so long.

After class, a number of girls came up to her. Some were crying.

And Sharon brushed away their tears.

She wonders, sometimes, what to tell her children, and when. She has told Cristen a little bit, when Cristen started asking questions. "We said, 'You know how Mommy and Daddy sing you songs and dance with you? Well, my mommy and daddy didn't do that.'

"She said, 'I think we should find them and make them apologize.'"

And she holds her daughter and thinks, well, child, I never got the apology, but I sure did find them, didn't I?

And she smiles that smile, as wide as the morning itself, and her daughter smiles back.

CHAPTER FIVE

"It's Time for You to Die Now"

Choosing a way to die, that's easy. It's choosing a way to live that's the difficult thing to do.

—CLINT EASTWOOD IN *THE OUTLAW JOSEY WALES*

There are two questions that everybody always throws at *America's Most Wanted*. One has to do with the criminal's rights, and the other has to do with the victim's.

On the criminal side, there's always the question: What if this fugitive we're chasing is living a nice, productive life somewhere? What if he's reformed, and will never harm anyone again? Aren't you destroying the life of a respectable member of society by bringing his past back to haunt him?

On the victim side, the question is: Where is the line? When are you helping victims, and when are you exploiting them? Can the number one victim's advocate show in America be sure that it's not making the same mistakes the regular media are making—the media who stick microphones in the face of grieving mothers and ask them how they're feeling as they see their children's bodies being carried into an ambulance?

Those two questions are central to everything we do at *America's*

Most Wanted. And never have they collided so forcefully—or raised so much heat—as in the case of Terry Wayne Hart.

I remember seeing our first version of the story. I was sitting in the office of the executive producer, Lance Heflin, asking one question: Are we sure we should be airing this?

And I remember his answer:

John, we have to.

■ ■ ■

The Country Club Apartments were no country club, but they weren't bad. They were clean, and safe, and a decent place to raise your kids, especially if you have to raise them alone. In the summer of '91, after her marriage broke up, Cathy Kennedy moved in to the apartments, in Oklahoma City, with her eight-year-old twins and her two teenage girls. It was the younger, Jerri, who had urged her mom to split up the marriage. In fact, Jerri, even though she was only fifteen, had moved out first, and stayed with a friend for a week until her mom followed suit and got settled at the apartment complex.

Jerri was, in a lot of ways, a typical teenager, a little awkward, a little self-conscious—but there was something about her, a sort of tough, grown-up veneer, that sometimes made her seem older. She wasn't a great student, had experimented with alcohol about as much as any fifteen-year-old, and liked to hang around the apartment complex pool. Jerri was a small, shy girl, with long dark hair threatening to cover her sad and sullen eyes, and speech without emotion or affect, all of which gave her the dark aura of a kid who wasn't quite as sure of herself as she wanted everyone to believe. But when she smiled, the dark air disappeared, like night disappearing in the morning, a sly, dimpled expression replacing the shy air with one of confidence.

Her sixteen-year-old sister, Jacqueline, couldn't have been more different. Jacqueline played by the rules; Jerri liked to break them and challenge her parents to react. "My older daughter was sneaky, but Jerri would bold-face do it in front of you," says Cathy. Jacqueline would sometimes quietly raid the stash of her father's snack cakes; Jerri would stride up and take one, then strut through the living room eating it.

Cathy knew she could only control Jerri up to a point. Her discipline was tempered with certain concessions: The two could smoke cigarettes together, for example, looking in that moment more like an older and younger sister than a mother and child.

Jerri did have one driving ambition: While her friends liked to listen to heavy metal music, Jerri was enamored of rap and hip-hop, drawn to the driving, danceable beat. She loved to dance, and hoped to one day open her own dance studio.

As well as she could dance, Jerri couldn't swim a lick. So she always hung out by the shallow end of the apartment complex pool, where the younger kids hang out. And if you saw her there, listening to her hip-hop, showing off the tattoo of a cross near her ankle as she stuck a painted toe in the water, afraid to jump in, the grown-up veneer faded away, and you would see a young girl without trouble, without concern, just another teenager on a hot summer day.

At the grown-up end of the pool, on some afternoons, a couple would show up. The woman was not remarkable. She was tall, somewhat heavyset but not terribly unattractive, with big, teased blond hair. Her companion was a good-looking young blond man whom you might not notice until he took his shirt off, and then you couldn't help but notice: He had a huge, intricate tattoo, starting on his right pectoral muscle, stretching up around his shoulder, and across his back. It was a massive hallucination of a tattoo, with a soaring eagle, mushrooms flying through clouds, swirls, designs, and interlocking patterns.

The couple would bring lotion, towels, two pool floats, and a cooler of beer mixed with tomato juice. Anyone with a trained eye, looking at the man's tattoo, would guess that this man had spent time in prison.

That guess would be correct.

■　■　■

Terry Wayne Hart stole a snowmobile in Alaska when he was a young teenager. But it was just the beginning of his wild ride. By the time he was twenty-eight, he'd been in detention centers and jails and prisons about as much as he'd been out of them.

Hart never took well to jail, never learned how to keep his nose clean, stay out of trouble, and serve his time. In one of his early stints, at the Pontotoc County jail in Oklahoma, records show he tried to slit his wrists. His brother, Mark, had hanged himself in a Florida prison in 1978; Terry was greatly affected by this, and feared that he was following the same path.

So when he finally got out of prison in 1990, and moved back with his parents in Oklahoma, they were hoping he'd clean up his act a bit. And at first it seemed as though he might. "He was a good boy," remembers his stepmother, Patsy, "but he didn't know how to act, he'd been in prison so long."

Terry, who had grown into a good-looking young man, with wavy brown hair and green eyes, started attracting women. Lots of them. They would come from as far as 150 miles away, from Kansas and the Oklahoma panhandle, to ride around with Terry, or hang out at the house and talk. "He was just making up for lost time, experimenting," Peggy says. "He wasn't in love with any of them." He wouldn't even kiss them, mostly; just talk with them.

And, of course, take their money.

"He was a con artist in ways, getting money off those women coming around," said Patsy. "It wasn't much, twenty dollars here, maybe a hundred."

For a short time he moved in with a woman who lived down the road. It didn't last long, and soon, in the fall of 1990, Terry was looking for a new target.

■　■　■

Things were quiet at Panama Red's: It was just after 8:00 P.M. on a Saturday night, and the bar wouldn't start hopping until after the band started playing. So when two women from a nearby apartment complex came by, they found the place pretty empty. A little country music on the jukebox, a little Budweiser on the floor:

nothing special going on. The women, Peggy Carothers and a friend, ordered a couple of beers, and settled in.

About half an hour later, two decent-looking guys sauntered in. They said something to a waitress, who walked over to the women.

"Those two guys want to know if they can come sit with you," she said.

Why not? thought Peggy. Peggy hadn't had the best luck with men. She has a nice smile and a soft voice, but hadn't had too many guys come into her life whom you could call charming. And Terry Hart, when he wanted to be, was charming.

The band started up, and Terry asked Peggy to dance. Later that evening, they went out to eat, and then back to Peggy's for a few more beers. The conversation rolled on into the night, and Peggy thought she'd struck gold. This is a nice man, she thought. This is a nice man who will treat me right.

Within a week, Terry had moved in with Peggy. A few days later, on October 15, 1990, Peggy was celebrating her birthday, and Terry took her out to Panama Red's. He had already taken to telling people they were married, and had even given her a ring that he expected her to wear all the time.

And the honeymoon lasted for months. He sent her flowers. He held doors for her. He went with her to church. He had found work painting and roofing, and was working hard.

One afternoon, while she was working at Favorites Restaurant, Terry showed up unexpectedly. He said he needed to drive a friend home to Lawton, but he never came back. He still hadn't come back the next night, either, and Peggy was a little miffed. So, at the end of her shift, when a co-worker asked her if she'd like to go out for a drink, Peggy said, sure. Blow off a little steam, maybe show Terry that he can't just come and go as he pleases and expect me to be sitting home waiting for him.

Peggy was halfway through a beer when Terry found her. He thought she was out trying to pick up men, but he didn't say so. He just told her to come home. He was short with her, and sullen on the ride back to their apartment.

And when they got inside, he balled up a fist, and hit her, harder than she had ever been hit in her life.

He blackened both her eyes. He broke her cheekbone. He beat her so badly that he was afraid to take her to the hospital. And so she sat, beaten and bloody and black and blue, and she looked across the room at the man she thought she knew, and she said to herself, well, the honeymoon is over.

"After that, he abused me all the time," Peggy said. And his abuse, strong and physical, was laced with the madman anger of a jealous rage. Peggy never gave him reason to distrust her, but his distrust grew stronger and stronger nevertheless. "He would come home, and check in the bathroom, to see if somebody had been there, to see if the seat was up. He'd see if there was hairs in the bathroom," she said. "Or, when he came home, he'd check the hood of the car to see if it was warm. He'd check the mileage. Or he'd check the gas and see if there was the same amount of gas as when he left for work. He'd think that I had been out running around somewhere. He'd check the ashtrays, to see if there was a cigarette or something there."

Once, her mother had been visiting while Terry was at work; she brushed her hair before she left, and when Terry came home, he found a hair on the bathroom sink. Furious, he demanded that Peggy tell him what was going on. He would not believe that the hair belonged to her mother.

"He started abusing me over it," she said. "He was accusing me that somebody had been there. And my mom even had to come over and tell him. And he still wouldn't believe it."

Terry, apparently, was slowly dipping back into the criminal life, as well. On April 11, 1991, he and a friend tried to rob an apartment building. But as the friend was handing a TV set out the window to Terry, an alert citizen across the street spotted them and called police. Terry was booked and released.

It might seem odd, but Terry was a very neat person. He kept his clothes and the apartment perfectly clean. He couldn't stand to see a dish sitting in the sink; he'd have to go wash it, dry it, and put it away. I've had forensic psychologists tell me this is not uncommon in violent men like Terry Hart. Their desire is to control everything around them, to control their world and the people in it. The obsessive neatness is just one outcropping of that desire for control. So are the violent outbursts, stemming from the same place—from an unstoppable anger at events that seem to be spinning out of control.

Sometimes, there was very little warning to signal that Terry Hart's outbursts were coming. Peggy would come home, and he would think she had been running around on him, but he would be really nice, really sweet, and Peggy would think, well, maybe it's going to be okay, but then she would look into his eyes, and see an evil look on his face, and know that she was going to get hit.

After the fury of these beatings was past, Terry would beg forgiveness, promise to return to church with Peggy, to change his ways; and Peggy, desperate to believe him, would give him one more chance. "One time, Terry beat me and I went to the hospital. I came back and I filed charges on him. And he called me and told me that he'd go to church and everything and he'd never hit me again. And we did. We went to church and he even went up to the altar, but it was all just a front."

As the summer wore on, Terry became worse. He had a November court date hanging over him from the unresolved burglary charge; Peggy thought, maybe this was making him nervous and more abusive, knowing that he would probably have to become a fugitive or go back to jail. Or maybe it was because he was drinking more.

The abuse got so bad that on August 17, 1991, after one particularly terrible incident with Terry, Peggy wrote a note and slipped it into a vase. Later she said she was thinking that if something happened to her, someone would find the note. Really, it was more like putting a message in a bottle, a lonely little cry for help, sailing it off of the frightening island on which she was marooned with a lunatic, wondering if anyone would ever read these words:

"I got up out of bed at 7:00 A.M. Terry gets dressed out of bed for work asking are you going to be here when I get home. Then he said how he was going to kill the Grays and Steve [friends of Peggy's and an ex-boyfriend from junior high school].

"And if I leave before November when he runs, he would kill my nephews and my family and have me killed. He said that he would have me killed and that he would be sitting in church for an alibi.

"He grabbed my hair and started holding me down, beating me. He put his hands in the back of my head and started beating me. I was scared. I didn't know what to do. Last night he made me wear a Teddy and told me I had to do what he told me.

"He needs help and he needs help bad."

It was a tiny chip of her pain, a fragment of her sad tale, that she had broken off, and placed as an offering in a hidden place. It was, in a way, her first tiny attempt to break away from Terry, at least in her own mind. But it wasn't enough to save her.

One day the next month, in September of 1991, Peggy was late coming home from work. When she arrived, Terry was already out on the lawn, pacing, and she knew something bad was going to happen.

Before she could get out of her van, Terry was at her door, pulling her out, pulling her into the house, where he began hitting her. "If you're going to act like a whore," he said between blows, "I'm going to treat you like a whore."

He pulled her back into the van, and headed for the highway. He told Peggy that he was taking her to a biker gang, and he was going to have them all rape her. And then he would have her killed.

He was hitting her the entire time, weaving all over the road.

They pulled over at a roadhouse, where a number of motorcycles were parked outside. Terry talked to some of the bikers, who, fortunately, would have nothing to do with his crazy scheme. So Terry got back in the van, and headed back up the highway, still pummeling his poor girlfriend.

He pulled into a gas station, and stopped the van. He took Peggy into the back of the van and began punching her, harder now, getting the leverage that he could not get while he was driving, hitting her so hard that she was about to pass out. Peggy's still not sure how she got away, but she found herself running toward the store, and a car door opened, and the driver said, get in.

She saw a gun in the car.

She saw Terry running after her.

She figured she would take her chances.

She got in the car.

It turned out that the gun belonged to the driver, a security guard, who told her he would take her to the hospital. As they drove off she looked back and saw Terry, in the parking lot, screaming, and shaking all over.

■   ■   ■

This is another one of those situations in which people start to blame the victim. They say, why didn't she just move out? Why did she put up with this sort of thing?

I've worked with hundreds of abused wives over the years, and girlfriends of abusive men, and I've learned one thing: People who have not lived in their hell cannot comprehend what that hell is like, what a terrible prison these violent men put them in. These brutal men, these cowards, who have to take out their violent rage on women too defenseless to fight back, have a need to control their victims, to exert total control over their movements.

It's not like these guys go to school for this, yet they all seem to play the game the same way. First, they find women who don't have the highest self-esteem to begin with. They begin by making the woman spend every waking minute with them; the guy pretends it's because he loves her so much, but really it's a way of isolating her from her family, her friends, her support group.

Once they have control, they begin picking fights, for several reasons: one, because they're bored; two, because they're excessively jealous; third, and most important, to show off their control, to exert it and flex it and strengthen it. All of this, of course, stems from their own deep-seated insecurity, their own lack of self-esteem. They fight, harder and harder, to exert control as a way of showing their strength.

Of course, it is never enough. They are trying to use the woman's forced affection and attention to make themselves feel less inadequate. They usually pour alcohol and drugs into the mix, trying to stem the pain of their own self-loathing. It never works, not for very long, so they try harder and harder to control their victims, hit them harder, beat them more violently. And still the insecurity increases, and so the rage increases.

And all the women say the same thing: The physical violence is terrible, but the emotional and mental abuse is worse. The controlling nature of these beasts is what becomes so horribly unbearable. They threaten everything imaginable: If you leave me, I will kill you, I will kill your mother, your brothers, your children, and you will be responsible for their deaths. And the women, barely able to think for the fear and the pain that is inflicted on them, and usually without the resources to find help (Where will I go? Who will help me get away?), can see only one choice in their own minds, to try to placate the beast, keep it at bay, keep it quiet, while they try to figure a way to escape an inescapable prison.

Some of the producers at *America's Most Wanted* have shied away from stories like Peggy's over the years, thinking that the audience won't be sympathetic to the victim, fearing that viewers will take the awful position of, well, if she's not going to move out, then she's bringing it on herself.

And I have to tell them, what about the women who do decide to move out? Where are they going to go? Get an apartment around the corner? So that a week later you can see him on the street and he will beat you senseless? Or move out of the city? And what if she doesn't happen to have the money, the planning ability, the stamina, and the mental preparedness it takes to pack up, leave your life, your friends, your family, everything you've ever known in the only place you've ever lived, move out of state, all alone, find a place to live, get far enough away that he will never find you—and still know, in the back of your mind, that no matter where you go, he will always find you? Who is that strong? Are you that strong? Could you do that?

And what if he does harm your family? How will you live with that?

This is the kind of mental prison that Terry Hart had placed Peggy Carothers in. He had threatened to kill her family if she left him. She was terrified.

But for all that, after this last beating, she had no choice.

She returned to Terry, after that scene in the parking lot.

But not for long.

■　■　■

On the morning of September 20, Peggy acted as cheerful as she could, as though she was happier than she'd been in a long time. But Terry seemed to sense something was wrong. "You'd better be here when I get back," he said ominously.

As soon as Terry was out the door, she called her brothers. They'd discussed this the night before, and were ready to spring into action. Peggy told them to move fast.

They came with a pickup truck, and within hours had loaded into it everything Peggy had, furniture, clothes, everything, and as they drove away, Peggy felt relieved. But in her head, over and over, she heard Terry Hart's voice: If you leave me, I will kill you.

They moved Peggy's things into storage, and Peggy went to stay at her mother's house. That afternoon, her friend Tawna came by. We're going out, she said. We're going out, and we're not talking about Terry. That's behind you.

They went to the state fair first, and played some games, and went on some rides, enjoying the feel of the sun on their faces. The sounds of children laughing and the low-key fun of a state fair made Peggy feel like she had traveled a million miles away from that prison she had been living in.

The women were feeling so good that they didn't notice a man, lurking behind a tent, watching them. Following them.

He followed them through the fair, and when they had had enough, and went downtown to Panama Red's, he followed them there, still hiding, lurking, stalking, waiting for the right moment.

But when the club's bouncer began to walk Peggy to her car, the man could lie in wait no more. He strode toward the bouncer, a massive blue tattoo showing around the edges of his muscle shirt, as he balled up a fist and hit the bouncer as hard as he could, and then began pummeling him.

Tawna saw Terry Hart do this, and she jumped on his back, and Terry punched her, blackening her eye. In the melee, Tawna and Peggy managed to get away. Tawna convinced Peggy to call the police, and then they went back to Peggy's old apartment, which was right across the street, to await their arrival—a bad move, in retrospect.

Perhaps she had had a bit too much to drink, and there was her own comfortable couch, friendly and inviting; for whatever reason, Peggy, feeling like nothing ever changes, lay down on the couch in the apartment she had just moved out of, and fell into a fitful, restless sleep.

■　■　■

On that same night, on the other side of the same apartment complex, Jerri Kennedy's mom had gone over to her boyfriend's house, leaving Jerri at home with her sister, Jackie. The girls and Jackie's boyfriend, along with the twins, had spent the night watching TV. Sometime around midnight, Jerri was getting bored, but not tired. The twins were sleeping, and Jerri figured that Jackie would probably not mind a little privacy. So she decided to take a little stroll around the apartment complex. The phone in the apartment was out anyway, so she walked down to the pay phones to call some friends, see who was still awake.

No one answered, and she turned around and started heading back to the apartment. She couldn't have been more than eight feet from her front door when she noticed a gold Pontiac Trans Am pass her from behind, make a U-turn, and park, facing her. As she walked up to the car, a man stepped out.

The man had just been in a fight outside a bar, his girlfriend had just left him, and he was not in a very good mood.

"Do you know Peggy?" he asked the girl as she walked by.

"No, I don't," she replied.

He asked again: "Do you know where Peggy is?"

Now she was getting a little weirded out. She noticed her sister, poking her head out of the apartment door, making sure Jerri was okay. She motioned to her sister that she would be right in. "I've got to go," she said to the man.

"Look what Peggy did," the man said to Jerri, pointing to a broken headlight on his car.

"Sorry about that, mister," Jerri replied. She started moving, slowly, toward her front door.

"Give me a kiss," he said to her.

Jerri said no, and began to walk past the man.

From behind her, she felt a pain, something tugging at the back of her head, and then she realized that the man had taken hold of her hair, and was pulling her backward, toward the Trans Am. He threw her across the hood.

"If you scream, I'll cut you," he said.

Jerri could not help herself. She began to scream.

From somewhere, a knife appeared, moving in a hard, fast motion, drawing a line along her hand, a line now marked in red.

Inside the apartment, Jackie heard the TV, and nothing else.

Now the man had his hand over Jerri's mouth, and was dragging her behind the apartments. He was strong and muscular, she was small and frightened, and he had no trouble tossing her around, tossing her to the pavement. He knelt, and pounded her head into the cement.

Somehow, she broke free.

She ran to the back door of one of the apartments, and banged on it, as hard as she could.

No one was home.

And in a second, she felt the tug at the back of her scalp, and knew that this time, she would not escape.

■   ■   ■

There is a drainage ditch that runs behind the apartment complex, down a small hill, out of the sightline of the mostly darkened windows. It is a concrete canal, about eighteen feet wide, with ten-foot side walls. The water is several inches deep in places. Bordering the canal is a fence to keep people out. It is through a hole in this fence that he he dragged her, through the knee-high weeds, down into the ditch.

"Sweetheart," she heard the man saying, "have you ever been raped or killed?"

And this frightened child, this innocent girl who had always been afraid to go to the deep end of the pool, now found her face an inch above the slowly moving water, smelling the damp muddy leg of a pair of denim jeans against her cheek, and now a great force behind her propelled her forward and down, under the water.

Jerri got up to run, but could not. She slipped and slid in the muddy creek. The man punched her, again and again, in the face, in the stomach. He was tearing off her clothes, and pounding her head against the cement retaining wall. She teetered on the edge of consciousness. She managed to break away, but in her confusion ran in the wrong direction, away from the apartments, and he caught her, and began his beatings anew.

His shirt was off now as well, and she saw a massive tattoo that reached from his chest around to his back, a blue hallucination of fierce eagles and roiling clouds.

He put her face in the water again, and, terrified, she pushed him away. He punched her and kicked her with the full force of mindless rage, and Jerri thought, I am going to die. I am going to drown. Or he is going to kill me just by punching me. She tried to fight him off, tried to grab his hair, anything, but it was like trying to stop a freight train with a pillow. Nothing she did seemed to have the slightest effect.

"How can you do this to me?" she pleaded, sputtering. "I've never done anything to you!"

It is the moment every crime victim comes to—pleading with the tormentor, trying to reach some human place, some tiny hidden bit of common decency.

But Terry Hart was too far gone. There was no humanity left. There was only rage.

"You're a whore," he told her. "If you're going to act like a whore, I'm going to treat you like a whore."

"How can you do this to me?" she cried.

"It's easy," he said.

And then Terry Hart raped Jerri Kennedy. And all the while, he called her by name.

Not by her own name.

He was calling her Peggy.

"You'll never leave me again, Peggy," he said, over and over, as he forced himself on the battered, bloody child. "You'll never leave me again."

■ ■ ■

When he was done, he said to her, "It's time for you to die now."

He put his hands on her throat, big, powerful hands. He began to choke her. Jerri frantically looked for options. How can I get away? She saw no escape, she saw only her life, passing away from her. It is not fair, it is not fair, it is not fair, she thought, and looked down at the man taking her life away, and saw his pants down around his ankles.

And, as she gasped for her last breath, the terror faded, and she had one crystal moment of clarity. She thought of her mother, and she remembered something her mother once told her, her mother, a strong woman, not given to sentiment or mincing words.

"If any guy tries to do anything to you," Mom had told her, "kick him between the legs."

Her face was beaten beyond recognition, she had been punched harder than most men could bear, she was bleeding, her face had been pounded into the concrete, and she had been viciously raped—but from somewhere inside, Jerri found strength.

Strength for one kick.

"I kicked him as hard as I could between the legs," Jerri said. "Then I punched him in the nose. And I pushed him off me. And I started running as fast as I could."

Terry Hart reeled, staggering backward, and Jerri seized the moment. She somehow jumped the wall, then ran blindly, as fast and hard as she could, and somehow, found herself at her mom's boyfriend's apartment, the apartment where her mom was spending the evening. She ran up the stairs, and pounded on the door for dear life.

No one answered.

"I was screaming," Jerri said. "I was thinking, Oh, God, this is the only chance I've got. If he catches me this time he will kill me. I didn't think anyone was coming to the door. I thought he was going to get me again and finish the job."

She pounded, and pounded. And then she heard footsteps behind her, and felt a pain at the back of her head, a tugging.

Terry Hart had followed her.

He had her by the hair.

He was trying to pull her back down the stairs.

Jerri, bloody, naked, and bruised beyond recognition, grabbed on to the steel railing outside the apartment door. Terri pulled harder, but Jerri held on and wouldn't let go.

Then the railing gave way, breaking off.

And at that moment, the door opened.

Jerri's mother, Cathy, came out, and did not comprehend what she saw. This beaten, naked girl at her feet, this wild man pulling on her hair.

Jerri was beaten so severely, her mother did not recognize her.

She did not recognize that this was her own daughter at her feet.

And then she saw the tattoo of a cross on the girl's ankle.

And realized it was Jerri.

Cathy screamed, and started pounding her fists onto the man's body, as he dragged her daughter away.

"It's all right," the man said. "This is my wife."

"Your wife?" Cathy screamed back. "You asshole, this is my daughter!"

There played out a macabre scene, a life-or-death tug-of-war, Cathy Kennedy and Terry Hart both pulling on the girl, fighting all the way down to the bottom of the stairs, Cathy letting go of her daughter to beat on the man, Terry barely acknowledging her presence, until finally he let go, dropping Jerri's head on the cement at the bottom of the stairs. He walked off, as though nothing had happened. A neighbor who had seen the fight approached him to try to stop him.

Terry just fixed him with his eyes. "You are a dead man," he said, then turned, and trotted off, into the night.

Cathy took her daughter up to their apartment, and dialed 911. As they waited for the ambulance, her daughter was screaming. Cathy wanted to watch for the ambulance, but Jerri would not let her go.

"She was in hysterics, screaming, Mom, shut the door, don't let him in, don't let him get to me, don't let him hurt me anymore," Cathy said. "And I tried to console her and said, 'There's nobody that's going to hurt you anymore, he's gone, you're here with me, I've got the door locked, nobody's going to hurt you.' And I started to go out the door, and she started to scream, 'Don't go out there, he'll hurt you, he'll kill you.' "

Jerri was taken to the hospital. As standard procedure, pictures were taken of her bruised face. Later, Jerri would ask to see the pictures, to see what she looked like that night. It was decided that they were too horrible to show her. She has not seen them to this day.

■　■　■

Peggy woke up on the couch to a strange sight: Terry was in the kitchen, washing his tennis shoes. She hadn't intended to return to the apartment that night. She hadn't intended to fall asleep there. But she had, and now here she was.

She told Terry that she was going to go back to her mother's house. That it was over between them.

He said no, we've discussed this. We're going to be together. We'll work it out. He was very calm now.

Often, after their most violent outbursts, these predators become very calm. They seem perfectly logical and sane. They return to the habits that are most familiar to them—in Terry's case, that would be washing and cleaning. They try to reorder the universe, to find a way to make it all right, in their own minds. Often they're able to convince themselves that the horrible crimes they committed never took place. I don't think that was the case with Terry Hart. I think he had just switched back into his controlling mode.

But this was not a situation Terry Hart could control. As morning broke, the word was all over the apartment complex.

A neighbor's child knocked on Peggy's door, saying that the neighbor wanted to talk to Peggy. Peggy went next door, and the neighbor told Peggy what she had heard: that Terry had raped a little girl, and that everyone was looking for him.

There's no way, Peggy thought. He was at Panama's, I saw him there, we fought. There's no way, she thought. Why would he rape a little girl?

She went back to the apartment. Terry was packing. She confronted him about what her neighbor had said.

He said he hadn't done anything wrong, but with the burglary charges hanging over his head he couldn't afford the heat. He was throwing things in the trunk of his car when a woman drove up, parking her car to block his from exiting.

She got out of her car.

She had a stick in her hand.

And fire in her eyes.

"If I was thinking straight I would have told the kids to call the police right then," said Cathy Kennedy. "But if I had been thinking straight, I would have took something with me. A gun, or something, and incapacitated him."

Instead, when Cathy had returned from the hospital, and some of the neighbor children told her that they had seen the car of the man who raped her daughter, that it was back at his apartment, she didn't think. She grabbed a stick and followed her instincts.

"He was carrying an armload of stuff and his girlfriend comes out a couple of seconds behind him, and I confronted him about it," said Cathy. A small but angry woman confronting a man strong enough to snap her in half, a man capable of terrible, terrible violence, as Cathy had been witness to just hours before. But she was too filled with anger to feel fear.

She told him that she knew he was the man who raped her daughter. He denied it.

She banged her stick on the hood of the car. "You're the one that did this to my daughter last night, you raped and beat my daughter up," she said.

"No lady, you're crazy, you don't know what you're talking about," he yelled.

"Take off your shirt," she ordered him. She remembered the tattoo. She was certain of that.

Terry Hart refused to take his shirt off.

"Terry, what is she talking about?" asked Peggy.

"She's crazy. Let's go," he said. He ordered Peggy into the car.

She saw the crazed look in his eye, and knew better than to argue. But in the car, she confronted him.

Why wouldn't you take off your shirt, she asked.

Because I didn't want her to see my tattoos, he admitted.

Peggy got Terry Hart to drop her off at her mother's house. He said again that he had not raped that little girl, and that he would return for her when the heat died down. He said he loved her. Peggy didn't even say goodbye. She just got out of the car. And as she watched the taillights of the gold Trans Am as it pulled away, she knew, in her heart, that she was through with him forever.

But this nightmare wasn't over for Peggy. There was something she had to do.

She had her mother drive her over to the section of the apartments where the little girl had been raped. They asked around, and found out which apartment she lived in.

Peggy went up and knocked on the door. The woman who answered was the same one who had confronted Terry in the parking lot. Peggy explained why she was there.

She expected the woman to be angry at her, but Cathy spoke to her with kindness. And then she took her in to see Jerri.

■   ■   ■

"I saw Jerri laying in bed. She was beat up real bad. Her whole face was blue. She couldn't really talk," Peggy said. "When I saw her, as abused as she was, I remember how Terry had abused me.

"I had looked just like her. He had beat me like a man, like he had been beating her. He just didn't stop, he wouldn't stop. And I could see it happening all over, him doing that to me, as what he did to her."

Peggy had to leave the room. Later, when Jerri was able to speak, the two women had their first conversation. Two women, brought together by an evil force, bonded by their contact with the same predator. Peggy, an insecure, grown woman, who had suffered his abuse for so many months; Jerri, a feisty young girl who thought she had nothing to fear.

"She told me that when he was raping her, he was calling her Peggy," Peggy said later. "That made me sick to my stomach." She felt that what had happened to this girl was her fault, that somehow she had caused this catastrophe. "I felt that if I hadn't moved out, none of this would have happened. I feel guilty for the little girl. It should have been me instead of her."

Again, that's part of the true evil of these men: In addition to the physical abuse, which in Peggy's case was not far from fatal, there was the psychological prison. She had escaped from the prison, just for a day, and look at what happened! Look at how this poor innocent child has been beaten! If I just hadn't tried to get away from him . . .

For Peggy, the guilt was compounded by the knowledge that, now that Hart was on the prowl, there was no telling whom he might attack next.

"He's evil," said Peggy. "He's very, very evil. He'll do anything. He told me that he would never go back to prison again. He's not afraid of nothing. He's not afraid of nobody. He's evil."

But she did not say this to Jerri. She tried to remain as calm and reassuring as she could be. So the woman and the girl talked, bared their wounds to each other, and each went away feeling a little less alone. But each, in her own way, had to live with the same fear:

What if he comes back?

■ ■ ■

In the weeks that followed, Jerri's wounds began to heal, slowly. Her physical wounds, anyway. Inside, she was ripped to pieces. And nothing was making those wounds feel better.

"All these people come up to me and say, 'You're lucky to be alive,'" she said. "I'd tell them, yeah, it didn't happen to you.

"You don't have to wake up at night in a cold sweat because you see his face in your dreams.

"You don't have to live with being scared to be home by yourself. Thinking that he's going to come back and get you again. And most people, they don't understand what you have to live through when something like this happens to you. Living the way I do, and the fear that I live in, you know, it's just like being dead. Nothing really changes. Everything is the same. You see the same things, you have the same flashbacks. And then you wake up the same, night after night, just seeing his face."

■ ■ ■

Terry Hart was a fugitive, and as the months dragged on, there was no sign of him. A source told investigators that Hart might be using the alias Randy Staggs. And the gold Pontiac was found in Jeffersonville, Indiana, four months after the rape.

But Hart was not found in Indiana. He had, however, clearly crossed state lines, meaning that the case could now become a federal matter, and in March, the Federal Bureau of Investigation requested and was issued a UFAP—a document charging Hart with unlawful flight to avoid prosecution.

The case, basically, was stone cold. Hart could be anywhere. He had the knowledge, and the skills, to blend in wherever he went, to find work and stay quiet.

It looked, frankly, like this might be one of those cases where the bad guy wins.

Fortunately, the case landed on the desk of a guy who likes to track men. And who doesn't like to lose.

■ ■ ■

Walt Lamar had been with the FBI for eleven years by the spring of 1992. But he did not come to the FBI by the most conventional of routes.

Lamar's father, Newton, was the president of the Wichita Indian tribe, and had become a well-known national leader in the Native American community. His mother grew up on the Blackfeet Reservation in Browning, Montana.

After little Walt was born, the family moved to the Wind River Reservation, where Newton became the chief of police. Walt loved it when his dad would put him up on the front seat of his 1954 Pontiac patrol car. "Dad had on his uniform and gun and he'd turn on the siren and the lights for me," he said. "I felt he had a pride in what he did."

That pride stayed with Walt, as did the pride of his grandfather before him: Walt's grandfather Ed Gobert had been the deputy sheriff in Glacier County, Montana. The handcuffs that Walt carries today are the same ones Grandpa Ed carried.

After college, Walt became a teacher on the Blackfeet Reservation. That's when he met Special Agent Chuck Choney, himself a member of the Comanche tribe of Oklahoma, who was working as a recruiter for the FBI. "He was a great big fellow, a decorated Vietnam veteran," Walt remembers. "I had a lot of respect for him."

Although law enforcement had always been in the back of Walt's mind, he'd never thought of the FBI until then. "To meet a guy like me that was in the FBI made me think it could be a reality for me," he said. "In the past, the agency had almost exclusively hired white males." There were few role models for women and minorities.

But Chuck encouraged Walt to try, and the challenge interested him. "I wanted to succeed for my family. I wanted to succeed because I am an American Indian."

After making it into the bureau, Walt got himself assigned to fugitive apprehension—something he seemed to have a special predilection for. It was almost a sixth sense—like the time he was hunting for fugitive Johnny Merrill.

"I was in San Francisco," he recalled, "and all I had was a months-old lead, a phone call made from the fugitive to his mother in Mississippi." But Walt decided to play what the uninitiated call a hunch. "The Tenderloin section of San Francisco is one place people on the run gravitate to. There are soup kitchens. I had a young agent with me, and I said, 'Let's go down to the Tenderloin and show his picture around.' We made a left-hand turn in, walked a half-block, and he walks right in front of us. I said, 'That's him, right there.' I walked up behind him and said, 'Johnny Merrill, you're the unluckiest guy I ever met.'"

It was the same when he was hunting fugitive Roosevelt Ferguson, wanted for capital murder in Arkansas. Walt went to an area of town where he thought Ferguson might be hanging out. "I saw three guys a half-block away, sitting on a stoop, and I said, 'There he is—the guy on the left.'" And as he walked up, he realized he was right. "What are the odds of that happening? It's more than just having a lead. It's a sixth sense. People say I have a golden horseshoe—that I'm always in the right place at the right time."

The right place—if, of course, you don't mind being shot at, as Walt has been, more than once. He is a careful hunter of men, but an aggressive one—and those of us who've gotten to know him know that he'll stop at nothing when it comes to tracking down his man. Walt has that mixture of cowboy and scientist, instinct and logic, aggression and precision, that makes for a good agent. "To work through the challenge of finding a person that doesn't want to be found, there is a certain exhilaration to the chase. And once the arrest is made there's a certain exhilaration because of the danger of the situation you were in. There is a heightened sense of awareness, an adrenaline rush."

Walt had been transferred to the Oklahoma City bureau a few months before Terry Hart's attack on Jerri Kennedy. The case was first assigned to Sergeant Scott Cannon of the Oklahoma County sheriff's department. The two men, both part of a multi-agency fugitive task force, had worked together before. Cannon had the strong instincts and the keen eye of a manhunter, too. When Walt was assigned to the case, the two men knew that together, they could find Terry Hart.

But they knew they would need some help.

■   ■   ■

In the afternoons, about once a week, reporters for *America's Most Wanted* gather around a table in the conference room to pitch their stories. The questioning is tough: Why should we put this guy on *America's Most Wanted*? Do we know he's bad enough? What do we have to tell the story with? Who will talk to us? Have we talked to the victims? Do they want their stories on television? What pictures are available? What video?

In the case of Terry Hart, the questioning was pretty intense. The victim was only fifteen years old. The reporter said Jerri was willing to go on air and tell her story.

Most TV shows would jump at the chance. Compelling television, they would say. But we were worried. Did the girl understand what she was getting herself into? That all her friends would see her and know she had been raped?

The reporter argued that the details of the case were already known in her area.

Some of the show producers argued that perhaps it would be better to put her in shadow—to silhouette or digitize her face, so that she could be heard but not recognized. Even though we had the victim's consent, they argued, the viewer might think we were exploiting this girl's pain for the sake of ratings. It would make us seem more sensitive if we put her in shadow, and it might spare the victim some suffering.

This argument was offered to Jerri Kennedy.

And in her soft, eloquent voice, with her clear and simple logic, she explained: It was important that she not hide in shadows, she said. Because she wanted to send a message. That she wasn't the one who had to hide; Terry Hart was.

"I think most girls are ashamed of what happened to them," she said. "They are embarrassed, they are going to think it's their fault. Because they might have been wearing something wrong, or doing something wrong. But you know, it don't matter if you are wearing a real short skirt or kissing on everybody. You don't deserve to get raped. It don't matter what you're doing—no one deserves to get raped."

She said she wanted to do whatever it takes to find Terry Hart—not just to exorcise her own demons, but to take a very real demon off the streets.

"If they catch him on *America's Most Wanted,* then I think some of the nightmares will stop, because I'll know he's not on the streets. And I would hate for someone to go through the same thing I went through.

"It's hard to live, knowing he's still out there. I know he'll do it again, and again, and again, until he dies."

There are still those who question our decision to let Jerri go on air, full-face, with her name superimposed on the screen.

But I think that Jerri had the answer. I find such strength in the courage of girls like this. I'm so proud of Jerri for her bravery, to stand up and say, I didn't do anything wrong. She lived in fear of Terry Hart, and she had to believe, as she spoke to us, that he would be watching. And this was her one chance to say to him, as she said to all the world: The hell with Terry Hart. He hurt me. But he did not break me. He took something from me. But he did not break my spirit. I will prevail over Terry Hart. He will be captured, and I will be the one who led the team that took him down.

It was a message that I knew so many viewers would draw strength from. In the end, you have to make your decision not based on who's going to think you did wrong, but what you know in your heart is right.

There was no question. We would air the case. Jerri would go on air. And we would find Terry Hart.

■   ■   ■

The producers decided to reenact the case. Cases like this are difficult to reenact, because they force us, once again, to walk a very fine line.

You see, whenever we do a reenactment, there are two forces at work. We want to show how heinous the crime is; but we don't want to put on a program that's too violent. However, when we do tone down the violence, we always get heat from the police. "You didn't show how violent that guy was," they'd say. "How horrible the crime was. How mutilated the victim was. Nobody's gonna want to turn this guy in 'cause you didn't make it look like he did anything all that bad."

I have to admit, I'm sympathetic to their point of view. I hate portraying these guys as anything less than the animals they are. But we know that, to keep people watching the show, and to keep it on the air, we can't portray the crimes in all their gruesome detail.

In this case, I felt that there was no question that we'd have to tone it down a lot. "The scene of a mother, with her naked, beaten daughter, playing tug-of-war with a rapist—how do you put something like that on TV?" said Gary Meyers, the director of the reenactment. "It was really just so bizarre."

Gary was in charge of all the little details of putting together the reenactment—finding a creek in which to stage the rape scene, for example, involved testing the water in a laboratory to make sure it was safe; shooting at night meant stretching light cables near the water, a dangerous task if not done right; the creek they found had no path like the one Jerri ran along, so a path had to be cut.

Reenacting the surrounding events was pretty routine; we showed Jerri hanging out by the pool, afraid to go in the water. Gary made up an actor with Hart's elaborate tattoo, because we felt it would be an important part of catching him. The makeup people used a special semipermanent ink, which lasts about five days, and worked with photos of Hart and tattoo templates borrowed from a friendly tattoo parlor.

Peggy came on camera to tell about Hart's constant abuse, and we showed how she finally got up the courage to move out. The reenactment scenes were intertwined with the interviews with Peggy and Jerri. Both women were strong on camera; clear, precise, and unafraid.

Reenacting the crime was the tough part. It was physically very taxing on the actors. We couldn't ask the young actress who was portraying Jerri to keep her head under water as many times as would be needed to complete the filming; so in some of the shots, when you see Terry Hart appearing to hold Jerri's head underwater, it was actually the director's head. Gary subbed in for the actress, so as not to wear her out.

All that night, and over the next week, Gary continued to struggle with the question of how much of the violence to portray. "I feel we need to show the horror of the crime that was committed," said Gary. "I think the more people are emotionally involved in the case, the more they will want to go out and get the guy. And after I read the case file on this case, I didn't care about anything except getting this guy caught."

After much back-and-forth discussion, Gary did tone the violence down to a great degree. In addition to the obvious need to keep the actress clothed, we decided not to make her up to show how horribly disfigured and bloody the victim was after the attack, and to suggest, rather than directly portray, the brutal violence of the attack. When Gary was done with his work, we toned the reenactment down much, much more in the edit room. In the end, I think the product was powerful but tasteful.

Not everyone agreed.

"I thought it was a bunch of bull," Cathy said when she saw our reenactment of her daughter's attack. By toning down the violence, and by staying away from portraying the horrific bruises and blood, Cathy thought we did her daughter a terrible disservice, masking and ameliorating Terry Hart's brutal nature. And she let us know, in no uncertain terms.

Maybe she was right. I gotta say, we've been at this for ten years, and we still fight about it all the time. How much is too much. How much is not enough. All I know is that we try to put on a program that people can watch, and that can do some good; and we try to walk that fine line as best we can.

On September 4, 1992, we aired the case of Terry Wayne Hart. I was hoping that we'd made the right decision, and that in the end we would be proven right by finding closure for Cathy's daughter.

Well, she found closure, all right.

But not in a way anyone could have expected.

■   ■   ■

Everyone on the hotline that night was happy to see Walt Lamar back again—especially the hotline chief, Sharon Greene.

Sharon is a feisty, fiery woman with a never-say-die attitude. Whenever she thought we had a good chance of catching a fugitive, she'd fight like crazy to get the case on the air as fast as possible. Sharon always pushed herself hard—and pushed the cops hard, as well. Often, when cops from small towns come to *America's Most Wanted,* and the tips start pouring in on the night of the broadcast, they're a bit overwhelmed. "Hey, these look like good leads," they'll say. "I can't wait to get home and start checking them out tomorrow."

And Sharon, politely but forcefully, will say, well, why don't we call on this one right now? Here's a tip in San Francisco that looks good. Why don't you call the FBI there right now? Here's the name of the agent. Here's his phone number (she never needs to look these up; she has a Rolodex embedded in her brain)—hey, why don't I dial it for you? Here, it's ringing.

And before they know what hit them, the befuddled cops have their fugitive in custody.

But the cops and agents who really know what they're doing are the ones that Sharon is happiest to work with. And Walt Lamar really knows what he's doing.

Sharon and Walt had first met in our studio on the case of Kelly "Sunshine" Loyd, a woman wanted for running a sex ring that lured underage girls into prostitution. Often, we'll keep some telling clue about a fugitive off the air, to help us sort out the good tips. In the case of Kelly Loyd, we had kept back the one clue we knew would catch her: the tattoo of a teddy bear on her butt. After the broadcast, Walt and Sharon sat back, and waited for some guy who'd been with her and noticed this unique marker. Sure enough, some guy called up and said, "The only difference between the woman I know and the woman you're looking for, is mine has a tattoo of a teddy bear on her ass."

"Walt was totally jazzed about it," Sharon remembers. "It was just a great capture."

■　■　■

On the night of the broadcast, Sharon led her staff of twenty-four operators up into a tiny, hot, windowless room, where they crammed together to watch a tape of that evening's show, and go over the case sheets, to familiarize themselves with the cases, which clues were airing and which were being held back.

They filed down into the studio, where the hotline calls would begin coming in in about an hour. Agent Walt Lamar and Sergeant Scott Cannon came in shortly afterward; Sharon ran to greet them, then settled into the work of the evening. Walt and Scott sat in a row of folding metal chairs against a side wall and listened, along with the cops who were in town on the other cases, as Sharon gave the speech she'd given so many times that she knew it by heart:

"Welcome to *America's Most Wanted*," she'd begin. "I want to start by explaining the process and procedures for our hotline." She'd work through the details of how the hotline operators would screen calls when the show aired, how the tip sheets would be distributed, and then explain what the officers might expect.

"Before ending each and every call, the operator will ask each caller, 'May we give your name and number to a law enforcement agent should they wish to call you back for any additional information?' Ninety to ninety-five percent of people will leave their information depending on the type of case it is. The operator will also characterize the caller, since you aren't able to speak to every person, such as nervous, scared, sincere, serious, etc.

"If an operator gets a tip that's really hot, then the operator will raise their hand and ask for the appropriate case agent. Please proceed over to the operator. They will brief you on their conversation thus far and release their phone and seat over to you. I encourage all of you to walk around the set tonight.

"These tip sheets will be collected throughout the night and distributed on the table to your left. If your fugitive is not captured tonight, any tips received over the weekend and on Monday will be FedExed to you Monday night. If you don't receive a FedEx by Tuesday morning, please let me know. After that, any tips received will be mailed to you at your office. If it's hot information we will fax or page you directly.

"We have several operators that speak Spanish if you need them.

"There are two phones for you. Also, I have pens, paper, a fax, a law enforcement directory, and atlases. If you need something else please let me know.

"Before the end of the night we also ask that each of you fill out a confidentiality form. It is to keep all of this information and callers' identity confidential. It can be used for law enforcement purposes only. I am going to get out of the way so you can watch the show and we'll call you as we need you. Thanks, and good luck!"

Walt Lamar and Scott Cannon settled back as 9:00 P.M. rolled around and the program began airing. They were watching it on a big rollaway monitor in front of the folding metal chairs. Beyond the monitor, they could see the buzz of activity as the hotline began ringing on the cases that had come up on the show first. One by one, the cops around them began to be called away, pulled into the rapidly expanding web of hurried conversations, papers passed across tables, leads being checked and faxed, and always, on each of the twenty-four telephones sitting on long tables in the studio, their little black lights blinking, and everyone wondering, which of those little black blinking lights will turn out to be the call that leads to a capture?

Finally, the Terry Hart reenactment came on, followed by the "wanted sequence," in which we showed photos of the real Terry Hart, including a picture of that telltale tattoo, and gave the aliases he'd been known to use, including Randy Staggs. "At first I didn't think it was going to happen," said Walt. "Then the hotline started up."

Operator after operator furiously scribbled down the information coming from the callers. Soon Walt and Scott were sorting through dozens and dozens of leads. Too much information to process, and yet nothing quite concrete enough to move on.

And then Walt started noticing a pattern. In among the nearly one hundred pink sheets piling up in front of him were several numbers from Tennessee, especially the Knoxville and Nashville areas.

At first, Walt liked the Knoxville tips. But then the Nashville tips seemed to be a bit more specific.

One caller said he'd seen Hart in a Shoney's in Nashville. In Clarksville, an hour to the northwest, someone said he spotted him smoking a cigarette at a construction site. Back in Nashville, someone thought he saw him in a truck, fishing around the river. In Lebanon, about half an hour to the east of Nashville, someone saw him in a retail store; also in Lebanon, a delivery man for Delta said he'd delivered a battery to Hart, but that he wouldn't sign the delivery slip.

Those are what we call good director tips—they can send an investigation in a certain direction—but not good locator tips—in that they're hard to follow up, and usually don't locate a fugitive without other information. What if that really was Hart at that Shoney's? What then? Just because he ate there once doesn't mean he'll eat there again, and it's certainly not a good bet that he's eating there right now. So with tips like these, you tend to focus your attention on a given area, and stay alert for more information, but you're certainly not ready to call out the dogs.

Still, Walt's sixth sense was telling him that this was their man, that he was in Nashville or near it. Walt walked over to the side table, picked up one of the phones, and called an FBI agent in Nashville. He told him what was going on, and faxed him some information so the agent could follow up—including photos of Hart, and the *America's Most Wanted* case sheet with all the relevant details.

Walt went back to the hotline. The calls had slowed down. In all there would be eighteen calls from the Nashville area. Clarksville, Nashville, Lebanon. Somewhere, in one of those towns, Walt was sure, we would find Terry Hart.

■   ■   ■

It was at the Wrangler nightclub in Lebanon, Tennessee, one cool October night in 1991 when Tricia, an elementary-school librarian from a nearby town whose family was well known and well respected in the community, was approached by a young man she hadn't seen around before. His name was Justin Kimball Botkin, he said, and he was new in town. And he was cute.

Tricia (she requested anonymity, so we've changed her name for this book) and Justin began dating. Dating consisted of spending time with her family, and going to church. The relationship progressed quickly. That spring, Justin found work at Contractors Heating and Cooling, which did a lot of heating installation and air conditioner work in the Nashville area. Lois Miller, an office administrator with the company, remembers interviewing him; after getting the pertinent information out of the way—he showed her his Tennessee driver's license, along with the social security card in his name, Justin Kimball Botkin—they chatted. She remembers him as being well mannered and nice looking. Supervisors said he was interested and worked hard. The rumor around Contractors was that he had met a nice young schoolteacher and was in love.

James Brandon, Botkin's supervisor, said Botkin kept a low profile. "He didn't carry on and raise Cain, he wasn't lazy, so that wasn't outstanding. He didn't try to shun work, he didn't fuss and argue with anybody."

Justin Botkin had a fairly weak explanation when Tricia, who had by then become his fiancée, learned that he also carried identification under the name Mark Warren Hart. He told her that that was his birth name, but that he was in the process of legally changing it because he disliked his family, who had abandoned him as a baby.

So Tricia came to know him as Justin Botkin.

But soon, on one fateful evening, she would come to know him as Terry Hart.

Tricia married him on August 8, 1992, at the wedding chapel in Springfield, Tennessee. The marriage license listed his name as Justin Botkin. They moved into the Continental Apartments in Lebanon, an inexpensive two-story red-brick barracks of a building.

They had been married less than a month when Tricia came home from work on the evening of September 4. She said hello to her husband, who was on the couch watching television, and went upstairs to take a bath. The television was turned to Fox. He was watching a rerun of *Married with Children*. The Bundys were arguing over whether to redecorate the bathroom.

Toward the end of the show—Al Bundy was losing the argument—there was a commercial break, and a promo for that night's Fox prime-time lineup came on.

"Fear stops most rape victims from reporting the crime," the narrator said. There was video of what appeared to be a young man and a teenage girl approaching each other on a street. Then another voice came on, a woman's: "After he got through raping me he said, 'It's time for you to die now.'"

"Tonight," the narrator continued, "you'll meet a courageous sixteen-year-old who's fighting back with the help of her mother— and the accused man's ex-lover!"

A face appeared on the screen. It was the face of a woman Hart had struggled with on a porch, late one night, a year ago. "I have to confront this guy for what he's done," she was saying. It is not clear whether Hart recognized this face. But he most certainly must have recognized the face that came on next: It was his ex-girlfriend, Peggy. "When I saw Jerri abused as she was, I remember how Terry abused me," she said.

How Terry abused me.

Terry.

And the man who was calling himself Justin Botkin knew that this story was about him. Just then he heard his wife coming out of the bath, and weighed his options.

"Watch *America's Most Wanted* tonight on Fox," the voice-over was saying.

That would not be the option he chose.

■ ■ ■

There's one odd set of circumstances that has happened to us so many times that the reporters have a name for it: They call it the Chinese-food capture. It was in our second year that we got a good tip on a fugitive and sent FBI agents to a motel room. There they found the TV on Fox, the *TV Guide* open to *America's Most Wanted,* and the Chinese food on the table still warm. It was obvious that the fugitive had seen himself on the show and taken off, not even taking the time to turn off the television.

That is the option most often taken by fugitives who see themselves on the show: Get up and start running.

It was another option open to Terry Hart.

It was also not the option he chose.

When his wife came down the stairs, she saw him in the same spot he'd been in before, in front of the television, still on Fox, now starting a *Cheers* rerun. He told her that he wanted her to go out and get two large pizzas. She didn't feel like it, but he was adamant.

Tricia left the apartment a little after six-thirty and ran a few errands. She went to Wal-Mart and bought some makeup. Then she realized she didn't have enough cash left to get the pizzas, so she headed back home.

She got there at 8:40 P.M.

And she found out the option he had chosen.

■ ■ ■

Lois Miller, the woman who had talked with Justin Botkin at Contractors Heating and Cooling, was watching *America's Most Wanted* with her husband. When the Terry Hart story came on, she thought he resembled one of the boys at work, but then she thought she was probably mistaken. So she didn't call.

But Billy Willeby did. Billy said he was a heating and air technician, and worked with Hart. At 8:54 P.M., his time (9:54 in our studios) he called again, with the phone number of Hart's employer. Another caller, a teller at First American Bank in Brentwood, Tennessee, said Hart had cashed checks under the name of Randy Staggs.

The hotline operators who took these calls immediately called Walt Lamar to their stations. The FBI agent knew we'd moved from the "directional" tips to the more "locational" ones—and that his hunch had been right. Randy Staggs was the alias Hart had used; someone was using the alias Randy Staggs near Nashville; we had a lot of calls placing Hart in the Nashville area. It's not Aristotelian logic, but it's a damn sure bet—we've got our man. "It wasn't a positive identification," said Lamar, "but we knew it was him."

Now we just had to catch him.

Walt wanted to locate Hart's employer, to have someone show him a picture of Terry Hart and see if he recognized it. From there, we could get an address from the personnel files. Since it was after hours, the agent in Nashville was having trouble locating the owner of Contractors Heating and Cooling.

No good new clues came in from the West Coast airing of *America's Most Wanted.* A little after 1:00 A.M. eastern time, the hotline operators began filing out. Sharon Greene, Walt Lamar, and Scott Cannon sat slumped at the side table, where the phones are set up for the cops to use. They were feeling a little deflated. They'd been so close—but never got that final call that would put Hart away. "I was sure we were going to catch him," said Lamar. "But didn't think it was going to happen that night."

Around 1:30 A.M., the room was silent. The three agreed to give up for the evening, and to resume the hunt in the morning.

They were out of the studio, and didn't hear the ringing of one of the phones on the side table. A stagehand who stayed behind to close up did hear it, though, and, seeing no one around, picked it up. After a few seconds he came trotting out to find Sharon and the two law enforcement officers, who were halfway to the parking lot.

"Sharon," he said. "There's a call for you."

Sharon exchanged a glance with Walt Lamar, then walked back into the studio and picked up the phone.

Walt saw Sharon's jaw drop.

"Walt, you better take this," she said. "It's the Lebanon police. They say they think they've got our guy in the morgue."

■   ■   ■

When Tricia returned home, she didn't find her newlywed husband, Justin, sitting in front of the television where she'd left him. Instead, she found a note. It read:

"The reason I sent you to get a pizza, is because I am on america's most wanted. I seen the previews while you was in the bathroom.

"I am wanted for rape. I am so sorry, I wish I had more time.

"Well you can find my body by the dirt road that run's by the apt. By the dumpster.

"Also this is the best that I have ever had in life. The church, you, and the family. I have prayed not to bring shame on any of you.

"Also I wish to be buried here. But I will understand.

"I've got to go.

"Love,

Terry Wayne Hart."

Tricia was frantic. First she called a friend in a nearby apartment who walked down the path until there was no more light to see by. But she could not find Hart. Tricia called the police. Sergeant Mike Owen and a patrolman searched the wooded area behind the apartment, and a little farther along the dirt path than the woman had walked, in a clearing where the trees gave way to low bushes, scrub weeds, and patchy grass, lay the body of Terry Hart, on his back, with his eyes open, blood coming from his mouth, from his ears, and from the back of his head. By his right hand was a .357 Smith and Wesson revolver. Sergeant Owen felt for a pulse. There was none.

■   ■   ■

Before he killed himself, Terry Hart had made one last phone call. About 7:00 P.M. that evening, after sending Tricia out for pizza, he'd called the only other woman who'd ever really loved him. He called his stepmother, Patsy Hart. She was sitting on a recliner in the den while her husband, Terry's father, was upstairs taking a thirty-minute nap after work when the phone rang.

She was glad to hear from Terry; he hadn't called since he left Oklahoma rather suddenly. She'd had mixed feelings about the whole matter: She didn't believe he would commit rape, because, she said, "he could get any woman he wanted."

If only it worked that way.

Terry told her he was going to slit his wrists. He didn't mention *America's Most Wanted,* but he did refer to the rape, and told her that the inmates in prison don't take kindly to child rapists.

He's right on that count.

She told him the Bible said you couldn't go to heaven if you committed suicide. He sounded matter-of-fact, taking care of details, and asked her not to request that his body be returned to Oklahoma. He kept trying to hang up; she tried to keep him talking.

Eventually he got off the phone. That night, she saw *America's Most Wanted,* and the story of the man she considered her son. The next day, she got a call at work: Terry had carried through his plan to kill himself. She drove the eleven miles home. Terry Hart's father was there.

He dealt with the news stoically.

"He's a man's man," she said. "He holds it in. He acted quiet. I asked if he wanted to go down there, and he didn't."

■　■　■

Sharon Greene sat down in a corner of the studio, stunned, consumed by a torrent of disbelief and guilt, not listening as Walt Lamar got the details of Terry Hart's suicide. He had faxed Hart's fingerprints to Tennessee, to check against the body. The FBI there had faxed him the suicide note. And then he went down a checklist of the mundane details that follow such an enormous shock. The business of being in law enforcement is often a series of surprising jolts followed by a mountain of tiny details. Details are the way cops deal with the moment. Also macabre jokes. It's not disrespectful; it's just a way of dealing with a job that involves dealing with death so often. Laughter is a life-affirming action, a ritual of separation, like whistling past a graveyard.

Sharon is not a cop, and she had no idea how to deal with the moment. As Walt talked and joked on the phone, she withdrew to a place inside herself.

"It really freaked me out," she said later. "I couldn't believe that someone would actually commit suicide because of our show. That *America's Most Wanted* could have that kind of impact."

In her four years on the show, there had been so many captures that she had begun to take them for granted. It was almost like a giant high-stakes game, a national game of cat and mouse. She had, it appeared, developed the thick skin of a cop. But this was something she was not prepared for.

"Now it wasn't a game anymore," she said. "I felt I was partly responsible. I didn't know what to do with all these feelings."

Walt saw the young woman sitting off on the side of the room. He knew what she was going through. It was like seeing a rookie cop doing her job, then going off in a corner to contemplate the enormity of that job. He sat down beside her.

He spoke in a tone that cops call straight-up: sincere but not syrupy. Compassionate but not condescending. He was just going to tell it like it was.

"Sharon, let me tell you something," he began. "Listen to me. Everyone makes choices. You aren't responsible for those choices. They are.

"Terry Hart chose to brutally rape this girl. He chose to run. And now he's chosen to take his life. Everyone makes choices in life, and that's what it's about."

He continued to talk to her, in almost fatherly tones, until he saw a flicker of understanding. It was a tiny moment, and yet it was a turning point, a defining moment in her career: the moment in which she began to understand that if you're going to do what you believe in, then you are going to have to live with the consequences of those beliefs.

"It started to become clear to me," Sharon said, "that people make choices. Terry Hart made his choices; I made my choices. We all make choices.

"My choice was to look at it not that I was responsible," she said, "but that I was a part of a company that represented law enforcement and victims of crime. And that's my choice. And you know what? It's a good choice."

It is something that everyone who deals in such a high-stakes world as law enforcement, such a life-and-death world, has to come to terms with: You can't get lost and hypnotized by watching the ripples that spread out from your actions, and wondering which of those ripples cause which reactions. You can only do what you believe is right, and hope for the best.

■　　■　　■

Peggy Carothers was sad when she heard the news about Terry Hart—but not overly surprised. "The reason why I think he commited suicide was, for one, I think he didn't want to affect his new wife," she told our crew when they arrived. "But also in prison, if you go in there with those kinds of charges, the inmates don't take a liking to that. He told me before that he had two counts of burglary two and he didn't want to do time. He talked about committing suicide then, too. He talked about it whenever he was in a bind—like when he was behind in his bills. That's when he would start thinking those crazy things."

Peggy was probably once childishly pretty, but in this moment, even though her face was covered in pancake makeup, thick mascara, and blue eyeliner, she looked washed-out, tired. She picked up a picture of her and Terry, and began to cry.

"I've had people call after they heard what he did, and they said that he got what he deserved. I don't believe that," she said. "He didn't deserve to die for that. He needed help. That little girl didn't deserve what she got either. It's just a bad deal that happened. I wish it never happened to her. I wish it would've happened to me instead of her. I still think about her all the time."

■　　■　　■

At first, Jerri Kennedy didn't believe it when her aunt called with the news. Her initial reaction was one of anger: "He took the easy way out," she said. "He made me suffer, then he takes the easy way out. He didn't get what he deserved for what he did to me."

It had taken about a month after the rape for Jerri's face to heal enough so that she could return to school. She stayed with it for just about a week, but was afraid to walk to school alone and dropped out. At least, that was the reason she gave herself; more likely it was her myriad emotional scars that caused her to withdraw. She was still having trouble sleeping at night, because she felt she needed to stay up and protect herself. So she stayed up all night watching television, then slept all day, sometimes in the closet.

When she did sleep, she would wake up screaming. She went nowhere alone, always having to be in the company of her mother and friends. She had panic attacks several times a week. When she has a panic attack—and they can come anywhere, anytime—she can't breathe. She jumps at every noise. She took to drinking and drugs to quell the pain and anger.

She was headed the way I've seen so many crime victims go— they never really recover, never really find their way back to the world. They withdraw from their friends, from their families, have only minimal conversations. Their world becomes an interior world, a tiny place filled with pain and sorrow. It's so heartbreaking to see a child so young, so innocent, fall so far.

Then, somehow, she started climbing back.

She began spending time at the home of a friend, Priscilla. She'd actually recovered enough to sleep over at Priscilla's house; they'd watch TV, and hang out, and talk to boys on the phone.

One of those boys, named Phillip, was twenty-one, and just out of the military; he was part Native American, tall and dark, and Jerri liked him. They talked for hours on the phone—although she never told him about the rape.

The day Phillip was to move to Florida, Jerri got the news: she was pregnant. She didn't feel close enough to Phillip to ask him to stay, but a few months later he came back, and the two were married in July in a big wedding at her mother's church.

It was by no means an easy road back for Jerri. Marriage and motherhood were too much for her; she was still living with the rape, still living in her interior world. The next years were a roller-coaster: Jerri broke up with Phillip, moved, and got pregnant again.

Strangely, this tumultuous time was when she says she stopped living with the rape. It was almost as though she'd become too busy, too entangled in her life, to deal with the pain anymore: "It didn't fit into my schedule," she said.

She and Phillip reunited; now they and the two children live together, happily, back in Oklahoma City. The younger child, Emily, is two years old at this writing; Alexis, the child Jerri and Phillip had together, is now four years old, with long dark hair and olive skin, and is like her mother was as a girl: brash, hyper, and the bolder of the two little sisters.

During the day, Phillip works as a bricklayer, and Jerri brings the kids over to her mom's. They don't talk much about the past.

Jerri's first reaction to the suicide had been anger; later she started to feel guilt. "I felt horrible," she said. "I felt like I pulled the trigger myself. I felt like I murdered someone. I would never have wished that on anyone. I just cried."

Her panic attacks have subsided; but recently, she was driving to her mother's house in her '97 Saturn when one came over her. She started to hyperventilate, and things started to go black.

Luckily, she got over to the side of the road, and her panic attack subsided.

The panic attack was emblematic of the legacy Terry Hart has left behind for Jerri Kennedy: The rape still causes her moments of rage and pain, forcing her to stop, collect herself, and go on with her life.

■　　■　　■

There remains, then, only one question: Had Terry Hart really reformed? Were we wrong to air his story?

The press had a field day with this one. They love tearing down

America's Most Wanted, and the headlines were screamers. "TV Show Blamed in Suicide." "Telling a Story versus Telling Too Much."

All day, I was pummeled with questions. Don't you feel awful? Here this guy was, living a totally reformed life, going to church, and you go and ruin everything and force him to kill himself. Don't you think *America's Most Wanted* is becoming like Big Brother? Don't people have a right to another chance?

Well, let me tell you something.

I feel sorry for a lot of people in this case.

I feel sorry for Peggy Carothers, who was taken in by this guy, beaten, tortured, every day, and who feels guilty that it wasn't she who was raped and beaten within an inch of her life instead of that little girl.

I feel sorry for Jerri's mother, Cathy, who will never get over the torture of having to play tug-of-war for her little girl's life.

I feel sorry for Jerri, who had every right to live a normal life, and has to consider it a triumph that she can drive all the way to her mother's house without blacking out, who had to go through so many years of self-torture before she could start her own life again. Jerri, who's trying to raise two beautiful little girls as best she can, and not let her pain rule her family's life. I know that she will triumph, that she will survive, because she is tough. Because she is honest. Because she stared into the face of the abyss, the dark interior place that so many victims retreat into and never return from, stared straight into it, began to let herself fall, and said: No. I will not fall. You will not consume me.

I don't know why some crime victims fall into that place and others don't. I know that I fell deep into that depression, and I don't know what—other than the love of those close to me—pulled me back. I just know that we are blessed to be able to carry on. In this way, Jerri is blessed, too.

So there are a lot of people I feel sorry for in this case.

But Terry Hart?

No way.

And I'll tell you why.

First, there is the question of reform. I can't believe the press is so ready and willing to accept that he had reformed, whatever that means, just because he went to church a few times and hadn't beaten anybody up lately. I think he was just a time bomb waiting to go off again, a rerun waiting to happen. Remember that Peggy Carothers had a three-month honeymoon period with Terry Hart before he started beating her. How long were Tricia and Terry married? Less than a month.

So her folks thought he was a nice guy? So did Peggy's folks. So he'd started going to church? Well, remember what Peggy said: "One time, Terry beat me and I went to the hospital. I came back and I filed charges on him. And he called me and told me that he'd go to church and everything and he'd never hit me again. And we did. We went to church and he even went up to the altar, but it was all just a front."

Terry Hart lived in the place between his cunning and his rage; perhaps the rage had subsided, gone into a bit of remission after his last violent attack. But I've dealt with hundreds and hundreds of these cases, and I've never seen one of these guys cured by the very crime that gives vent to his rage. If anything, I would predict that Terry Hart's next outburst would have been more violent. These guys think that a violent outburst somehow lets off the pressure, like taking the lid off a boiling pot. It doesn't. Sooner or later, there's going to be another explosion.

Remember, in his suicide note, he apologized to his wife, not to his victim. In the end, he showed no remorse, no understanding of what he had done. And where there is no remorse, and no understanding, then there is no redemption, and no reform. There is only recidivism—the crime will happen again.

But even if you do believe that Terry Hart had reformed, there is another question that you must answer: So what?

I know that sounds cruel and heartless. But you haven't seen the pictures of Jerri Kennedy's face after the rape. You haven't held the hands of a mother whose daughter has been destroyed. I do not believe that people who commit these crimes have the right to pardon themselves. God can absolve Terry Hart; the state can decide not to prosecute Terry Hart; the victim can find it in her heart to forgive Terry Hart; but Terry Hart does not have the right to pardon Terry Hart. He does not have the right to say, I committed this crime, but I think I've turned into a pretty nice guy, so I hereby grant myself immunity from prosecution, on the condition that I will never ever do it again, cross my heart. And that's good enough for me.

Sorry, but Terry Hart did not owe a promise to himself, he owed it to Jerri Kennedy, he owed it to you and to me. You know what? If he had really reformed, then let him stand up like a man. Let him turn himself in, do his time, make moral restitution, and go on with his life. Terry Hart hadn't reformed. He was watching out for number one all the way, and when he could find no other way to protect himself, he went on to the next life.

And finally, if none of that makes enough difference, then it comes down to this.

It comes down to what a seasoned FBI veteran told a young hotline supervisor the night Terry Hart committed suicide.

Everybody makes choices.

I did not put that gun in Terry Hart's hand. I wanted to hunt him down so that he could stand trial for the crime he was accused of, and if he was convicted I wanted him to serve his time. I wanted Jerri Kennedy to see that the justice system works, and that no one gets to attack a perfectly innocent young girl and get away with it.

That would have been my choice.

Everybody makes choices.

Terry Hart made his own.

CHAPTER SIX

The Most Wanted Man in America

There is no hunting like the hunting of armed men.

—ERNEST HEMINGWAY

In the early days of *America's Most Wanted,* when we had just a skeleton staff and a skeleton budget, we had to be careful about which cases we chased after. We usually looked for stories that were at least six months old—thinking that if the cops hadn't caught the fugitive by that time, he might never be brought to justice without our help.

This was a business decision as well as a manhunting one: True, these were the cases where we were needed most. But also, we couldn't afford to be halfway through filming a reenactment and have the guy get caught before we went to air, in which case we'd be forced to throw all that production away. (It happened often enough to give our accounting folks gray hair anyway. But we tried to avoid it if we could.)

As the years went by, we expanded our mission. As you've seen in earlier chapters, we started taking "hot" cases, handling them in a news fashion, and trying to jump on the killers' trails before they got cold.

That aspect of the show started taking on more and more importance—partly because Lance Heflin and several of the producers had a news background, so they loved being in the thick of a breaking story; and partly because the cops started realizing how helpful we could be, and how quickly we could react, on a breaking case.

That led us into some big manhunts.

And, finally, into our biggest manhunt ever.

We found ourselves smack in the middle of the hunt for a serial killer, who was carrying out a killing spree across the country. We knew who he was, and we knew that we were in a race against time.

Before it was over, we'd be in the same city as the killer twice, and possibly three times. We would come within twenty minutes of catching him. He would strew clues in our path, and we would go on twenty-four-hour alert, waiting for the next sign or sighting, hoping that we could pounce before he could kill again.

When the manhunt started, we were virtually alone on the case.

By the time it was over, everyone in America knew the killer's name.

■　■　■

Andrew DeSilva lived so close to the upper echelons of the gay world he could almost taste the eight-hundred-dollar-an-ounce caviar. He was a likable, good-looking, twenty-seven-year-old gigolo with a taste for fine wine (though he rarely drank), an eye for fine art, and a hunger for the fine life. He managed to find rich older men to support his flamboyant lifestyle—flying him to Paris when he wanted, giving him the money and cars he needed, dressing him in the clothes that showed off the exotic good looks he'd inherited from his Philippine father and the thin, muscular body he'd honed in gyms up and down the California coast.

But it was the next step up, the very highest echelon of the gay world, that he courted: the fabulously wealthy in Hollywood and around the country who had the beautiful homes in Key West, Fire Island, Miami's South Beach, Long Island's Hamptons. It was this velvet world that he lusted after, occasionally getting himself invited to a party where he'd see some movie mogul with a new young lover, a lover who would be kept until his looks faded, and if he was smart he'd land the lovely parting gift of a condo and a Porsche. DeSilva was well aware that the life lasted as long as the looks, and at twenty-seven, he feared his looks were fading, and his luck was running out.

DeSilva had just lost his last rich lover (he only got the Infiniti, not the Porsche), and things were not going all that well for him—though you wouldn't know it from the going-away party he threw for himself at California Cuisine, his favorite San Diego restaurant, on April 24, 1997. His last sugar daddy had left him to foot the bill for his lifestyle alone, but on this night he was all smiles.

He gathered his friends, gave away some of his fashionable clothes and a designer watch, and laughed the night away as he spoke of the new start he was going to give himself in San Francisco, after taking care of some business in Minnesota.

The only hint that something was wrong—the ominous note at the end of the lilting song—was when he said, to the gathered crowd, "Everyone has their own idea of who they think I am. Nobody really knows me. Nobody knows who I am."

It's true. Some of them didn't even know that Andrew DeSilva wasn't his real name; it was his stage name, the gay world being his stage.

His real name, which he still used often, for business transactions and the like, was Andrew Cunanan.

Back when he'd attended the exclusive Bishop's School in La Jolla, California, Andrew Cunanan had been voted least likely to be forgotten.

And soon, he would fulfill that prophecy.

■　■　■

The "business" Cunanan had to take care of back in Minneapolis involved a former lover, David Madson. Madson, thirty-three, a well-respected and successful architect, had the wide-open face, the upright stance, and the intelligent charm that marks a successful

Midwestern businessman. He looked the way a firm handshake would look if you put a good suit on it. You can only assume that Madson's affair with Cunanan was his walk on the wild side: Cunanan was flamboyant, with a huge personality and huge appetites—especially for the more violent and kinky forms of sadomasochistic sex ("He was the tying-up-and-whips type," one friend told *Vanity Fair*). And then, according to several sources, there was Cunanan's drug dealing to contend with.

Madson must have been initially thrilled by the wildness and danger as much as he was later put off by it. Eventually, it all became too much for the more straitlaced Madson. Here he was, well respected in Minnesota, part of the establishment, very together, learning that his lover was not who he thought he was, that he was really just a glorified street hustler putting up a good front—and not just a street hustler, but a dangerous one to boot.

The more he learned about Cunanan's life, the less comfortable he felt with it, until finally he broke off their relationship.

That was two years earlier; but while he had succeeded in kicking Cunanan out of his bed, he hadn't managed to get him out of his life.

Cunanan still visited Minneapolis, seeing Madson and another friend there, Jeffrey Trail, whom Cunanan described as his best friend, sometimes as his brother. Trail, another clean-cut good-looking Midwesterner, had graduated from the naval academy, was a Gulf War veteran, and was even more straight-up than Madson. Trail often let Cunanan stay at his home, although he objected to what he reportedly said was Cunanan's sideline of drug dealing. Some reports said that Trail had become Madson's lover; actually, it appears that they were just friendly acquaintances. Either way, their well-tailored worlds did not leave much room for Cunanan anymore. And I think that the rejection by the two of them was, for Cunanan, the last straw.

Cunanan flew to Minneapolis on Friday, April 25, 1997. He hooked up with Madson, and they went out with a female friend for drinks at a restaurant called Nyes'. The next night, Madson and

Cunanan went drinking and dancing at a place called the Gay Nineties. Trail was away for the weekend, so Cunanan stayed part of the weekend with Madson and part of the weekend at Trail's empty apartment. This may be when Cunanan stole Trail's prized, rare, .40-caliber gun.

Cunanan, calling from Madson's, left this message on Trail's machine on Sunday: "Oh, J.T., where are you? It's eight-twenty, so please give me a call when you can. . . . Okay, bye-bye. Let me know if you are still coming. I really want to see you. Bye-bye."

Trail returned home on Sunday and got the message; that evening, he went to Madson's apartment.

He was never seen alive again.

■ ■ ■

It was Sunday night. Madson was probably out walking his dog, Prints, leaving Cunanan and Trail alone in the apartment.

A neighbor heard an argument.

Cunanan was in a rage.

He did not reach for the .40-caliber gun.

He reached for a claw hammer.

Cunanan swung the hammer at Trail, who deflected the blow with his arm. Again and again Cunanan swung. Finally, one of the blows hit Trail in the head. He crumpled to the floor, and Cunanan stood over the man he used to call his best friend, and hit him again and again; some news agencies reported that there were twenty-seven blows, although police said the skull was so badly shattered that it's hard to tell exactly.

Cunanan rolled Trail's body up in a rug, and dragged it behind the sofa.

It was probably at this point that David Madson came home.

■ ■ ■

This is a murder of rage, a hot-blooded murder. You cannot bludgeon someone to death with a hammer coolly and calmly. It takes adrenaline and heat and rage to grab, to hold, to strike, to hear your victim's screams and strike again; it takes enormous physical exertion to kill a man this way. This murder, whether premeditated or not—I don't think it was—showed all the signs of pent-up rage finally exploding, taking with it the man who perhaps had been the kindest of all to the man Cunanan used to be.

But that Cunanan was gone.

Now Cunanan the Gigolo had been replaced by Cunanan the Killer.

Although police believe Cunanan killed Trail on Sunday in Madson's apartment, a strange fact popped up: Madson and Cunanan were seen walking Prints Monday and Tuesday. Meaning they were living, for two days, with a dead body in the apartment.

I'm piecing this together from facts we learned later, and the events are open to interpretation, but here's what I think happened: Cunanan had snapped. He had killed Trail, and now was holding Madson hostage. (The fact that Madson was not complicit in Trail's murder was officially confirmed by police later on.)

Two pairs of handcuffs and three large wads of duct tape were found in Madson's bedroom; at first, police thought these were the accoutrements of a weekend's sexual escapades.

Or maybe Cunanan used them to keep Madson in control.

Or maybe Cunanan just used Jeffrey Trail's gun to achieve that end.

This macabre situation—Madson forced to live in his apartment with a dead man and his killer—couldn't last long.

Many have speculated that Cunanan killed Trail in rage, then killed Madson to cover up the crime. I don't think so. I think that killing Trail didn't satisfy Cunanan's rage, but rather unleashed it. I think Madson was Cunanan's true target—the one he most wanted to take out his rage on.

And soon, he did.

Cunanan and Madson drove in Madson's red Jeep Grand Cherokee to Rush Lake, northeast of the city. Cunanan shot Madson three times, then dragged the body of his former lover into the tall grass and left it there, and took off in the Jeep. Fishermen found Madson's body on Saturday—possibly five days after he was killed.

That gave Cunanan a big head start.

Plenty of time to head for his next destination.

Turns out, Cunanan was headed for Chicago.

Turns out, so was I.

■   ■   ■

Back at the *AMW* office, Donna Brant was holding down the fort. She'd been with the show almost from the start, and was one of the best reporters we'd ever had: She'd cut her teeth on the assignment desk at NBC, and had an incredible eye for detail. She reminded me of a lot of the cops we worked with: She was easygoing and loved to swap war stories when we'd go out for drinks with the cops at the end of the night—but when a crime went down she was all business, holding everyone's feet to the fire to make sure we had every detail buttoned down right, passionate about pursuing the truth.

She'd just been promoted to become one of the show's producers, the position we call managing editor; more of a newspaper term than a TV term, at our shop that's the person who handles all the breaking news. She had the background for it, the training in it—and boy, was she going to need it.

That week, Lance Heflin and I were headed out of town, to do the show from Chicago. We were going there to cover some big local crime stories the staff had come up with. But when we arrived Sunday night, May 4, there was a new case breaking, a murder discovered just that morning that had Chicago in an uproar.

Marilyn Miglin, a cosmetics mogul, had come home early that morning from a business trip to Canada, expecting her husband, Lee, a prominent real estate developer, to pick her up at the airport.

He never showed up.

When she got to their home in the Chicago area known as the Gold Coast—a secure retreat for the fabulously wealthy—she noticed some more odd things. The front gate wasn't locked—that wasn't like Lee—and the curtains were pulled shut. Inside, she found a half-eaten ham sandwich on a counter, and dirty dishes in the sink—not like Lee at all. There was stubble in the sink from an electric razor and next to it . . .

Oh, my God.

A gun.

Marilyn called the police.

Then she looked frantically for her husband.

In the garage, she found a terrible, terrible sight. It was her beloved Lee—his face wrapped in a bizarre mask of duct tape, covering all but his nose, giving him the appearance of one of the men in those S-and-M videos that Andrew Cunanan liked to watch. His chest was a mass of dark, dried blood, showing where he had been stabbed, over and over, with a pair of garden shears. His throat had been severely sliced with a saw, as though the killer had tried to decapitate him.

Police determined that after the murder, the killer apparently amused himself, entering the Miglin mansion, coolly helping himself to an apple and making himself a ham sandwich in the kitchen, going into the bathroom for a shave. The gun found at the scene was not the rare .40-caliber that had been stolen from Jeffery Trail, which had been used to kill David Madson. That would not surface again until later.

When he was done, the killer stole Miglin's leather jacket, wristwatch, and two thousand dollars in cash, along with Miglin's dark green 1994 Lexus.

He left behind the car he had arrived in.

A red Jeep Grand Cherokee.

■　■　■

After some fast and furious phone calls, Donna was on the case: She assigned a local producer in Chicago to "crash" a story on the Miglin murder. It was the biggest story of the year in Chicago: Miglin, seventy-three, was a famed philanthropist at the top of the city's ladder of power and prestige; the murder struck Chicago as other cities would be rocked if the victim were a Rockefeller, a Getty, a Trump. Chicago mayor Richard Daley held a press conference to eulogize his good friend Lee. "He was very successful, but he gave back to the community, we all know that. [He and Marilyn] were wonderful Chicagoans."

There was much anguish, but so far, no suspect; at that point, it was a brutal, painful, unsolved murder.

But as the hours ticked by, a name would emerge. The story of two bizarre gay murders from Minneapolis would hit the wires. And Donna would realize she had something much, much bigger on her hands.

The red Jeep found abandoned near the Miglin place was traced back to David Madson—linking the Chicago killing to the two murders in Minnesota.

By now, Cunanan's name was beginning to surface. It came out that Cunanan had left a ton of evidence back at the Minnesota crime scene—most important, a gym bag with his name printed on it. And there was the neighbor who saw Cunanan and Madson walking Prints together the day after Trail was killed in Madson's apartment.

And, of course, he'd left all that evidence at Lee Miglin's house: the teeth marks and saliva on the apple and sandwich, the DNA-traceable hair clippings in the sink. Not to mention the red Jeep.

He was committing murder, and he clearly did not care who knew it.

Nobody had a warrant out yet on any of the murders: not Minneapolis, not Chicago. But Cunanan's name was becoming linked to all three. He was, it appeared, a serial killer, who just happened to have struck in the town where *America's Most Wanted* had shown up.

We usually won't put someone's face on the air if police haven't charged him yet. I remember someone walking up to us in an airport in the early days of the show, wishing us well but warning us, "*America's Most Wanted* is an awfully big gun. Be careful where you point it." That's always stayed with me, and we've always tried to make sure that the cops were sure—that they weren't guessing at the killer, hoping we'd catch their suspect and that they could wring a confession out of him after he was caught.

But even though Cunanan wasn't charged, all my senses were

telling me, this is the guy, and this guy is dangerous, and if we pussyfoot around and wait to nail down everything to our satisfaction, he's going to get away, and he's going to kill again. We're going to have a serial killer on our hands and it's going to be our fault if he strikes again because we didn't move fast enough.

I got on the phone with a good friend, Robert Ressler, a former forensic profiler for the FBI. He'd helped the show out many times in the past; he'd also interviewed most of the nation's serial killers, including Ottis Toole, the man who I believe killed my son. I told Ressler what we knew so far about Andrew Cunanan. I wanted to know what Ressler thought of Cunanan, and what Cunanan's next move might be.

Ressler surprised me. First, he said, Andrew Cunanan is not a serial killer.

"How can you say that?" I asked. "He's killed three people in the last week."

Ressler laid it out for me: Serial killers are usually totally remorseless, cold-blooded, and methodical. Guys like Toole and Henry Lee Lucas are the aberration—90-I.Q. guys who stumble along through dumb luck. Most serial killers are smart, the Ted Bundy type, the ones who believe they don't have to live by the rules of society. They usually have a very distinct need to kill, in a very distinct pattern, the way an obsessive-compulsive must walk down the street in a certain way or open a door in a certain way. A serial killer might have the urge to kill, say, a dark-haired teenage girl, and once that urge is satisfied, he will go into hiding for a while, appearing calm and quiet and polite, until the need arises again.

Cunanan, he said, seemed smart, but not methodical. He's what is called a spree killer, Ressler told me. Something has snapped in him, and now he's on the loose. He's not a calculating killer, but he's a spree killer. The murder of Trail didn't stop or satisfy anything, it unleashed something. He's not motivated by some long-standing internal perversion that builds up steam like a pressure cooker, finally exploding in a predictable pattern. He's actually more dangerous: a spree killer with a taste for blood. He's over the edge and he's not coming back. And, until he's caught, he might strike anywhere.

In any case, Ressler said, you better get after this guy fast. He's narcissistic enough to think he can outwit the police. And maybe he's smart enough to actually do so. He's going to kill again. Guaranteed. He's changing cars after each murder, and picking up money along the way, and he knows his way around a lot of the big cities of the world, so he's not going to be easy to find.

But you better find him.

■   ■   ■

The story Donna and her team put together was powerful but careful. It carried the discordant images of a high-profile murder: photos of the smiling, tuxedoed Miglin juxtaposed against his shocked, grieving wife. Their upscale home, and the team of police searching through the garbage behind the house for clues. We told the tale of the Miglin murder as an unsolved case; at the end of it, we noted that the red Jeep was found at the scene, that it was connected to the Minnesota murders, and that it may have been connected to the Miglin case.

We put up Cunanan's picture. We said he was the prime suspect in the Minnesota cases, and that he might be the prime suspect in the Chicago case.

We knew we were going out on a limb.

We also knew that if we didn't, another life could be lost.

We had moved as fast as we could.

But we hadn't moved fast enough.

■   ■   ■

There was one important clue in the case that we were withholding from our reports.

On Thursday, two days before our broadcast, Cunanan used the cell phone in Lee Miglin's car. Police traced the signal to western Pennsylvania. The hunt was on. We had our first good clue as to where he was headed.

In our briefing for the hotline operators just before the show went on the air, we would relay this information. This would be the kind of clue that could help us sort out the hundreds of tips that were sure to come in. We could give our operators an area to focus on. We wouldn't report the clue about the cell phone on air, of course, because we knew Cunanan could very well be watching the show, and we didn't want to tip the cops' hand on the best clue they had going. That phone could be their homing device to bring them right in on Cunanan.

Unfortunately, the rest of the media weren't so circumspect.

The first reports about the cell phone were attributed to the *Chicago Tribune,* but as early as Friday morning, they were all over the place, especially—because of the Pennsylvania calls—in Philadelphia: Lee Miglin's killer was using the cell phone in the stolen car. The cops think the media learned about it by intercepting an unscrambled police radio report.

Maybe the information was leaked.

But it was out there, for anyone to hear.

Including Andrew Cunanan.

And, apparently, he heard it.

He ripped the cell phone out of the Lexus.

And then he made his next move.

■　■　■

That Friday was a rainy day, so there were few visitors to Finn's Point National Cemetery in Pennsville, nestled in the swampy marshes of southern New Jersey. It is one of the most quiet and isolated spots in all of New Jersey, this cemetery, one of the few places in the country where Confederate and Union soldiers are buried in the same ground; beyond the granite cemetery walls, history buffs tramp around Fort Mott State Park.

When tourists would make their way to the cemetery, William Reese, the caretaker, a gentle, bearded man, didn't mind showing them around, first pointing out the mass graves of 2,436 Confederates, their names listed alphabetically on plaques surrounding an obelisk; then pointing out other monuments. "Over there are 135 Union guards who died along with them," he told one visitor. "Now, over here are thirteen Germans who died at Fort Dix, where they were POW's during World War II."

But there was no one to escort around that day. Listening to the falling rain, Reese was quite alone, sitting in his office with the light on, reading his Bible and listening to a Christian radio station. His red Chevy pickup was parked outside. He must have been smiling and welcoming when he heard a knock on the door.

He had no way to know that the visitor was there to make an exchange.

The visitor would give up his green Lexus.

In exchange, he would take the red Chevy.

And William Reese's life.

Reese was found shot with a .40-caliber handgun. The shell casings and bullet jackets matched those used to kill David Madson.

And after killing this innocent man, Andrew Cunanan—who just days earlier was using a cell phone that had police bearing down on him as though he were sending out a lighthouse beacon—now was back in the shadows, headed for who knows where.

And our best chance of catching him was gone.

■ ■ ■

Every once in a while, a new Fox executive comes up with the exciting idea, why don't you guys broadcast the call-in tips live from the hotline? Why don't you let the viewers watch as the tips are coming in?

This is why.

I remember sitting at home watching a TV show, once, with a live call-in about the Green River killer, and one of the callers, apparently quite sincere, was saying, my lover matches the description of the killer, and I thought, what if this guy is right? And what if the killer is watching the show? This caller is a dead man. As our ability to instantly communicate grows, so should our sense of responsibility. You can't just go out there and say, the FBI is tracking the killer's cell phone. Yes, it's a big scoop, and everybody pats you on the back and says what a great, aggressive reporting job you're doing, and you go home feeling all proud of yourself.

And then a guy who never hurt anyone in his life, a family man whose hobby was getting together with his wife to make crafts and sell them, an innocent cemetery caretaker with a two-year-old daughter, reading his Bible on a rainy Friday afternoon, loses his life.

And I don't care what you say about the public's right to know, and the media's right to report—nothing, nothing makes up for an idiotic mistake like that, an idiotic grab for readers or ratings. It's just irresponsible of the media to act so recklessly. That's a big gun you have there; you have to be careful where you point it.

I was angry. I blamed the media for the death of William Reese.

So did Lee Urness.

Lee Urness is a cop assigned to the FBI Fugitive Task Force in Minneapolis, a senior special agent who coordinated the Cunanan search from the Minnesota end. He'd first heard about the case back on Friday, May 2, after Trail's body had been discovered, and while Madson was still a missing person.

Lee was sitting in his police car, looking at data on the mobile terminal, when he noticed that the Minneapolis police department was investigating the homicide of a man named Jeffrey Trail. Lee called them and said, if you get a fugitive, let me know, I'll do whatever I can to help. He left his name and number with the homicide division. Before the warrant on Cunanan was served, Lee found himself immersed in the case.

Lee had been in law enforcement in Minnesota for twenty-six years. His kids take up most of his time, but he does like to hunt, and every summer the Minnesota native takes a fishing trip up near the Canadian border, as far away from telephones as he can get.

That summer, there would be no fishing.

And the only hunting he would do would be for Andrew Cunanan.

Lee was pissed off when he heard about the slipup that had led to Reese's death. "I called everyone and told them, from then on, work on a need-to-know. If you're using a cell phone it better be digital. If your radio is not digitally encrypted don't say anything on the radio. If you have a hot lead go cover it, don't even call me, I don't need to know."

After that, as the hunt went on, Urness would only talk to *America's Most Wanted.* On every big news story, there's usually one news agency that takes the lead. We're not used to being in that role on a breaking news story: We're a relatively tiny outfit. There's only forty people working for *America's Most Wanted* all together, versus hundreds at the big networks. But Urness trusted us, and after the rest of the media had leaked the cell phone lead, he trusted no one else.

The loss of the cell phone had been a crushing blow to the investigation. Now all eyes were on the *America's Most Wanted* broadcast that Saturday night, May 10, to see what we could turn up.

We didn't turn up Cunanan that night.

But we did turn up more than a hundred leads, which we passed on to the cops.

We also turned up something else.

We turned up Cunanan's roommate.

■　■　■

We sent a local California producer to talk with the roommate, then sent our correspondent, Lena Nozizwe, out to San Diego to follow up. We were hoping to find out whatever we could about Cunanan. I thought Lena was the perfect person for a mission like this—aside from the fact that San Diego happened to be her hometown, and she was well known there, Lena has a way of getting people to open up to her in ways they don't open up to other people. The previous week, she'd been following the murders of rappers Tupac Shakur and Biggie Smalls, and had an exclusive interview with Biggie's mom, a powerful, painful, emotional interview.

Lena noticed one similarity between the rap murder story and the Cunanan murder story. On both, she felt oddly alone, not elbowing her way through the usual media hordes. I have to be blunt: We all knew the reason. It was, we believed, because the victims in the first story were black, and some victims in this one were gay, and we've always found that the mainstream press isn't as quick to pick up on crime stories where the victims aren't straight, white, and middle-class.

Her feelings were confirmed when she talked with Cunanan's roommate over lunch. He felt that the police hadn't taken him seriously because he was gay; and that the media hadn't taken the story seriously enough because the first victims were gay.

He had a point: Here was a quadruple murderer running free on the streets. Sure, the press was covering the story. But that pack mentality, that frenzy that turns a story into the Big Story wasn't present, not by a long shot. The coverage was still mostly local in the areas most affected: Minneapolis, Chicago, New Jersey.

As lunch wound down, Lena called for the check—and an odd thing happened. "We were joking around. I had just done the story on Biggie Smalls, with his mom, and there's an expression I picked up there. Instead of saying, 'Are you thirsty? Are you tired?' they'd say, 'Are you straight?'—like, are you okay.

"And we were done, and I said to him, the roommate, 'Are you straight?' And he looked at me and said, 'No!' And we both started laughing."

It was a comfortable relationship, the kind that can form in the middle of a terrible, tense situation. The roommate was happy that *America's Most Wanted* had been so quick to jump on the case, and that we were following up so thoroughly. He still loved Andrew, he said, but if Andrew had done what they say he had done, then he had to be caught.

He invited Lena back to the apartment—to Cunanan's apartment. It looked the way apartments do when the police get through with them: as though a chimney had exploded. There was black fingerprint dust everywhere, on every surface, on every glass, counter, table, book, and candlestick.

Slowly, Lena entered Cunanan's room. What she was looking

for, she wasn't sure: some clue to who he was. Some clue to his identity. Some clue that might catch him.

What she found was a mess: piles and piles of magazines strewn everywhere. Cunanan's collection of sadomasochistic videos, tapes with titles like *Roped and Delivered.* A closet stuffed with designer clothes and expensive shoes. Someone had written in marker on the mirrored sliding closet door, "Thanks for the great party."

One of our crews had already been in the apartment—it was the *only* crew to gain access to the apartment at that point—but Lena was still being careful. The San Diego police were done with the scene, but the Minneapolis police were on their way down to take a look for themselves, and Lena had arrived before they did. "I didn't want to touch anything, for fingerprints," Lena remembers. "I found a box of handcuffs next to the bed, but didn't go inside the box because of the fingerprints. The police had already been there, but I thought, more important that the case be tight than for me to get my paws on things."

Now came the important part. Lena's crew arrived, and she set up to do the interview with the roommate. He wanted his identity concealed—but he concealed nothing about Andrew Cunanan.

■　■　■

"Could the guy you know commit these despicable crimes?"

"When I think about it, it's just amazing to me. I've never seen any type of aggression from him, or hostility. When he's irritated at someone, that's all it is; it's just irritation, and it never goes past that."

"Is there any doubt in your mind that he committed these crimes?"

"It's hard to believe what's going on—but I do not doubt that it is Andrew who is doing this, after all the evidence that I've heard, all that I've seen, I have to believe it."

"What was Andrew Cunanan like to live with?"

"Well, he's not a clean person [laughs].

"The thing is, Andrew is a night person, extremely. He gets up, at the earliest, three or four in the afternoon. I have normal hours, and I'm going to make noise, but nothing wakes him up. Then he's up until four or five in the morning, until the drugs wear off. . . .

"Just sitting at dinner with him—I can't begin to tell you. It's just such a trip. It was like he entered another world, and you never knew where it was gonna be. It was so entertaining. He's so charismatic, he can pull anything off. He really can. He's like Ferris Bueller in real life—everyone loves him."

"What are his identifying traits? Describe him."

"Well, for the average person, Andrew is gonna look very normal. He's very poised, extremely intelligent. He will always have a newspaper in front of him. He loves to read constantly. He's gonna follow everything that's being said in the newspapers, or watching TV, he monitors it very closely. He's ahead of everyone right now, and it's not by mistake.

"Any videos that he would rent would be with bondage. It would not be any normal sexual videos at all. He'll be in leather shops, all that sort of stuff.

"He's very, very clean-cut. Looks very Jewish, so to speak. No accent whatsoever. If he does get in a crunch, he speaks French fluently, so he might try to, you know, come across as a foreigner. He is definitely not Caucasian, so he can come across as some other race if he wants to.

"He will always have around him a cigar, if he can. He smokes expensive cigars, and he will always be drinking non-alcoholic stuff: cranberry juice, or Coke, or water. He desperately needs a group surrounding—he needs interaction—that's the type of person he is. He thrives off it, so he won't be by himself very much.

"He does have an extremely boisterous laugh. That can't be taken away. That's his notoriety. It's one of those type of laughs where you hear it in a restaurant and it seems so obnoxious—you can't stifle that, and you'll be able to hear it for blocks away when he laughs."

■   ■   ■

It was a good amount of information, one of the more detailed portraits of a killer we've been able to paint. A lot of times, the family and friends of the fugitive won't cooperate, and the police can't learn anything about his background, and we wind up going to air with nothing more than "smokes Marlboros, drinks Budweiser, two-inch scar on his ankle." That drives me nuts. But here's one of the most important cases we've ever handled, a spree killer on the loose, and here's someone willing to give us every possible clue you could ask for.

Other people in San Diego who knew Cunanan provided more clues. I was psyched: Once the cell phone fell through we lost Cunanan's trail, but the hunt was heating up again. With all this information, I thought, we have a much better chance of picking up his scent again.

We were focusing on places with big gay populations: New York, San Francisco, Miami, Key West. The cops also thought there was a good chance, since he was both world-wise and fluent in French, that he had fled to a French-speaking area, the nearest and the most likely being Quebec.

We happened to be doing the show from the streets of San Francisco that week—one of Cunanan's possible hiding places— and I was half feeling like we were going to bump into him. I was so pumped by all the information we had gathered, I told Lance, "I'm sure we're gonna catch this guy this weekend."

I felt almost certain of it. This guy was moving like a jungle animal, leaving all sorts of tracks behind as he killed. We knew the path he had taken thus far. And we knew him. We had good photos, good clues, and a good idea of some of the places he might be. There was no way he was staying out.

When we aired the show, we got a lot of what seemed to be solid tips. Cunanan was last seen in New Jersey—had he turned north or south? We got excited about good tips up and down the East Coast, and passed them on to the cops.

But when the weekend came and went, and still none of the tips had panned out, I could almost hear that laugh of Cunanan's, that laugh the roommate told us about, that mocking, braying cackle.

I thought, either this guy is incredibly lucky, or this really is one of the smartest men we've ever hunted.

I thought again about what the roommate had said:

He's ahead of everyone right now.

And it's not by mistake.

■ ■ ■

As the weeks wore on, Lee Urness, the Cunanan task force coordinator back in Minneapolis, pored over the *America's Most Wanted* tips. We kept hoping he'd pull a rabbit out of a hat—give us a location to definitely focus on—but Lee was smart, and cautious. "The one thing I could never do was say for certain he was on the eastern seaboard. I refused to, because if you get tunnel vision, you're shot. Also, I didn't want the news media to broadcast it."

When he should have been fishing up near the Canadian border, Urness was sitting alone, reading over his eight legal pads filled with notes (much of which he didn't put in his formal reports, after the cell-phone leak).

"Sometimes I read them over at night—what did I do? What did I forget?" Urness said. "It was an obsession with me, because I have to figure out what should be done, what hasn't been done, and tie it all together. I kept looking back."

Lena's report had aired on June 7. On that broadcast, we named Cunanan our Public Enemy Number One. Two weeks later, the FBI would name him to their ten most wanted list. That's a big step. It brings with it a huge influx of money and manpower—and ensures that Cunanan's picture will be sent to every cop shop in the country.

But much to our amazement, Cunanan managed to stay on the run. By the end of June—two months after the first murders—we still couldn't say for sure which city he was in, or which coast he was on.

The gay communities in big cities helped distribute his picture. Between their efforts, the FBI, the local media, and *America's Most Wanted,* his picture had been everywhere. But he looked a little different in every photo—and not different enough in any of them.

"The big thing is, he looked pretty much too normal," Urness said. "The pictures started going out right away. But he had a lot of luck, and he's an average-looking guy. I kept thinking, 'Why doesn't he have a big scar on his forehead? Why didn't he have red hair?' "

Cunanan sightings were everywhere; but it was almost impossible to verify them.

Even Urness himself, who carried a picture of Cunanan with him everywhere, thought he spotted Cunanan. But even he, a trained detective, couldn't be positive.

"In Minneapolis, at lunch one day, there was a guy who was an identical ringer. I realized the eyewitness leads will be really tough if a guy with the picture in his pocket, looking at the picture, looking at the guy at the next table—if he can't say yes or no, what's the general public to do?"

One of the strangest moments of all was when there was a report that a man, closely resembling Cunanan, had been spotted at the Mazza Gallerie, a chic shopping mall in Washington, D.C.

It stands a block away from an Italian restaurant, That's Amore.

Where, to celebrate the fact that Fox had just picked up the show for another year, the entire staff of *America's Most Wanted* had just sat down for lunch.

■   ■   ■

Well, almost the entire staff. A few minutes earlier, a D.C. cop had showed up at our office to ask for a photo of Cunanan. Donna Brant wanted to know why she was asking for it.

That's when she found out that Cunanan had been seen. And that she wasn't going to get to the luncheon.

While Donna worked the phones, Lena and a camera crew raced to the shopping center.

"I ran down the street," Lena remembers. "I was thinking, most people would run away from a killer, and here I am running toward him. I went to the Neiman Marcus, and went to someone I knew who frequently helps me in the bag department, and the guy said, 'Yeah, I saw someone who looks like him.' " Lena started checking in other stores nearby—"and they told me the police had put them all on red alert."

Word reached the staff at the restaurant in mid-toast. It was an eerie moment. Everyone started looking over their shoulders—thinking, wouldn't that be the end, if Cunanan walked in here.

Was it really Cunanan? We'll never know. A lot of these sightings were tantalizing but unconfirmed.

It was getting so frustrating. We were all thankful that Cunanan hadn't struck in several weeks. But at the same time, we all knew this story wasn't over, not by a long shot.

And unless we could come up with something solid, he was going to strike again.

We couldn't have been more correct.

■ ■ ■

From our hotline, enticing tips kept surfacing. What about this one, spotting him in New York? Or how about this one, that he had stolen a black Pathfinder outside a disco in Boca Raton?

Those might or might not have been solid. But we would learn later that a few of our tips were right on the money.

Tips saying that Cunanan had gone underground, hiding among the gay community in Miami's South Beach.

South Beach was a perfect place for Cunanan to hide. The glittery, glitzy, gay, party-till-dawn atmosphere has, in recent years, attracted a large, wealthy, and wannabe-wealthy crowd of pretty boys, rich men, and elite supermodels, drawn to a place that has taken the undisputed title of the American Riviera. Under the archways of art deco, under the cool neon that gives a surreal glow to the hot night, Cunanan could blend in with the waves of young men cascading down the Ocean Drive promenade along the beach, flowing in and out of gay bars until dawn, perhaps taking one last desperate stab at finding the life he'd long since lost, perhaps just planning his next kill.

On May 12—just three days after the murder of the New Jersey caretaker—Cunanan checked into the Normandy Plaza hotel, not exactly one of the high-rent hot spots in South Beach. Clearly, he was running low on funds. Twice, Cunanan almost got caught in South Beach, before he could strike again. The media would make a lot out of these incidents, and criticize the cops mightily; but from inside the investigation, I can tell you that the cops, the FBI, and the other Florida law enforcement on the case made all the right moves. These are the things that just happen, and you can't do anything about.

The first positive sighting came in early July at a pawn shop in Miami's South Beach. On July 7, apparently desperate for cash, Cunanan walked into a shop bearing an orange sign with plain lettering: "Cash on the Beach—*Empeños*." He took out a plastic bag, withdrew a gold coin, and handed it to the woman behind the counter. She asked for his ID, and had him fill out a form; the name at the top, written clearly and legibly, is Andrew Phillip Cunanan. He also, by state law, had to leave a print of his right thumb.

He took his $190 and walked out. The law requires that the form he filled out be submitted to a law enforcement agency. It was.

It sat in someone's in-basket, unnoticed, until it was too late.

The media who tried to make a lot out of that were, I believe, taking a cheap shot. Thousands of those forms flow into police stations every day. They're mostly there for reference, on small larceny or gun charges. Say I think you stole a stereo. If I can go back through the records and prove you pawned the stereo, that's a good document for me to bring into court. But it's clerical people that sort through these papers as they flood into the police station, not detectives looking for hot clues. Talk about a needle in a haystack. There's no way you could have expected the Miami Beach police, or the FBI, to have noticed that sheet the day it came in.

The second sighting came at the Miami Subs Grill, right around the corner from the Normandy Plaza—the result of a tip to *America's Most Wanted.*

"I don't want you to think this is a hoax or anything," Kenneth Benjamin, a worker at the sub shop, told the police, "but there's a guy in my store who resembles someone I saw profiled on *America's Most Wanted.*"

He was so sure he had Cunanan, and so detailed in his description, that the cops took him very seriously. Cunanan had cut his hair very short, but for Kenneth, there was no question.

The Miami Beach police sent uniformed officers to the scene; meanwhile, the dispatcher stayed on the line with Kenneth. Keep him busy, Kenneth was told.

Keep him busy.

Imagine yourself in that sub shop: You're staring at a man you have seen on *America's Most Wanted*. You know he's killed three times already. What if he catches on? What if he turns on you?

Kenneth was frightened—but he was brave. He did whatever he could to try to keep Cunanan in the store. The moments that passed seemed like hours, and he thought, where the heck are those guys already?

And then Cunanan split.

Again, the media had a field day with the cops—how could you let him slip away after a tip like that?—but you have to understand two things. One, we'd had hundreds of tips like that one, and rather than criticizing the Miami police, I've congratulated them for managing to pick this tip out of the crowd so quickly. Remember, they weren't even sure that Cunanan was in South Beach yet, and he had committed no crime in Miami—yet here they were, taking this one particular tip very, very seriously. The cops, the records show, were on the scene in just minutes. But how long can you expect a guy behind a counter to stall someone in a sub shop?

Two, it's so easy for a young, crew-cut gay man to disappear in South Beach. Go one block from the Miami Subs Grill and you're in a river of bodies, there's a hundred shops you could slip into. They canvassed the area, but Cunanan was gone.

So there was no way of making sure that this was Cunanan.

Still no proof that Cunanan was in South Beach, any more than we could be sure he had been across the street from the *AMW* luncheon in Washington, D.C.

The proof would come four days later.

In the worst possible way.

■   ■   ■

Fashion designer Gianni Versace was, in the words of one foreign journalist who worked with us on the case, "the man who could make ordinary people dream." He was the very icon of the high life to which Andrew Cunanan aspired: Fabulously wealthy, extraordinarily extravagant ("He could spend three million dollars in a day," his accountant told us, "and I wouldn't realize it until I had to pay the bills"), surrounded by the ultra-ultra-chic, he was at the nexus of the fashion and the rock-and-roll worlds; it was he, as *Vanity Fair* would note, who with his designs could make Princess Diana seem deliciously tarty or Courtney Love respectable and elegant. Of his four astoundingly opulent homes, the most unusual, I thought, was in South Beach, located on the art deco strip otherwise exclusively populated by the best restaurants, the fanciest clothing emporiums, and the hottest bars. He became a regular fixture on the South Beach scene. Yet he and his gay lover were, by all accounts, perfectly faithful; the locals would often see them, with Gianni's sister, out on the beach in the late afternoon, the perfect family living the life of dreams.

Had Versace ever met Andrew Cunanan? I think it's unlikely. Eric Gruenwald, a San Francisco attorney, says he knew Cunanan well in the early nineties, and remembers an encounter at a chic nightclub: "There was a private room, I guess they refer to it as the VIP room," Eric told us, "where apparently Versace was, and at some point during the evening he met Versace in the VIP room. He didn't at first believe it was Versace. He told me that he said to Versace, 'Yeah, right, you're Gianni Versace. And I'm Coco Chanel. Nice to meet you.' "

Other reports also surfaced, tying the two together. None of them are really verifiable.

None of them really matter.

Maybe there had been a chance encounter or two, maybe not. If so, those encounters contain no answers, no explanations, just a bit of irony.

There can be no real explanation for what occurred next.

■   ■   ■

The rumors of a Versace link to the Italian Mafia were long-standing and thoroughly unproven. But the events of July 15, 1997, certainly added fuel to the fire. Versace went to the News Cafe early, as was his habit, for an espresso and an Italian newspaper, and was returning to his fabulous estate.

A woman passing on the street recognized him and smiled. He smiled back, then turned to walk up the front steps of his home. The woman, not ten feet away, turned back to look at him one more time.

This is what she saw:

A young man, dressed like a tourist in a tank top, shorts, and a baseball cap, rushed toward Versace. "He pointed his gun with his arm very stretched out as Versace was placing, or trying to place, his key in the lock," she told police, in a statement obtained by the *Miami Herald.*

Versace did not see the young man, who now had the black gun barrel close to Versace's left ear. He fired twice.

The gun went "Tatt! Tatt!" the witness said. "There was no smoke, there was no nothing. It was a precise shot."

Versace collapsed, on his steps, in a pool of blood. The shooter placed the gun in a black backpack, then walked down the street and into a parking garage. Onlookers pursued him, but stopped when the young man turned, took out his gun, and pointed it at them.

He then went to a red Chevy pickup in the garage, changed his clothes, and fled on foot.

It was the pickup that once belonged to a nice cemetery caretaker from New Jersey, shot dead by a .40-caliber bullet on a rainy afternoon.

Inside the pickup, a short while later, police found the eye-glasses, clothing, and wallet of Lee Miglin, the slain Chicago businessman.

They also found the pawn ticket for Miglin's coin.

And they found some of Andrew Cunanan's clothes, personal papers, and passport.

Once again, he'd left calling cards.

The international press was almost disappointed. The Mafia conspiracy theorists had been salivating at the thought of a mob hit on Versace.

But this was not a mob hit.

This was the spree killer, totally out of control.

■　■　■

I was in Vancouver, British Columbia, still working the *America's Most Wanted* road show with Lance, when Donna Brant called him from Washington. She was the producer in charge back at the studio—in fact, she was the *only* supervisor back at the studio: The two other show producers were both on vacation out of the country, and Lance and I were on the road. She called as soon as she heard about Versace. She and Lance had developed a running joke about how Cunanan sightings were everywhere. "Maybe Cunanan killed Versace," she joked. "Yeah, right," Lance laughed.

A few hours later, nobody was laughing.

Lee Urness was at a gas station in Minneapolis when the news went down, getting a cup of coffee to go. "I got the page—I've got an alphabetic pager, so they can type messages to me. Basically, the message was, 'Versace killed in Miami with a .40-caliber, is it Cunanan?' So I ran outside to my squad car and got on the phone on the way to my office."

He had to ask who Versace was; he was told he was a big fashion designer, and that he was gay. Everything started clicking; Urness knew right away that it was Cunanan. When it was all over, he'd ask himself the question, how could this be? "After Versace was killed I really looked back. What the hell, how could he have been in Miami and I didn't know this? Hindsight is great—but there's nothing I didn't do."

■　■　■

When Versace was killed, the media went into full frenzy, and when it was revealed that Cunanan was the prime suspect, the madness focused on the only people who'd been chasing him from the start.

It started at a press conference, where the FBI was being taunted by the media. They were asked, why the hell didn't you tell the public that a spree killer was on the loose?

And they replied, we did. We put him on our ten most wanted list, for chrissake. He's been aired several times on *America's Most Wanted*.

Now the media, who were way behind on the story, realized that *America's Most Wanted* was their way to catch up.

"Our phone did not stop ringing," Donna remembers. "Everybody had called us, *Prime Time Live*, *20/20*, *Nightline*, *The New York Times*, *Time*, *Newsweek*, *Entertainment Tonight*, *Extra*, *American Journal*, you name it, everyone had descended on this office, wanting our stuff." Terribly shorthanded, Donna and a production assistant, Evan Marshall, fielded all the calls—at the same time that Donna was furiously putting together a Cunanan update for that week's show, which I would introduce from Vancouver. It was a madhouse. Donna remembers, "At eleven-thirty that night, I said to Evan, 'Do you hear that?'—The phones had finally stopped ringing. It was unbelievable."

That Saturday night, everybody and his mother and his mother's FBI agent were in our studio as the tips were coming in. Several shows had sent camera crews, and even though Donna had explained to them that we have to protect our tipsters' confidentiality, each time she'd turn around she found a producer trying to shoot close-ups of the tip sheets. "Get your cameras off those tip sheets!" Donna was calling out, shooing the cameras away, swooping up the tip sheets, and generally trying to keep order in the chaos.

When the uproar died down, we reassessed the situation.

Cunanan had taken the dangerous risk of pawning the gold coin, so he was clearly out of money.

He had left the red pickup behind, so he was clearly out of transportation.

He had left his ID and passport, so it was unlikely he could leave the country.

His face was everywhere, so the chance of making another getaway was nil.

He had committed his most brazen act. He had nothing to lose.

This was a man ready to make his last stand.

It appeared that he would make his last stand in South Beach. So that's where we took the show.

■   ■   ■

On the flight down to South Beach, I was reading all the papers, trying to get caught up on the story—and getting pretty disgusted by all the speculation.

The big theory was that Cunanan had AIDS, and that somehow this murder spree was a means of extracting revenge.

That was nonsense. First of all, everybody we talked to— everybody who knew him—swore that Cunanan not was HIV-positive. They assured us that they would know; he was not the kind of person who could keep that information secret from everyone. And what sort of odd revenge would this be, anyway?

The other speculation was that the Versace killing was somehow connected to Versace's supposed mob ties. Back in 1994, a British paper said, without sources, that the house of Versace was tied to a mob money-laundering scheme. Versace sued, and won a settlement and retraction from the paper, but the speculation never quite died down.

I didn't buy the mob story at all.

Once you pushed aside the hysterics, the picture seemed fairly clear.

Cunanan was pushing thirty. His looks were failing, his easy money was getting harder to get, he had fallen off the A-list for big parties and probably off the B-list too. His dream of sleeping and charming his way to the top was slipping away. The world, little by little, was rejecting him. The great Andrew DeSilva, whom everybody wanted to be around, was turning back into little Andrew Cunanan, the drug dealer and street prostitute whom nice people didn't want to have around.

The last chance he had, and the last rejection, was David Madson. I think Madson came to symbolize all the rejection Cunanan was facing. And rather than be a man, stand up to the reality around him, Cunanan turned himself, in his own mind, into the victim. And just like a little kid who stops crying when he thinks Mommy can't hear him, Cunanan's hurt feelings meant nothing unless he could show them to Madson. That's why he had to go to Minneapolis.

I don't know if he went to Minneapolis with murder on his mind; but I do think that when he arrived, and found out that neither Madson nor Trail really had any room in their lives for him anymore, he snapped. Cunanan's rage had been growing like a jet engine revving up. I think Jeffrey Trail was just unlucky enough to be standing on the runway.

I think Madson, as I said earlier, was the prime target. Cunanan, like every coward we've profiled on *America's Most Wanted,* fell into the self-pitying syndrome: If I can't have you, no one will. It's the most common motive in domestic crimes on *AMW;* it forms a perfect explanation of what happened in Minneapolis.

After that, I think it becomes a survival game. He has tasted blood, and it has changed him. I don't care how smart and educated and sophisticated he's supposed to be: At that moment he turns from the predator into the hunted, and he will do anything to keep himself alive and free. I think Lee Miglin was an easy target for quick cash, nothing more; the speculation about possible ties to Cunanan are painful to his family, and it's time for them to stop. The cemetery worker was a means to an end, nothing more. Cunanan didn't have to kill these men, he didn't have to torture them, to get money and cars. But the taste of blood changed him, and he became an animal, outside the laws of civilization, outside the laws of logic.

I think in desperation, his paranoia, his fear of rejection, grew, until he decided: Let me make my name. Let me go down not just as a spree killer, but as an assassin. Let my name be linked with a great gay man forever, in death, as I desperately wanted, but could never achieve, in life. "At this point," said one of our sources who had been close to Cunanan, "it's a game for him. It's a thrill ride. He probably views himself as a dead man walking, and this was a stunt. His next stunt will be bigger, and better, in his eyes."

What that all meant to me was that Cunanan had no capacity to reason, no ability to feel remorse.

He truly had nothing to lose.

It was time for the final showdown.

■ ■ ■

Our team was working around the clock, both in Florida and in Washington, everyone running on pure adrenaline, putting in the twenty-hour days that news people always complain about but secretly relish, that thrill of being in the middle of the hunt for a story—but in our case, it was much stronger, because we were literally in the middle of the hunt for a killer.

We were invited to the Cunanan command center in South Beach, a huge room with two long desks, on which were two long rows of personal computers. We were the only media allowed in, and when I got there, and saw what was going on, I thought, these guys are doing it right.

The Miami Beach police, the Florida Department of Law Enforcement, and the FBI were all working closely on this case. Sharing information. Sharing manpower. There was none of the ego that can get in the way of an investigation. In my last book, I went public with my anger at the Hollywood, Florida, police, who, I believe, botched the investigation into my son Adam's death—because they were too proud to call in other law enforcement agencies. But this was truly a team effort. And I was proud to be considered part of the team.

We'd set up camp at the Pelican Hotel, and flew in every freelance producer we could to help on the case. Lance decided to devote the entire show to Cunanan.

On the night of Wednesday, July 23, we were planning to work on a story about the bars we believed Cunanan might have been hanging around in—Liquid, Twist, the hottest hot spots on the gay scene. But first, I was scheduled to interview a good friend of the show, Richard Barreto, the Miami Beach police chief.

Barreto wasn't doing interviews. He'd been fried by the media on the pawned coin, and since then he'd basically frozen out the press. Miami was in the middle of one of those media swarms that you see at events like the O.J. trial, and on top of that he was trying to run an investigation; I could only imagine what the chief was going through, and I wouldn't have been surprised if he canceled.

But at 5:00 P.M., there I was, in Barreto's office, just settling in to talk about the case. We were going over the details—just that afternoon, the FBI had released ballistics results showing that the .40-caliber bullets recovered in the Madson and Reese murders matched the bullets that killed Gianni Versace—when the phone started ringing.

I could tell by the look on his face when he picked up the receiver that he was on to something. He was telling everyone, stay off the scanners, stay on the cell phones.

What they were saying: They had someone trapped on a houseboat. They said the caretaker of the houseboat had been approaching the front door when he heard shots fired. Miami Beach doesn't have a SWAT team anymore (more budget cuts), so they were calling in the metro Dade SWAT team.

The story would not necessarily be a big deal, in the scheme of things, in a big city.

Except for one thing.

The caretaker had gotten a glimpse of the guy on the houseboat.

He gave a description.

It matched the description of Cunanan.

■   ■   ■

We turned on the TV.

It seemed like only minutes before the media had live satellite helicopter shots of the houseboat. Barreto was saying into the phone, cut the power to the houseboat! He could be watching this! He'll see the SWAT team move in!

I'm thinking, if it is Cunanan on the boat, he's armed, he's trapped, he's got nothing to lose—those helicopters are going to get those SWAT guys killed!

I watched as Barreto put the plan in place: The street was blocked off; the SWAT team would move in from boats on the water side when the time was right.

Barreto was incredibly calm. He's a tall, distinguished gentleman, not given to fits of emotion, but even still, I couldn't believe how calm he was staying. It's a standoff, he explained. Nobody's going anywhere. He decided not to make a statement to the media, but to run the operation for a while from the office, then head down to the scene.

I told him I'd meet him there.

■   ■   ■

When I got to the houseboat, I saw the media madhouse on one side of the road, and the houseboat on the other. To my surprise, I was waved past the police line. And when I got out of the car, the reporters started screaming at me. Later, I'm told, this scene played live on Miami TV: "Something is happening! Someone is pulling up! It's . . . It's . . . John Walsh????"

The scene had the unreal glow that only high-powered TV lights, a hundred screaming reporters, hovering helicopters, and a possible murder can create. I didn't have time to sort it out. Barreto had apparently left word to let me through. Al Boza, the Miami Beach public information officer, spotted me and filled me in. "John, we've got a body on the second floor," he said. "Part of the face is blown off, so we can't make a positive ID."

Listen, I asked, I'd love to give something to our Fox affiliate across the street, do you mind if I tell them this? It would be a big scoop for them.

No problem, said Boza. Just don't quote me.

What developed was one of the strangest scenes I've ever been part of. On the one hand, all the media are screaming at Boza, at the top of their lungs: Why are you letting John Walsh through? We're the real journalists! He's just got a cop show!

And I'm thinking, as my kids would say, well, duh, when are you going to figure *that* one out?

But they're screaming bloody murder—until I get close to them. Then, suddenly, it's "Oh, Mr. Walsh, can we have an interview?"

I talked to Fox first, then CNN, and some other media outlets that have been helpful to us in the past, and I told them what I knew. Yes, there is a body. No, we don't know if it's Cunanan. The homicide guys are on the way.

I went back to the boat—to a chorus of more screams—and I ran into Barreto. I asked him, what do you think?

"Ninety-nine point nine percent it's Cunanan," he told me. "He killed himself."

We have a fingerprint from the body, he told me. And we have the fingerprint from the pawn ticket, and one from his California driver's license, but John, you know how long it takes to run a print. I can't say anything until I'm sure.

But we think it's Cunanan.

I looked up at the boat.

So that's the final play, I thought.

That's the last move.

Take the easy way out.

■   ■   ■

Dawn was breaking, and the media pack was in a frenzy every time we moved a muscle. All through the night, they'd been airing reports—it might be Cunanan, we think it's Cunanan, who knows if it's Cunanan. The police still haven't matched the prints, so they haven't announced anything.

I asked Barreto, can I go over and tell people what's going on?

I'm not having a press conference for two hours, he said, until we're sure. But you can go over there.

By now, the media mob had grown to gigantic proportions. I hadn't slept all night, and I was doing a hundred interviews. I thought some, like Matt Lauer from the *Today* show, were doing a nice job of reporting. I thought most weren't.

As the morning wore on, I heard more and more questions from interviewers that, frankly, I thought were just dumb. Maybe I was getting grouchy from lack of sleep, but I was beginning to get upset.

All of these reporters seemed to be so sympathetic to Cunanan. All these passionate, soul-searching reporters were asking, why did he do what he did, why did he take his own life, it's a shame for it to end this way. What a terrible ending. Now we'll never know. What a tragedy.

And, on one of the interviews, I finally blew up.

This isn't a tragedy, I said.

I'll tell you about tragedy.

First of all, he saved the taxpayers of the state of Florida millions of dollars. They don't have to foot the bill for a trial, and his victims don't have to fly to Florida to sit through the trial and watch some lame defense attorney explain that he committed the murders because he was gay, because he was fat, because the other kids made fun of him when he was six years old. All those lame excuses. I said, you know what, the psychiatrists can take pieces of his brain, they can study his background, they can worry about him all they want.

I worry about the victims.

You wanna talk tragedy?

The tragedy would be to force Lee Miglin's family to sit through that trial and hear how Andrew Cunanan tortured their father and wrapped his face in duct tape and tried to saw off his head.

That won't happen now.

The tragedy would be for the family of Jeffery Trail to sit and listen to the gruesome details of how Cunanan beat him to death with hammer, with forensic experts explaining how pieces of his brain wound up on the floor. The tragedy would be for the parents of David Madson to sit through the details of the two days that their son, witness to the aftermath of one murder, must have known he would be next, until finally he found himself staring down the barrel of a .40-caliber pistol.

That won't happen now.

The tragedy would be to watch as the Versace family saw its name dragged through the mud in an American courtroom as another celebrity-crazed lawyer threw out all the sick allegations you know would come out in a media-circus trial like that one would be.

Thankfully, we would be spared that spectacle.

Andrew Cunanan knew what he had done. So Andrew Cunanan tried himself, found himself guilty, and gave himself the death penalty. I'm not sorry for that. Not one bit.

I don't know how long I went on, but I know I felt good when it was over. I took the little microphone off my lapel, and looked at the media horde on one side of me, and back at the houseboat on the other.

I knew that for the media, this story was over.

But this story wasn't over.

For the family of Jeffrey Trail, for the family of David Madson, for the family of Lee Miglin, this wasn't over. For the widow and the beautiful two-year-old daughter of William Reese, this wasn't over. For Gianni Versace's lover, and his sister, and all the people whose lives he touched, this wasn't anywhere near over.

I knew those people had a long, long road ahead. They had a lot of grieving to do.

But when I saw them wheeling the body of Andrew Cunanan out of the houseboat on a stretcher, I thought, well, maybe for the victims the story isn't over, in some ways it may never be; but at least now, the grieving, and the healing, can begin.

CHAPTER SEVEN

The New Warrior

Everybody knows that if we put enough light out there, we're going to get her back.

—EVE NICHOL, MOTHER OF POLLY KLAAS

Rage, rage against the dying of the light.

—DYLAN THOMAS

You'd think a kid would be safe at home. Maybe not on the street walking to school. Maybe not in the playground. Maybe not even in the front yard. But you'd think that in your own house, once you've locked the doors and checked the windows, a kid—your kid—could be sure that no monsters could get in to hurt them. What America learned from the tragic story of Polly Klaas was that you'd be wrong.

And yet there is another lesson that the Polly Klaas case has for America, and it's one that many may have missed.

One of the reasons people find *America's Most Wanted* inspiring is that we try to focus on ways that good can come out of tragedy. I won't lie to you: I'd give up everything, in a second, if I could have my boy Adam back. But I know that's not possible, and so I've had to do what I can to make some sense out of the most senseless act in the universe.

The murder of a child.

I saw everything that the rest of the country saw in the Polly Klaas story: the terror of a parent's worst nightmare, the horror of learning that she did not survive, the disgust at listening to the pitiful excuses in court of the monster who abducted her.

But I also saw something else in the world that surrounded Polly.

It was something I saw in her father.

As the case wore on, I saw a father's rage grow. I saw a father's pain consume him. I saw a father's anger burnished, and hardened, and tempered, until it took on a shape, a form, as tough as steel, as cold as ice, as sharp and unforgiving as a saber.

In the end, I saw someone emerge from the darkness of despair.

In a way, I saw myself.

■   ■   ■

It was still a month away, but kids in Petaluma, California, were already getting excited about Halloween. There are seasons in Petaluma, a small town forty minutes north of San Francisco, on the edge of wine country, unlike the relentlessly cheery year-round sunniness of the lower part of the state. On this Friday, October 1, 1993, you would have noticed just the slightest hint of the changing season in the air as you walked the streets of this town that relishes its piece-of-Americana image, an image so pervasive that Ronald Reagan filmed his "Morning in America" campaign commercials here.

That day, people were already beginning to put out carved pumpkins on their porches and hang little ghosts and goblins cut out of white paper on their front doors. At the local junior high school, at noon, a beautiful, laughing little girl named Polly ate her lunch and chattered away with her friends.

Polly Hanna Klaas had a sparkle in her soul that showed in her eyes and her smile: A perceptive child who appeared to be perpetually laughing, she also had a serious and focused side. She played the piano and clarinet, favoring Bach and *Phantom of the Opera*. She liked to record herself, then play it back and do a duet with herself.

Polly's mom, Eve Nichol, and her dad, Marc Klaas, had been

divorced since Polly was three. Mom was remarried, Dad was about to be; and although Polly lived with Mom she loved them both, got along with both, and got to spend a lot of time with both. She was a happy, loved, and secure child who was afraid of only two things: She feared the dark and she feared strangers.

Eve remembers Polly coming home that day in a great mood. Eve, Polly, and Polly's little sister, Annie, had pizza. Then, Polly asked if two friends—Kate and Gillian—could come for a sleepover. Mom made a deal—she could have the sleepover if she cleaned her room.

Before long, all three friends were giggling on Polly's bed.

Eve and Annie went to bed around ten o'clock. Annie had been kicked out of the girls' shared bedroom for the night so that Polly and her friends could stay up late by themselves. "I read for a little while," Eve recalls now. "And then I guess I just drifted off."

As the father of a murdered child, I've often thought about the hour, the moments, just before the unimaginable takes place and your child is snatched away from you forever: If only we could freeze time at the instant when the child is still safe and do something, anything, to prevent what is going to happen. If only time could have stopped before my son Adam's killer walked into the store where Adam was with his mom. If only time could be pushed back to this moment. Every parent who has had a child go missing revisits this moment, the moment that you are drifting off to sleep and your child is okay. You return to it again and again, as though you are a spirit floating over your old self, yelling, don't go to sleep! Don't go to the office! Go to your child's room and hold her as tight as you can and don't let go! Don't let any strangers come into the house! Please, let me stop time right in this moment!

But time did not stop that night.

And a stranger came.

■ ■ ■

"That night," Polly's friend Kate said later, "we were having a real good time."

Preparing for Halloween, they tried on different costumes,

including Mickey Mouse ears and deer antlers. The room was filled with their high-pitched squeals of glee.

"Then," says Polly's other friend, Gillian, "when Polly opened the bedroom door to go into the living room to get sleeping bags, there was a man standing there holding a knife. He told us not to scream or he'd cut our throats."

The man, who had a broad face and thick, unkempt graying hair and a beard, pushed his way into the bedroom and tied up Kate and Gillian with electrical cord and strips of cloth. He told them not to look at him and to keep their eyes on the floor.

"He told us that if we said anything he'd slit our throats and to lay face down on the floor," said Kate. "He kept talking to us the whole time, reassuring us that he just wanted money and he wasn't going to hurt anyone."

"Then he asked why there were so many people there," said Gillian. "He figured out that it was a slumber party and asked who lived there. Polly said she did, and he asked where all the valuables were."

Polly showed the man her jewelry box—it held a few trinkets and twenty-seven dollars she had saved—but he took none of it.

Instead, he started to leave.

Pulling Polly along with him.

She began to cry and pleaded with the stranger—but not for herself. Her two friends remember what she said.

"Please," she begged the stranger, "don't hurt my mother or my sister."

The man didn't respond to Polly. He told her friends to count to one thousand, and when they were through, Polly would be back with them.

But Polly never came back.

The two terrified seventh graders waited until they thought the intruder was gone and then struggled out of their bindings. They ran through the house, looking for Polly, but she wasn't anywhere to be found. Finally, they burst into her mother's room.

Polly's mom remembers Kate calling, "Eve, wake up, Eve. A man came into the house and tied us up."

Eve asked Kate where Polly was.

"She's gone." Kate told her. "He took Polly."

Frantically, Eve Nichol dialed 911. And then as she raced around the house and the yard, searching for her daughter, hoping that maybe—somehow—Polly was still nearby, Allen Nichol, Polly's stepfather, picked up the phone and called Polly's dad, Marc, who lived in Sausalito, about an hour south.

"It was about ten-thirty at night when he called," Marc says. "He told me Polly had been kidnapped and it just blew me away. I had a very difficult ten minutes, running around the house shrieking and screaming."

"And then," Marc continues, "somehow I had the presence of mind to call the FBI. I stayed up the rest of the night with my fiancée, Violet, trying to come up with some plan of action, knowing that we would be going to Petaluma in the morning."

It was in these moments—and the moments that followed— that Marc Klaas's rage began to be born.

■   ■   ■

At around midnight that night—as Marc was frantically getting ready to head to Petaluma—a homeowner named Dana Jaffe, who lived in a wooded area in nearby Santa Rosa, made a call to the police. Her baby-sitter had just been approached by a weird, disheveled man who had popped out of the woods. Dana called the Sonoma County sheriff's department, who sent two deputies to investigate. What they found was a man named Richard Allen Davis—a man with a broad face and thick, unkempt graying hair and a beard. His beat-up little white Pinto was stuck in a ditch. They asked him what he was doing, and he said he was sightseeing.

He's sightseeing.

It's midnight and he says he's sightseeing in the woods.

The deputies were suspicious; they tried everything to detain him. They gave him a Breathalyzer test. He passed. They ran a computer check. He had a long rap sheet, but he was out on parole and there were no outstanding warrants. They looked into his car. They saw nothing.

They had the street-smart sense that good cops do—the gut feeling that the guy is dirty—and the rap sheet bolstered their suspicions. But there was nothing tangible to run him in on.

And they couldn't hold him on suspicion of kidnapping, or question him about it—because they hadn't heard about any kidnapping. They hadn't heard about it, even though it was ninety minutes after Polly's disappearance had been reported to Petaluma police.

The reason they didn't know: The alert on Polly was broadcast on only one police channel; the two deputies were on another channel.

So they never heard the alert.

A lot has been said about the law enforcement effort on this night, and I'll come back to it later, but I want to make one thing clear right now: In this moment, the guys on the front line did all they could do. I know they're haunted by this moment, just like the rest of us. But they were not at fault. They questioned the guy for more than half an hour, just on their gut suspicion. Then they had no choice. There were other calls to answer.

They did what the situation called for.

They helped the guy get his car out of the ditch, and he drove away.

They couldn't have known.

They couldn't have known that Polly was less than one hundred feet away.

Bound, but not gagged.

And, possibly, still alive.

■　■　■

That Saturday was a day off for the *America's Most Wanted* crew—we aired on Tuesdays that year, but gave the staff the weekends off—so it was quiet around the studio. The set where you see me standing when I host *America's Most Wanted* has kind of an eerie, unreal feeling to it on those days when the crew isn't around, like the lights and the TV monitors and the walls themselves aren't fully part of everyday reality until we all show up, throw the switches, and use the airwaves to send out our message about hunting down the bad guys again. It's like a carnival in the morning, or a ventriloquist's dummy with no hand up his back—it seems frozen, in limbo, just a little ominous, but also kind of peaceful.

I was in the studio because Michelle Hord, our missing-child coordinator, had asked me to come voice a missing-child alert on a case out of Illinois. We'd made an agreement between the show and the National Center for Missing and Exploited Children to quickly get public service announcements out to all affiliates—Fox or otherwise—whenever a child goes missing. The case we were working on seemed pretty hopeless, to be honest, but you don't think about that. You put the alert out on the airwaves, you get people to air it, and you hope for the best. I was trying to move things along as quickly as I could; both Michelle and I were going to a big black-tie event downtown that evening, to celebrate our two hundred fiftieth capture, and I knew she'd want to get the heck out of the office and get ready.

I liked working with Michelle. She had just taken the job of missing-child coordinator that summer. She was only twenty-three years old, but wise beyond her years, and she truly, truly cared about missing kids. She was like a lot of the young people who come to work on the show—excited about working on a national TV show, but maybe just a bit leery of the mission, until they get the feel of what it's like to help a victim in need.

Michelle had come around quickly. I've always preached that when a child goes missing, the first forty-eight hours are crucial, and when Michelle took on the missing-child coordinator job, she took that on as her mantra. "It was an awesome responsibility," she said. "I felt like if I didn't get the announcement out in twenty-four hours, that would be the twenty-four hours that made the difference."

We had just finished putting the missing child PSA together on the Illinois case when the phone rang. I was a bit curious—who would be calling on a Saturday?

It was Ken Carlson, a freelance producer we work with on the West Coast.

He was speaking rapidly.

At first, Michelle was a little annoyed. "I was going to go get cute for this big party," she said later.

But all that faded, quickly, as she heard what Ken had to say.

A child has been abducted. It is not a parental abduction. It is not a runaway. The child has been snatched from her own bedroom. There is reason to believe the child is alive. The community is mobilizing.

They need your help.

■   ■   ■

By Sunday, in Petaluma, an unprecedented volunteer search effort had begun to take shape. A local print shop owner, Bill Rhodes, offered his facilities to print up flyers, and then he began to bring in other people and businesses. The print shop became the headquarters of the search effort. By that afternoon, six hundred volunteers were out combing the rolling hills and fields around Petaluma, and more were in the volunteer center—many with their children in tow—making calls and working the copiers. There was just something about Polly, and about Petaluma, that brought everyone together. As one woman said, as she carried a box of copy paper into the center, "I just feel like she's my child, too, and we have to get her back. I think everybody here feels that way."

We'd already gotten a quick PSA on Polly out to all the TV stations in a three-state area, and started working the case for that Tuesday's show. There was also a new ally in the fight, one most of us hadn't even heard of, and one I don't think we'd ever really used in a missing-child case before. Something called the Internet.

A local computer salesman, Gary French, brought his expertise to the search by creating a digitized version of the missing-person flier being distributed all over northern California. He was posting it on electronic bulletin boards all over the country—and all over the world. "We were on CompuServe, Prodigy, and AOL," Gary told one reporter. "We set up an E-mail address and sent information out about Polly on LISTSERVs and newsgroups. Every way you could access the Internet and its users, we took advantage of. We had to. We wanted everybody, everywhere, to be looking for Polly."

Marc Klaas was smart. Whenever there's a missing child case, and the parents are divorced, suspicion falls on the father. He didn't hesitate: He marched right in to the cops, said ask me all your questions, get this out of the way, so we can get the hell on to the business of finding my child's abductor. I know, firsthand, how tough that is to do—to face the fact that people are wondering if you abducted your own child—but he did it, and he was very, very cooperative, and he got everyone past it. That helped focus the investigation early on. It was a crucial step.

In Petaluma, in her small, gray-green Victorian house, Eve Nichol lit a candle and placed it in the window. A candle for Polly. To light Polly's way home.

That Tuesday, just four days after Polly was abducted, *America's Most Wanted* went on the air with the Polly Klaas abduction as our lead story. We had her picture, and a sketch (albeit not a very good one) of the abductor based on descriptions from Polly's friends. We also aired some home video of Polly that the Klaas family had given us. There was something about this child, something about the video of Polly in a blue tunic, so alive and full of joy, acting in a school play, calling out as she pranced across the screen, "I am Pegasus, the winged horse"—something that made her more than just a grainy picture on a missing-person flyer. Sometimes people see those flyers and don't connect to them, don't really notice them, but this video brought Polly to life, it made you see her: a real kid with a great smile and long, wavy brown hair, a kid with a real life and real parents and friends who loved her. And all of us—me, the staff of *AMW*, the people of Petaluma—we just had to get her back.

Everyone remembers when the whole nation followed the Polly Klaas story, but it's easy to forget that in those early days—in those crucial early days—no one outside California was paying any attention to the case. I was hoping that somehow, our story would help attract some national attention, to get her picture into the papers and onto the local news nationwide.

We got lucky.

One person who was watching *America's Most Wanted* that night, and who felt a deep connection to Polly, was actress Winona Ryder. Winona grew up in Petaluma. She had gone to Petaluma Junior High, Polly's school, and had shared Polly's dream of being able to act. Winona realized that dream, and she wanted to give Polly a chance to live out her dreams, too. And, as Winona said, she was lucky enough to have the resources to help. She offered a $200,000 reward for Polly's safe return.

Winona also taped an announcement about Polly, footage that we later aired on our show. Standing in the volunteer center, wearing a long-sleeved green T-shirt and looking frail but determined, Winona Ryder faced a TV camera and spoke from her heart:

> Hello, I'm Winona Ryder, and recently in my hometown of Petaluma, California, Polly Klaas was kidnapped at knifepoint from her home. Here's a photograph of Polly and a sketch of the man who kidnapped her. Please be on the lookout for both of them. We need your help to bring Polly back home safely.

It did the trick. Winona's presence brought a big article in *USA Today,* and a mention on the *Today* show, which led to a lot of national attention. And the case became the nation's case, Polly the nation's missing child. Other celebrities joined in: Robin Williams also taped an announcement about Polly, pleading for information about her and about the many other missing children all over the United States. *America's Most Wanted* kept the story on the air every week. We were determined that no one would forget about Polly Klaas.

■ ■ ■

Michelle headed out to Petaluma. When she got there she found a crazy media mob scene. It's the double-edged sword that the parent of a missing child must come to grips with: Without the media, you have no chance of finding your child. But with the wild screaming packs of reporters and their video cameras, flash cameras, microphones, and tape recorders camping on your lawn, you can barely hear yourself think. You feel, God bless them for what they're doing to find my child—but man, when you put so many of them together, they do become a frightening mob.

One of the things I'm proudest of about our staff is that they understand they have a job to do—but the victim's family has a much more important job to do. If we're helping the family, then dig in; if we're not, then get the hell out of the way.

I think victims' families understand that about us, and it's why we're able to work together so closely on missing-child cases. Before the national media caught on to the story, Marc and Eve knew we were there for them; and later, with the media pack howling at the door, Marc and Eve appreciated Michelle's low-key, what-do-you-need approach.

"We were very frightened in the beginning," Marc said. "It helped that *AMW* came in so early, because we knew they had a reputation for helping to find criminals, so we were very grateful and hopeful. And Michelle was very kind."

"I tried to remember, at all times, what they were going through," Michelle said. "You're seeing them in the toughest part of their lives. There are so many difficult demands on the family. Who wants to become a TV star because their kid's missing? I tried to be delicate."

She became their ally, even helping Eve sneak out the back door when the media were camped out front and she didn't have the strength to talk to them one more time.

One of the things Michelle became sensitive to was Eve's desire to keep life from becoming too crazy for her other daughter, Annie. After all, she had just had her sister disappear, and she was a frightened little girl who needed her mom more than ever.

"I definitely saw the pull between doing what she needed to do, and trying to maintain a sense of normalcy for Annie," Michelle said. "I would come over without my pad or the camera guys, and get out the LEGO set and sit on the floor and play with Annie, so she wouldn't think of me as just this media guy."

And she wasn't. As time went by, the case began to have an effect on Michelle, too.

"At night," she remembers, "I began dreaming about Polly being okay. It was devastating. I wanted so much for her to be okay, because I had such a connection with her mom and her sister."

By day, Michelle played the part of the seasoned journalist. By night, back in her hotel room, her true feelings came through. "Every night," she remembers, "I'd go back to my hotel room and cry and call my mom in Connecticut. I had to lean on someone. This really makes you realize how important family is."

■   ■   ■

There was another frustration we had to deal with. Police had brought in a sketch artist to take descriptions of the abductor from the two little girls who saw him. To be frank, it was a lousy sketch.

Eventually, Jeanne Boylan was called in. Jeanne would later become a key member of our *America's Most Wanted* forensic team: She's a sketch artist nonpareil, who has made a career of capturing, on paper, the true likenesses of criminals when others have failed. When she first began doing this kind of work in Oregon, she became frustrated with the standard procedure for developing a composite sketch—showing witnesses pictures of possible suspects, or offering them pictures of sample eyes, noses, and chins to build a face from. "I found that using that system really tended to lead the witnesses," Boylan says.

Over the years, Boylan has developed a technique all her own, one she describes as aiming to capture the brain's snapshot of something seen under traumatic circumstances. Recovering this kind of image, she explains, "is like taking a fifty-cent piece and tossing it into eight feet of water. It remains intact in the water, but the water creates distortion. So you have to reach down through that distortion."

Armed with Jeanne's new sketch of the kidnapper, the search took on renewed energy. By late October, the makeshift group of volunteers that sprang up the day after the disappearance had coalesced into a well-oiled machine. And volunteers kept coming into the center to help with the effort. "I'd show up here every morning, expecting to be alone," Marc Klaas said. "And then people would start showing up. They'd come in by themselves, with their friends and with their kids, and just get to work."

It was a sight to behold. As you walked in, you noticed that the air was bustling, hopeful, almost cheerful. The entire huge office was ringed with posters, images of Polly, bright rainbows, pictures drawn by local elementary school kids; one typical picture showed a girl holding a flower and read, in a child's scrawl, "Polly, this is a picture of you and I hope I can see you soon, love, Jorie and Jenny." Read another: "We miss you Polly! We really do!"

New volunteers who walked into this bustling scene immediately got blue ribbons (modeled after the AIDS ribbon) pinned to their lapels, and were put to work. The focus of the room was a group of long tables, with volunteers stuffing envelopes—young and old, all kinds of people, getting out mass mailings in English and Spanish. On another long table were mounds of food, donated by local bakeries and restaurants. Next to the computers on which the electronic bulletin board was coordinated hung a huge map, showing the poster distribution. In the back was an administrative area for coordinating fund-raising efforts—at one point there were twenty-three different fund-raisers being coordinated at once. There was also a big hotline area.

It was like a small business that had sprung up overnight, a business with one purpose: to find a single little girl. It is one of the most hopeful parts of the long, dark hours we all put into finding missing children—to see communities come together, rally together, work together, for a common goal.

I remember one volunteer in particular who talked to us. Her name was Barbara Zanussi. "I came out because four years ago, my nephew, Jacob Wetterling, was taken at gunpoint in a similar situation," she said. I knew that case well; we'd done it several times on the show. "It's been four years for us," she said, "but I truly believe that if you can get the word out, and get as many fliers out, the sooner Polly will be able to come home. I look at the posters around the room, and it is in a way like reliving a nightmare. But at the same time, it's an outpouring of hope."

I couldn't believe she was there, that she would put herself through the torture of bringing up all those memories; and yet, in another part of my heart, I knew exactly why she was there. All of us, in the terrible club of parents of children who have gone missing, want desperately to see one of these stories turn out differently.

Maybe this one, you think. Please. Let it be this one.

And then you try to shake off the simultaneous feelings of hope and hopelessness, and just get down to doing the work, and dealing with the matters of the moment that crop up in front of you. And in a missing-child case, you never know what's going to happen.

With all the activity and controversy and movement, all the volunteers and posters and flyers and TV coverage, you always felt like something was happening, something was pending, something was cooking.

And I remember thinking, this is what we've worked for, Revé and I, for all these years. Everything is being done right. All the politicians in the state are taking this seriously. The Adam Walsh Center, and the Center for Missing and Exploited Children, had been involved and kept everything moving right, right from jump street. *America's Most Wanted* hadn't waited for its next broadcast, it had sent the TV alerts out right away.

No one was letting the story die.

There was only one thing that did not take place.

Polly did not come home.

■　　■　　■

As the days turned into weeks with no break in the case, the toll on Polly's family just kept getting worse. Unless you've been in this situation—and God forbid you ever should be—you just can't imagine what happens to you.

"My life has been totally impacted, totally changed," Marc said. "This is a cause that I have to devote myself to now. I have to totally direct my efforts toward finding my daughter. There has been no other focus in my life since she was taken."

"It's wearing on all of us," Marc's father, Joe, told reporters.

"We all seem to be picking on each other, and we realize that. We're so angry, but it's only safe to be angry with each other, with people you love. We're trying to hold it all in, but it's hard."

Then, on November 28, that break we all wanted finally occurred. Dana Jaffe, the same property owner who had reported the trespasser in the woods on the night Polly was kidnapped, was walking in those same woods. She came across an area about one hundred yards from where the deputies had interrogated the man—and noticed some things the deputies hadn't.

She called the police, who arrived on the scene to find several suspicious items—a black sweatshirt, some strips of cloth, and an unrolled condom.

The police sent the material to Washington, D.C., to be analyzed by the FBI. By the next day, they had linked the evidence to the kidnapping—and to Polly. The strips of cloth were torn from Polly's nightgown (and, it would come out later, were used by the kidnapper to tie her up).

So now that they knew the scene of the crime, they went back and looked up the records on who had been at the scene that night.

The man who had been sightseeing in the woods at midnight.

Whom the deputies had helped when his car got stuck in the ditch.

Richard Allen Davis.

The FBI was quick to locate Davis, arresting him in Ukiah, California, on November 30. He was brought back to Petaluma, where he was initially held on a drunk driving charge, to which he pleaded guilty. This was a pattern of Davis's, as we later found out: Plead guilty to a lesser charge in hope of weaseling out of a more serious one.

So far, he was saying nothing about where Polly was.

Details about Richard Allen Davis were beginning to come out—details that made me sick to my stomach. This animal was a repeat offender who had spent sixteen of his thirty-nine years of life in jail.

And not just for petty crimes: Davis had previously abducted and tortured three different women—beating one of them with a poker—and was still let out by the system to walk the streets. To walk Polly's street in Petaluma.

Marc Klaas felt like howling at the moon. I did too. How long, for the love of sweet God, how long will we continue to ignore the violent offenders who prey on our wives and our children? I'll be damn honest with you—it makes me crazy when I hear judges pass mandatory life sentences for drug dealers, knowing full well that when the politicians go away and the prisons are full and the judges order a lowering of the prison populations because of overcrowding, that it's these maniacs, these predators, these vile perverts whom we will open the gates for.

"It was one of the most bitter lessons I've ever learned in my life," Marc would tell me later. "That the criminal justice system is there to serve the predators. That it's there to serve the criminals, not to serve society. It was at that point I determined that I had to do something to change that situation, to make people aware that this was going on."

In my heart—although I wasn't breathing a word of this to anyone—I feared the worst. I've learned that there are two kinds of pedophiles. There are those who let the child go, because they haven't yet progressed to the "violence point." They're cowards, and that works in your favor. They are virulent molesters, but they haven't yet tasted blood, and they believe that therefore they have not crossed a certain line, that they are not really all that bad, and they convince themselves—for a while—that they will not cross it.

But I was thinking, a guy that's got the balls to break into a house at night and start waving a knife around, a guy who has beaten a woman with a poker within an inch of her life, this guy is way past the point where he's afraid of violence. This is a dangerous, weird, sick individual. This perverted, twisted monster who invaded a slumber party and dragged a little girl off into the night—I know this is not a heartsick father who lost a kid in a custody battle, and is now gonna find a child to take with him to Disneyland.

I just prayed my gut feeling was wrong.

A few days later, Michelle Hord was at Eve's house. Annie came and sat in Michelle's lap. Annie knew that police had found the man who had taken her sister, but that he wouldn't say where her sister was. She had drawn a picture of Richard Allen Davis behind bars, with lots of spiders and snakes. "This is what I want to happen to the bad man who took Polly," she said.

On the afternoon of December 4, Michelle had another date to talk with Eve. She kept calling the house, but no one was there. Finally, Eve's husband answered.

"This is not a good time," he said.

Michelle knew.

She drove to the house.

The candle in the window, which had burned since the day Polly disappeared, was out.

With tears welling in her eyes, she decided to just drive on.

■　　■　　■

Michelle drove to the visitor's center. By the time she arrived, the police were getting ready to hold a press conference. Earlier that day, Richard Allen Davis had finally given it up. Davis had led the police to Cloverdale, California, about thirty miles from Polly's home. There, in the woods near Highway 101, they found the remains of a beautiful little girl. She had been strangled to death.

It fell to Sergeant Mike Kerns of the Petaluma Police Department to utter the words that no one wanted to hear.

"Polly Klaas," he intoned, "is dead."

■　　■　　■

People ask me all the time why I call parents of murdered children, or go to see them when I can, and I always explain that it's because no one did it for me. No one knew how. There is that moment, once you know for sure that your child is dead, when you sink into a hole that you just know you'll never get out of, and you wonder—maybe for the first time since your child was abducted—now what happens to me? You feel so horrible, so alone in ways no one can share with you, that you wonder, will I make it? Am I going to kill myself so I don't have to feel this way anymore?

I dread those calls. But I know I have to make them.

So that night, I called Marc Klaas.

What I mostly wanted to tell him was that, no matter how indescribably awful he felt, he was going to survive. He *could* survive. And to honor Polly, he *had* to.

I laid it out straight for him: I said, no one's going to tell you this, but you're *not* going to be okay for a while. You're going to stay in the worst depression and anger that anyone's ever felt. You're going to lose most of your friends, because they just don't know what to say to you, and you make them feel uncomfortable. These are normal things. Expect them. Be ready for them.

I told him that his health was going to go to hell. That he had to learn to eat right, and to exercise, because your natural tendency is going to be to not care about anything and to drink too much and eat crap, and when you're in a depression it's hard to get yourself to the gym, but you have got to keep up your health, or you won't be able to do anything else.

And then we talked about Polly. About what a beautiful, special child she was. How very talented she was. How happy she made everyone feel.

"Marc, you can't just dwell on the last day of her life," I said. "You have to think of all the good times you had with her. How lucky you were to have that child for twelve years."

"John," he said, "she was the light of my life."

"She still is," I said.

■   ■   ■

That night, on the phone, Marc also talked about how now, at least, with Richard Allen Davis in custody, there would be some justice for Polly. I had to tell him, though, from my experience with these kinds of cases, that the trial, if anything, was going to be harder than all the weeks of waiting to find out what had happened to Polly. And that the promise of swift justice guaranteed by the founders of the American judicial system had been corrupted long ago: Now that the lawyers and the courts were involved, it would probably take years for the case to come to trial. And, unfortunately, I was right. Marc's opportunity to face Richard Allen Davis in court was still two long years away.

■   ■   ■

A month after that phone call, I got to meet Marc in person, when I was doing a Geraldo Rivera show, his annual special devoted to missing-child issues. I've always respected Geraldo for the way he deals with these specials, helping us to get missing kids' faces out there and gain attention for our various missing-child causes and legislative fights. He always lets me bring whatever cases I want to, and he treats the issue with dignity and respect. Geraldo had asked me to ask Marc if he'd come on the show. I assured Marc that this would be a good venue, that he would be treated right, and that it might be a good chance to say some of the things he wanted to say.

So that's how I got to meet Marc Klaas. My first thought when I looked at him—I've never told Marc this, and I hope he forgives me for saying this now—was that, here is a guy who's not going to make it. He looked gaunt, and jumpy, and pale—just raw, like he was absolutely on the edge. People with me said, he looks like you looked, John, back in 1981. He was drawn and distraught, fearful of the moment, fearful that it would bring back all the pain of losing this child that he absolutely loved. I thought, no matter what I say to this guy, he's never going to be a whole person again.

The first time Geraldo asked him a question, he blurted out a thousand things: a long run-on answer trying to hit every point at once—what the cops did wrong, how hard it is to lose a daughter, how Richard Allen Davis shouldn't have been on the streets, why we need a three-strikes law, everything.

He was sitting next to me, and during a commercial break, I leaned over, and told him to try to slow it down—we'll get it all out. Just slow it down.

But he'd shown me something. I saw it, and later Geraldo told me he'd seen it too.

This man had the passion.

The passion to see that justice is done for his daughter.

The passion to make change happen, for missing and exploited children everywhere.

And I thought, you know, maybe he's gonna make it after all.

■   ■   ■

In the months that followed, you could see the change taking place in Marc Klaas. He was becoming galvanized for his crusade. Five days before Christmas, he went to the White House for a solemn meeting with President Clinton.

"Mr. President," Marc began, speaking to a man who is also the father of a teenage girl, "let me tell you about my daughter . . ."

Marc's message to the President was a plea for Clinton to lend his support to legislative efforts to pass what was then a revolutionary concept: the three-strikes law. Under the provisions of this proposed statute, Richard Allen Davis, who already had three convictions for violent crimes, would never have been free to walk into Polly's neighborhood—or any child's for that matter—because he would have been subject to an irrevocable life sentence after his third violent offense. Clinton heard Marc, and agreed with him, adding Marc's message to his State of the Union address, which he delivered to the nation just a month later.

"Violent crime and the fear it provokes are crippling our society," the President told the country. "Those who commit crimes should be punished, and those who commit repeated violent crimes should be told: 'When you commit a third violent crime, you will be put away for good. Three strikes and you are out!'"

While the lawyers for the state and for Richard Allen Davis continued to file motions and justice continued to be delayed, Marc tried to keep his anguish focused outward, which pushed him on. He began traveling the country, speaking to large groups and small ones—talking to even one person at a time, if that's what it took to draw attention to the problem of how lenient we are with criminals and how easy it is for them to prey on our children.

At first, Marc delivered his message as a member of the board of the Polly Klaas Foundation, the private, nonprofit organization that had grown out of the group that led the search. But in 1994—and this is another one of those strange twists in the case that could just break your heart—he was actually asked to leave the foundation because the other board members felt that the activities of the father of the murdered child their organization was named after didn't fit in with theirs.

"I wanted to be proactive," Marc explains, "and I guess they didn't see things that way. It's great to put out flyers, but there are lots of organizations that do that. I wanted to keep the kids *off* the flyers. Initiate programs that protect children."

Marc and I talked often during this period. I tried to offer him encouragement, helping him through some of the legal mazes of trying to get legislation passed, that sort of thing.

Once, when he called me, I tried to encourage him to lose his anger at the police. I know it well; I've got a ton of anger at the Hollywood, Florida, police for the way they screwed up in Adam's case. But if he's going to try to work to change the system, he can't alienate these people. And really, the system let him down, but these cops did the best they could. How would you like to be the cop who stopped Richard Allen Davis that night, and had to live with the fact that you might have saved Polly Klaas's life? They're people too, and they looked long and hard for Polly, and you have to get beyond the anger if you're going to try to get them to change the way they do things. And you can't burn the bridge, because that doesn't help the next child. And now you have to help the next child.

In later years, Marc told me that was the most important advice he'd heard. He also told one of our staffers something about that conversation that I had forgotten.

"I remember what John called me," Marc said.

"John told me I was the new warrior on the block."

■　■　■

The new warrior still had his most difficult battle ahead. The lawyers appointed by the state to represent Davis—saying that the publicity that surrounded the case would deny their client a fair trial—had argued for and received a change of venue. The trial was finally slated to be held in San Jose.

Everybody says, okay, no big deal, right?

Well, did you ever consider what this does to the victim's family?

Here's a trial that's going to cost the taxpayers of California three million dollars, to care for and feed Richard Allen Davis, and make sure he's got the proper legal representation. Fine. But what about the victims?

Except for when she had to testify, Eve Nichol could not bring herself to attend the trial of the man who had killed her daughter. But Marc, his mother, and his father moved to San Jose for the duration so they could be there every day. Even if they wanted to, the citizens of California could not help Marc or his parents with their expenses—state law decreed that all the citizens' resources were needed to defend the smirking child killer.

God bless our criminal justice system.

One of the effects of a crime that you almost never hear about is the financial burden it places on the victims' families. After my son Adam was killed, my wife, Revé, and I were so devastated, so lost, that it was impossible for us to live anything like a normal life for a long, long time. As a result, I lost my business, our house almost went into foreclosure, and our debts piled up sky-high. Many of the same things happened to Marc. He had owned and operated a lucrative car rental business; he never set foot back there after the day Polly was kidnapped. To this day, he and his wife, Violet, live almost solely on her modest income as a real-estate broker. And for the right to be present at the trial of the man who murdered his daughter, he would pick up the tab himself.

The trial of Richard Allen Davis finally got underway on April 16, 1996. From the first moments, the Santa Clara courtroom was crackling with tension and pain. Marc and three of Polly's grandparents sat in the front row, clutching each other as the prosecutor, in his opening statement, recounted the terrible details of how Richard Allen Davis strangled their precious angel. Davis himself sat just yards away from Marc Klaas, and Marc stared daggers at the hulking form in a long-sleeved black T-shirt, the graying bush of black hair stretching down over the collar in back. "If I had a gun," he told a reporter that day, "it would have been a bullet boring a hole in the back of his head."

The courtroom sat hushed as the prosecutor played the 911 tape of Eve Nichol's call on the night of the abduction. It was the first time Marc would hear the chilling, frantic conversation, as Eve's voice filled the courtroom—"She is not here!—I didn't hear anything!"—and then little Kate got on the phone with the dispatcher, calm and mature at first, then finally breaking down, saying she wanted to call her mommy, and Marc thought, yes, and at that moment, that is what Polly wanted, too.

The lawyers were predicting a long trial. Judge Thomas Hastings told the jurors: "You will be with us for some period of time."

Although Davis had previously admitted to killing Polly, his ploy at the trial was to say that he remembered very little about the crime and couldn't offer any motivation—except that maybe he was high on alcohol and pot. Still, the defense didn't try to pretend that Davis hadn't killed Polly. "The evidence in this case will be overwhelming that Mr. Richard Allen Davis did kill Polly Klaas," his lawyer told the jury. What he would try to do was lead the jury away from finding "special circumstances" in the murder—special circumstances that would make Davis eligible for California's death penalty.

This meant, among other things, that the defense was going to argue that Davis had not sexually assaulted Polly.

When Polly's body was found, it was so badly decomposed that clear evidence of sexual assault was not obtainable.

Prosecutor Greg Jacobs countered the defense move by reminding the jury that Davis had admitted to the rape. The defense countered by saying that the Petaluma police had coerced Davis into making that part of his confession.

I'd heard that dodge so many times before. I knew it was absurd on the face of it, but I also knew that this line of argument would make the trial not only excruciatingly long, but painful.

You see, that's something else you don't hear about much when you read about these kinds of trials in the newspapers or see them on TV: the emotional torture they are for the families. In the case of Polly Klaas, because the prosecutors had to prove that Davis had sexually assaulted Polly, Marc and his family had to sit through detailed testimony about how Polly's decomposing body had been found with her skirt pulled up and her top undone. They had to hear about the condom. And they had to listen to a discussion of how, sometime in the many weeks she had lain alone in the woods, her head had been detached from her body by animals.

"Would you like to sit through the minutes of your daughter's death?" Klaas asked later.

But he had to. He had to sit through all of it for Polly.

If Richard Allen Davis was going to be in that courtroom arguing for his life, then, by God, somebody was going to be there for Polly, because she couldn't be there herself. And so I will sit, thought Marc. As long as it takes.

"Our commitment is to take care of Polly's business." Marc explained, "and that's what this is. This is Polly's last business."

Don't think it's not important for the family to be there. And I'll tell you this, the defense attorneys hate you being there. They know the effect it has on the jury. They want this fight to be the state versus Richard Allen Davis—a person versus a government. They want the jury to see Richard Allen Davis as a person, but they don't want the jury to see Polly Klaas as a person. If you can bring the humanity of the victim into the courtroom, in any way, you hurt the defendant's case.

I remember, back before *America's Most Wanted,* we belonged to a court-watchers group that handed out a "Cracked Gavel Award" to judges who went easy on pedophiles. We'd sit through trials on a regular basis. At the end of one trial, the defense lawyer said to the judge, "I'd like John Walsh to stand up." I did. He then made a motion to have his client's conviction dismissed—on the basis of the fact that my presence in the courtroom prejudiced the jury! The judge, I'm happy to say, threw the appeal out. But it taught me a valuable lesson: Defense attorneys notice who's in the courtroom. And that means that juries notice, too.

The trial did, in fact, drag on for more than two months. Finally, on June 18, 1996, the jury told Richard Allen Davis what they thought of his flimsy defense: They brought in a sweeping victory for the prosecution, convicting Davis of all ten counts he had been charged with—including murder, kidnapping, and an attempted lewd act on a child.

The special circumstance.

Meaning he could be put to death.

■ ■ ■

As they led him from the courtroom, Davis greeted the jury's verdict with a sick gesture, a gesture no one who's ever seen it can forget.

Turning to Polly's family and the TV cameras nearby, Davis silently, menacingly, winked, blew a kiss, and extended the middle fingers of both his hands. The move brought gasps from the courtroom crowd.

"He was directing that at America," Marc Klaas said, and I couldn't agree with him more. "He is a contemptible little punk who has been flipping off the world his whole life."

President Clinton also saw that verdict—gesture and all—on TV. After the verdict came in, he spoke to Marc Klaas on the phone. "This does not make up for the past," Chelsea Clinton's father said to the father of Polly Klaas, "but our thoughts are with you. The country owes you a debt of gratitude."

Still, Marc Klaas's confrontations with Richard Allen Davis weren't over yet.

There was one more ugly, ugly scene to play out.

■ ■ ■

The penalty phase of the trial got started in the summer of 1996. Still trying to spare Davis the death penalty, the defense brought in witnesses to talk about Davis's difficult childhood, how his parents were divorced when he was young and how he felt rootless and abandoned ever afterward.

Gimme a break. This kind of whining makes me sick.

Thankfully, no one in the courtroom seemed particularly moved by the testimony.

But then came the victim-impact statements from Marc and his relatives, most memorably from her two grandfathers. It brought everyone—including spectators, some members of the jury, and even police detectives—to tears.

Polly's maternal grandfather, Eugene Reed, who had escaped first the Holocaust and then the blitz in England, recalled his beloved granddaughter: "She liked to tell jokes," he told the courtroom. "And she was particularly good at imitating foreign accents, especially mine." He went on to talk about the search for Polly. "It was just about the worst time we ever had in our lives," said this man whose own early life had been filled with horror. "In our old age, to be hit by this devastating nightmare and catastrophe of the death of our granddaughter. It's unbearable." He added that all he and his wife, Joan, have left of Polly are photographs of her, along with a bench they installed at their Pebble Beach home, facing the ocean, in Polly's honor. Because she loved the ocean so.

Reed's words were heartbreaking. But when Marc Klaas took the stand, what he said seared everybody's heart.

Describing the close and loving relationship he had with Polly, and the unfathomable void her absence had left in his life, Klaas said, "I can't sleep, I can't concentrate . . . everything is in ruins. I have nightmares about this case every night. Now, the only way I can visit my daughter is in my dreams."

■   ■   ■

On August 6, everyone filed back into the courtroom one more time, for the most portentous moment: Would the jury, in the end, buy into the argument Davis's lawyers had presented, an argument for leniency and pity, an argument that somehow a hard childhood entitled him to act out his problems by murdering a little girl?

The court clerk stood, and read the verdict:

The jury recommended that Davis be put to death.

It was now up to the judge to accept or reject that recommendation.

A month later, Davis was brought back to court to face sentencing.

And that's when he showed his true colors—the colors of bestiality and pain.

Davis, until now, had not made a single statement, even though he had plenty of chances. He could have testified at the trial, but didn't. He could have made a statement at the sentencing hearing, but didn't. He could have pleaded for his life, but didn't. He waited until the very last possible moment, to try to get the last word, to do the most damage he could do to Marc Klaas, to try to drive one more stake through this grieving father's heart.

And the judge allowed him to speak.

Davis launched into a long, rambling speech, criticizing police procedures and his own lawyers, and he again maintained that he hadn't molested Polly. As an attempt at proof, he uttered this putrid, vicious lie: "The main reason I know I did not attempt any lewd act that night," Davis told the court, "was because of a statement the young girl made to me while walking up the embankment: 'Just don't do me like my daddy.'"

The courtroom erupted in shock. Marc's mother let out a loud, long moan. A close friend of Marc's, San Jose city attorney Mike Groves, shouted, "Burn in hell, Davis." Marc tried to leap across the barrier separating him from Davis, but was restrained. Polly's grandmother wept in shock, as they dragged Marc out of the courtroom.

It was, in the end, one more act of violence, carried out by a violent man against a family that could not strike back.

I'm supposed to be on the side of law and order, I know. And all through the trial, I'd been counseling Marc to keep his cool—no outbursts in the courtroom. But never, in all my days of fighting for victims' rights, have I been so angry for the family of a murdered child.

So let me make a confession here.

I wish Marc could have struck back.

I wish he could have gotten in just one shot at Davis, so that all the years he has to sit in prison while he waits out his inevitable appeals, he could think about how Marc did extract some measure of justice from him, in more ways than one.

The image of Marc being dragged from that courtroom is one that will never leave me. Why on earth they didn't drag that scumbag Richard Allen Davis from the courtroom is beyond me, something I will never understand to my dying day. That that vermin can sit there and spout those horrible lies about the father of a child he murdered, and there is no mechanism to muzzle him; but let that father express the outrage that every decent human being in that courtroom felt, every decent human being who saw the moment on TV felt, and he is dragged from the courtroom as though he were the criminal. I thought it stunk to high heaven, and I thought it was the stupidest thing I'd ever seen a judge do to a crime victim, and within fifteen minutes I was live on CNN, saying just that. And then all the other media called, and I spent an hour on a live satellite feed venting my spleen. It wasn't a good move, politically. I was probably burning some bridges, in the same way that I was trying to teach Marc Klaas not to.

But sometimes you just can't be smart.

Sometimes you just go with your gut.

And when somebody sticks it to your friend, you gotta stick back.

■ ■ ■

In the end, I do believe Marc will get the justice he deserves. I have walked in his shoes, and he has walked in mine, and I know that there is only one thing that will bring him some measure of closure.

The jury had sentenced Richard Allen Davis to death, and the judge had followed their recommendation. Davis now sits in San Quentin awaiting execution.

After the guilty verdict was first announced in court, a reporter asked Marc if he wanted Richard Allen Davis to get the death penalty.

"I do want him to die," Marc replied. "I'm not a morbid person by any means, but yes, I do want to be there when they take his life, just like he was there when he took my daughter's life. I want him to be looking in my eyes when he goes down, just as she had to look in his eyes when she died."

I thought it was an enormously eloquent statement.

At *America's Most Wanted,* we were putting together our last story on the case, and we talked about ending our report with those words. But it's not that simple.

It was incumbent upon us to report that, with all the appeals open to him, it could be twelve years before that moment could possibly occur. Twelve years before the death penalty could be administered to Richard Allen Davis. Twelve years that Marc Klaas, and Eve Nichol, and all of us who cared about Polly, could wait for justice to be served.

Twelve years.

The length of a lifetime.

Polly's lifetime.

■   ■   ■

A month after the sentencing, Marc and I met at a restaurant in Sausalito. The producers had asked me to tape an interview with Marc about how his life had changed since Polly's death, and the directions he was heading in now. To be honest, I wasn't exactly looking forward to the interview, because I knew it was going to make me delve, once again, into all the feelings about my son Adam's murder that I will never resolve.

But I also knew that once we got started we would be just two fathers again, two fathers who needed to help each other cope with the death of their children. And I knew that could only be good for me, and for Marc.

I was upset with the field producer who had set this up and who had decided it would be a good idea for us to do the interview in a restaurant. It was a noisy and crowded place, not at all appropriate for what I knew would be a painful, emotional experience for both of us. Face it, I'm not a professional interviewer. This is not going to be Barbara Walters or Mike Wallace interviewing a crime victim. This is going to be two dads, opening their wounds, sharing their pain.

But once Marc and I greeted each other and got to talking, and the cameras started rolling, it was all all right.

I remember noticing, first, how different he looked from that first time we met—at that Geraldo taping way back when. He seemed healthy, robust, even; he was still that hyper, manic, slightly nervous guy, but his manner seemed more relaxed, more worldly-wise and a bit world-weary. He was still full of anger—as I am, still, after all these years—but the anger seemed tempered, more directed, more controlled. He seemed to know how to use it to make changes in a criminal justice system that is deeply flawed. And he seemed to be taking some comfort in the fact that Polly's case had changed the way many police departments handle missing-child alerts.

One example Marc told me about was that of Larry Hansen, chief of police in Lodi, California. Larry attended a seminar given by the Petaluma police about the Polly Klaas case, and what they had learned from it. Larry went away from the briefing thinking about how it was all very interesting, but of course, he'd never need to put the tips they gave him to use because nothing like a child kidnapping would ever happen in a safe and serene community like Lodi.

But then, just a few weeks later, it did.

In a case that bore an eerie resemblance to Polly's, a twelve-year-old girl named Katy was abducted from her home as her two horrified friends looked on helplessly.

Larry built on what he'd learned from the Petaluma police, using every means possible to get out a missing-child alert. There were no jurisdictional disputes and no delays—in just a couple of hours, Larry Hansen had called in the FBI and had 168 agents from à bunch of different law enforcement agencies looking for Katy. They set up roadblocks and alerted all the surrounding communities and cops, and they got that child back alive within twenty-four hours. Larry Hansen directly attributes the success of the Lodi police in recovering Katy to the lessons learned from what was done right—and wrong—in Polly's case. Marc feels very proud of that, like he had a hand in the rescue.

Like Polly helped bring that child home safely.

And he was right. In a very real way, she did.

We touched on a lot of things like that during the interview.

Marc told me about how he'd set up his own foundation, which he and his wife direct from their home, and how he's still traveling the country trying to educate parents and communities about how to keep their children safe. He told me that he was working on educating the public about how pedophiles use the Internet to lure children.

"I'm the grim reaper now," he said. "I represent a terrible reality that most people would rather deny. But on the other hand, as you are, I'm pushing for an agenda that allows our children to grow up into safe, productive citizens, and I think people are going to recognize that."

He told me that he'd learned the lesson I'd told him long ago—some of his oldest friends haven't been able to talk to him about what happened, and have fallen from his life. But there are other people, good people, who come up to him, and give him a hug, and say that they're sorry for what happened, and they thank him for his good works.

And then he went back to talking, as he always does, about Polly.

He focused, first, on what her friends said about the night that Polly was kidnapped, about how she'd pleaded with Richard Allen Davis, not for herself but for the safety of her mother and her sister.

"Polly left this world and faced her worst fears by putting the welfare of others ahead of herself," Marc said. "She showed an incredible amount of courage. She was an extraordinary person. In my mind, she is the most extraordinary twelve-year-old who has lived in this century. I think to find another child who had the impact of Polly one would have to go back to Anne Frank. I think the significant thing about Polly is that the world paid attention to her plight and good things have come from it. I feel privileged that I was able to spend twelve years with such an extraordinary person and that that person taught me more in those twelve years or even in her last moments than anybody else has ever taught me and that certainly my greatest teacher was a twelve-year-old girl."

I was finding it hard to speak, after that.

I told Marc that I feel that same way about my son Adam.

And I believe that Adam and Polly are in a better place and it's we, the parents, who are left behind to deal with the torture. I believe that Adam is proud of the things that I have tried to do and I believe that Polly is proud of Marc. So we have to keep up the good work, keep up the battle.

When I told Marc that, he smiled.

"Yeah," he said. "And they're both up there saying, 'Go get 'em, Daddy.'"

CHAPTER EIGHT

Public Enemy Number One

All things have second birth.

—WILLIAM WORDSWORTH

It ain't over till it's over.

—YOGI BERRA

This is the story of how it took two hundred thousand people to catch a single killer.

■　■　■

The morning of May 20, 1996, broke blue and glorious in Washington, D.C. It was going to be a bit of a scorcher, they were saying on the radio as I drove toward the Capitol; but I was just glad that it wasn't going to rain on our parade. This was going to be the greatest day in the history of *America's Most Wanted,* and I didn't want anything to spoil it.

The event was the brainstorm of Paul Sparrow, then the senior producer of *America's Most Wanted,* and Wanda Witherspoon, then our missing-child coordinator. They were the perfect team: Paul was the TV veteran, a tall, fast-talking producer with the metabolism of a hummingbird, who could keep a hundred things going at once. Wanda was a relative newcomer, but street-smart and victim-oriented; all the families of missing children loved her quiet, sensitive approach, and she had the organizational skills to move a small army—which was just what we were trying to do.

It had started six months earlier. We were just wrapping up a great story of two missing children, Eleazar and Adan Alvarado, who were found alive and safe by one of our viewers. We flew their families to where the kids were to be picked up. The footage of the family on the plane, the happy reunion, and the tears of thanks the family had for the tipster all formed such a joyous celebration that they gave Paul an idea.

Why don't we get *all* our missing children, and their parents, and the tipsters who reunited them—bring them all together, for one *big* celebration, one giant monument to hope?

The idea started to take off: Let's bring them all to Washington. Let them stand tall and be an inspiration for all the families of missing children out there, inspiration that there is hope, that there can be happy endings. And most of the families had never met the tipsters who brought their children home, never had a chance to say thank you face-to-face—what a great moment of healing and closure for them, and what a way for us to celebrate our triumph!

We started contacting the families, and making the arrangements to bring them to D.C. I loved the idea. This was the thing I was most proud about—the way *AMW* had become such an integral part of the search for missing kids. And I knew that none of these kids would be home with their families tonight if it were not for our hotline, and those tipsters.

Each of the kids, and each of the tipsters, had come to mean so much to us. Like Nicky Sullivan, the towheaded boy from Seattle whose abductor had taken him all the way to New York City. The celebration would give us a chance to reunite him with Ali Hassan, the New York hotel clerk who recognized him after seeing him on our show.

Nicky's mom jumped at the chance to meet Ali Hassan, and to meet all the other families with whom she shared this special bond.

We visited with her as she got ready to come to D.C. for the celebration.

"I'm anxious to see how those other families are doing," she said. "I don't think I'm going to get any sleep tonight."

I was looking forward to meeting Yemane Hughes, the smilingest kid who ever appeared on TV, and whose mother, Andrea, had gone through the most horrible ordeal. Andrea's ex-boyfriend had her locked up on bogus charges, and by the time the cops realized the mistake and let her out of jail, he'd kidnapped little Yemane and disappeared. An *AMW* viewer got him back.

"I just feel like I've come full circle," Andrea said when she got to D.C., "from being put in jail, to having my son back, and now this celebration for him. We just took the right steps, and God was with us, and God led us to John Walsh, and these are his children also."

It is very humbling to be thought of in such terms, and I do feel very attached to each of those children: to Brandy, and Kaitlin, and Bryan, and all the kids who were coming. I just couldn't wait to see them.

The official celebration was set for Monday, May 20. But over the weekend, as the families arrived in town, spontaneous little celebrations began springing up: The families toured the sights of Washington together, and found themselves in the company of others who had been through their same incredible torture, the torture of losing a child, and their same triumph, the triumph of finding that child again. Most of them had never had anyone to talk to about the experience who could share, first-hand, what they were going through. And so the bonds between the families formed easily and powerfully. They were filled, in the words of James Berryhill, one of the fathers, with "the fellowship and the blessing of being together with other families that have been reunited." And, of course, each of them sought out the tipster whose call to our hotline had brought home a child. The tipsters brought dolls and toys for the kids; the parents brought the tipsters their everlasting gratitude.

That Monday morning, Paul and Wanda were down at the Capitol early in the morning. The tents for the celebration were going up at the most historic site in America, on the expanse of lawn that stretches from the Capitol to the Washington Monument, and beyond the large reflecting pool to the Lincoln Memorial—the area known as the Mall, the site of so many famous moments: Martin Luther King's march on Washington, the Vietnam War protests, the Million Man March.

And now us.

Workers noisily unfolded hundreds of folding chairs under the huge tents, set up on the Capitol side of the Mall. People were arriving by the dozens: the families and their kids, congressional representatives and FBI agents, and reporters and photographers, nearly two hundred people by the time the celebration was about to get under way. Paul and Wanda had hired clowns to entertain the kids, and caterers to feed the crowd, and as the kids buzzed around, laughing and playing and spilling their sodas, it felt like a big birthday party was starting up.

The guest list for the event itself included law enforcement people and missing-children's advocates, who would speak about efforts to keep children safe. Senator Dianne Feinstein agreed to be the keynote speaker, and I was then going to get up and make a speech about how great it was to see all these kids together with their families.

This was, among other things, a day to show off to the world. I spend a lot of time lobbying Congress to pass laws to help protect missing children; I was glad we were doing this in the shadow of the Capitol, because I wanted the legislators to see, firsthand, what joy they can create, what utter happiness they can foster, when they help bring missing children home.

But it was, more than anything, an affirmation; an affirmation of hope, of faith, of the power of human beings to reach out and help one another, to reach into the darkest corners of despair, and bring a family back safely into the brilliant light of day.

So as I pulled up to the Mall, I was feeling great. I could see, from the little road that snakes through the Mall, the beautiful setup: the big, colorful tents, the huge stage covered with three-feet-tall building blocks in red and yellow and blue and orange; and at the entrance, a big sign, emblazoned with the name of the event that Wanda had come up with:

THERE'S NO PLACE LIKE HOME.

Paul, as usual, was talking a mile a minute when I got there, telling me the order of events, and who was in the audience. He'd just gotten started when one of our staffers told me I had a phone call.

"It's Chase Carey," he said. "He called your office. Your assistant gave him the number in your car. He says it's important."

I was a little concerned. Chase was Rupert Murdoch's right-hand man at News Corp, the company that owns Fox. He was in charge of running all of Rupert's enterprises, so when you get a call from him personally, it's like getting a call from Rupert himself: You know it is something big.

There was a rumor going around that they were thinking of cutting *America's Most Wanted* back to half an hour. That meant three things: One, that we could only do half as many cases, catch half as many bad guys, bring home half as many missing children. Two, our budget would be cut in half, meaning we'd have to fire a lot of staffers. And three, a move like that is usually a sign of no confidence—sometimes an omen of bad things to come.

I was supposed to fly to New York right after this event for the annual Fox rollout of its fall schedule the next day, and I knew they'd have to settle the hour-or-half-hour question before that, so I assumed that's why Chase was calling. I walked back to my car, and hoped for the best.

"Don't stay on the phone too long, John, we've got a lot to do," Paul called.

I got on the phone with Chase. I was hoping the news wouldn't be too bad.

In my wildest dreams, I couldn't have imagined how bad it would be.

Chase didn't beat around the bush. He got right to it. He said John, I don't know how to break this to you. This is one of the most difficult things I've ever had to do.

But *America's Most Wanted* is not going to be on the schedule for the fall.

He gave me a series of reasons: We can't rerun it, as we can with other shows; we have to produce a fresh show every week; the advertising dollars just aren't there to support it; it's more economical to have two half-hour comedies in your slot.

Outside the car, Paul was driving me crazy, pacing back and forth, knocking on the car window, pointing at his watch. It was time for the event to begin. I shooed him away, and listened to what Chase had to say.

"You should be very proud," he said. "Nine years is an incredible run on prime-time TV. We've been friends over the years, and this is an incredibly hard thing for me to do. I hope you understand. It's just business."

He was a real gentleman, and he handled the conversation with dignity. I appreciated the fact that he had called me himself.

I wanted to be professional; I listened to his reasons. I thanked him for keeping us on the air as long as he did. I said Fox was the network that had the guts to put this show on the air in the first place, that had the guts to try a victim and father with no experience as the host of a prime-time show; I thanked him for that.

But when I hung up the phone, it hit me.

We're not going to be on the air anymore.

Not as an hour. Not as a half-hour.

Gone.

Canceled.

Off the air.

I couldn't believe it.

I thought about our staffers, who'd become our family—and who would now be out of a job. Washington's not like Hollywood, where a show gets canceled and the staff just moves on to other shows. There's not that much network TV produced in D.C., and a lot of these kids would be out in the cold.

I thought about my family, my career—or my finished career, as of this moment. I thought of all those victims' families who'll have nowhere to turn now.

■   ■   ■

Paul knocked on the car window again.

I knew it was time to go.

But I couldn't get out of the car.

I waved him away again, and took a deep breath, and tried to gather my thoughts. I looked out across the lawn, and I could see those hundreds of people, smiling and excited but starting to get impatient, tapping their feet and looking at their watches. I knew somewhere out there Dianne Feinstein's people were getting nervous, because her schedule is so tight and they had to get her back to the Senate floor for a vote.

And I couldn't get out of the car.

How was I going to face all these people? How could I go out there on this joyous, joyous occasion, and not look like some sad, morose individual who'd just gotten hit in the gut by a freight train?

How could I tell them that the show that brought their children home was going off the air?

But how could I *not* say anything—how could I just keep this inside?

I've been a public speaker for a long time. I don't get those butterflies in the stomach—but then, for the first time, I didn't know how I was going to face that crowd.

America's Most Wanted was always so much more than a job to me. It was my calling, my platform, my forum for changing the world, my paean to Adam, my revenge, my solace, my sword. And on this, our greatest day, when I should be standing up there like Rocky Balboa on the steps of the art museum, my arms outstretched over my head in the sheer joy of triumph, all I could think of was, who's going to look for missing kids after this?

The parents of missing kids are going to be right back where I was when Adam disappeared; true, they have the National Center for Missing and Expolited Children, and their hotline, but they'll never have the power of those fourteen million viewers again.

I looked out at Paul, pacing around like a caged cat. I felt so bad for him. He was so proud of what he had pulled together for this day, of the human beings in that tent, alive because of us, because of our viewers; so proud of this marvelous celebration. He couldn't understand why I was making everybody wait. How could I tell him this was the end of the road?

I gave myself one of the famous pep talks my father taught me—the gut check. I grew up in a sports family, and my father said, when it's the fourth quarter, and you're tired, and the game is tied because your opponents are worthy, you go into overtime. Championships are won in overtime, when one team has just a little more in the belly than the other team—a little more stamina, a little more determination, a little more guts. And I said to myself, you gotta go out there. And you gotta keep the news to yourself. Don't tell anyone. Get a smile on your face. Let this be the joyous occasion it was meant to be.

So I stepped out of the car.

Paul wanted to know what Chase Carey said.

Nothing, I lied. Let's go.

As we walked to the stage, he had about fifteen seconds to try to brief me. I had no speech prepared, I had no notes. And there was no more time. I was just going to have to wing it.

He went up first, and introduced Dianne Feinstein. While she spoke, I tried desperately to figure out what to say.

Then she was done, and I got up.

And I looked out at that crowd. All those people, all here to celebrate the most important moment in their lives. A hundred shining, happy faces. It had taken the effort of dozens of people to get their stories on the air, to get their children home; but to them, I knew I was the touchstone, the symbol, the spokesman for the Team of Hope.

I couldn't let them down.

I saw the faces of all those children—Kristin and Kaitlin and Yemane and Nicky and all the rest—beaming up at me. And suddenly, I felt very calm, almost at peace.

It's the part of the mission that John Walsh is most proud of: *America's Most Wanted* has brought 23 missing children back home. On these pages are the faces of children who are still out there somewhere.

If you have seen any of these missing children, Call 1-800-CRIME-TV or 1-800-THE-LOST

Age Progression by NCMEC 9/27/97

AARON ANDERSON

Aaron's photo is shown age-progressed to 10 years. He was last seen playing in his yard at approximately 4:30 p.m. He has a small white birthmark on the lower right side of his abdomen.

Birth:	6/23/87	**Hair:**	Lt. Brown	**Missing From:** Pine City, MN
Missing:	4/7/89	**Eyes:**	Brown	**Age Missing:** 1 ³/₄ years
Race:	White	**Height:**	2'4"	**Age Now:** 11 years
Sex:	M	**Weight:**	32 lbs.	

Age Progression by NCMEC 2/14/97

SHAKEIMA CABBAGESTALK

Shakeima's photo is shown age-progressed to 14 years. She was last seen getting into a car with an unidentified male. She has a mole near the corner of her mouth and another below her neck. She has a double tooth on the upper side of her mouth.

Birth:	12/29/82	**Hair:**	Black	**Missing From:** Dillon, SC
Missing:	7/22/93	**Eyes:**	Brown	**Age Missing:** 10 years
Race:	Black	**Height:**	3'6"	**Age Now:** 15 years
Sex:	F	**Weight:**	65 lbs.	

AMBER BARKER

Birth: 10/14/87 **Hair:** Brown **Missing From:** Oklahoma City, OK
Missing: 12/18/97 **Eyes:** Brown **Age Missing:** 10 years
Race: White **Height:** 4'11" **Age Now:** 11 years
Sex: F **Weight:** 70 lbs.

Amber was last seen leaving a friend's house on her bicycle. Her bicycle was found in Denniston Park in Oklahoma City, Oklahoma. Foul play is suspected.

BRITTNEY BEERS

Birth: 8/1/91 **Hair:** Blonde **Missing From:** Sturgis, MI
Missing: 9/16/97 **Eyes:** Blue **Age Missing:** 6 years
Race: White **Height:** 4'0" **Age Now:** 7 years
Sex: F **Weight:** 45 lbs.

Brittney was last seen playing outside of the Village Manor Apartment complex in Sturgis, Michigan on the evening of September 16, 1997. She was last seen wearing a white tank top shirt with a possible floral design, multicolored shorts and white tennis shoes with purple trim. She is missing her four front teeth.

JESÚS De La CRUZ

Birth: 1/3/90 **Hair:** Dk. Brown **Missing From:** Lynn, MA
Missing: 9/28/96 **Eyes:** Brown **Age Missing:** 6 years
Race: Hispanic **Height:** 4'6" **Age Now:** 8 years
Sex: M **Weight:** 60–70 lbs.

Jesús was last seen wearing a white T-shirt, blue jeans, and brown boots. He has a scar above his left eye, and a pierced left ear.

KAREN GRAJEDA

Birth: 10/15/88 **Hair:** Dk. Brown **Missing From:** Tucson, AZ
Missing: 1/11/96 **Eyes:** Brown **Age Missing:** 7 years
Race: White/Hisp. **Height:** 3'5" **Age Now:** 10 years
Sex: F **Weight:** 50 lbs.

Karen was last seen playing outside in front of her apartment complex on W. Valencia St. in Tucson. She has dark brownish-black hair and her right front tooth is larger than her other teeth. She has pierced ears and was wearing a gold chain with a pendant on it.

STEPHANIE CRANE

Birth:	9/28/84	**Hair:**	Brown	**Missing From:**	Challis, ID
Missing:	10/11/93	**Eyes:**	Blue	**Age Missing:**	9 years
Race:	White	**Height:**	4'2"	**Age Now:**	14 years
Sex:	F	**Weight:**	85 lbs.		

Stephanie's photo is shown age-progressed to 11 years. She was last seen at approximately 6:00 p.m. walking towards the Challis High School. She has a cowlick on the right side of her hairline. She was last seen wearing maroon sweatpants and a maroon-and-white striped hooded shirt with the word "GIMME" on the front.

ERICA FRAYSURE

Birth:	5/6/80	**Hair:**	Lt. Brown	**Missing From:**	Brooksville, KY
Missing:	10/21/97	**Eyes:**	Blue	**Age Missing:**	17 years
Race:	White	**Height:**	5'6"	**Age Now:**	18 years
Sex:	F	**Weight:**	115 lbs.		

Erica was last seen in Brooksville, Kentucky on October 21, 1997. Her vehicle was found abandoned on an isolated road in Brooksville. Her purse, including her money and checkbook, was found inside the vehicle. Her keys were missing. She has a strawberry birthmark on the back of her neck.

Age Progression by NCMEC 2/27/97

MORGAN NICK

Birth:	9/12/88	**Hair:**	Blonde	**Missing From:**	Alma, AR
Missing:	6/9/95	**Eyes:**	Blue	**Age Missing:**	6 years
Race:	White	**Height:**	4'0"	**Age Now:**	10 years
Sex:	F	**Weight:**	55 lbs.		

Morgan's photo is age-progressed to 8 years. She was abducted by an unknown white male while she was playing at a ballpark in Alma, Arkansas. She has five visible silver caps on her molars. She was last seen wearing a green Girl Scout shirt, blue denim shorts and white tennis shoes.

Age Progression by NCMEC 4/9/98

SHANE WALKER

Birth:	12/7/87	**Hair:**	Black	**Missing From:**	New York City, NY
Missing:	8/10/89	**Eyes:**	Brown	**Age Missing:**	1 ³/₄ years
Race:	Black	**Height:**	3'0"	**Age Now:**	10 years
Sex:	M	**Weight:**	23 lbs.		

Shane's photo is shown age-progressed to 10 years. He was last seen playing with other children in a park located on Lenox Avenue between West 112th and West 115th Streets in New York City. He has a small scar under his chin.

TINESHIA JACKSON

Birth:	7/21/81	**Hair:**	Brown	**Missing From:**	West Covina, CA
Missing:	3/2/98	**Eyes:**	Brown	**Age Missing:**	16 years
Race:	Black	**Height:**	5'1"	**Age Now:**	17 years
Sex:	F	**Weight:**	155 lbs.		

Tineshia was last known to be in the company of a male acquaintance who has since been found deceased. She has a tattoo of her name on her chest and a tattoo of a rose on her left thigh.

CARITA JOHNSON

Birth:	11/27/81	**Hair:**	Brown	**Missing From:**	Kansas City, MO
Missing:	5/31/98	**Eyes:**	Brown	**Age Missing:**	16 years
Race:	Black	**Height:**	5'1"	**Age Now:**	16 years
Sex:	F	**Weight:**	105 lbs.		

Carita was last seen on May 31, 1998. Her vehicle was later found at a restaurant in Kansas City, Missouri. She has not been seen or heard from since. She has a tattoo of a rose on her right ankle and a scar on the left side of her face.

JEFFREY KLUNGNESS

Birth:	12/9/81	**Hair:**	Brown	**Missing From:**	Sumner, WA
Missing:	3/2/96	**Eyes:**	Brown	**Age Missing:**	14 years
Race:	White	**Height:**	5'10"	**Age Now:**	16 years
Sex:	M	**Weight:**	155 lbs.		

Jeffrey's mother was found deceased in her home on March 2, 1996. Child has not been seen or heard from since. He may go by the name Jeffrey Hayes or Stanley Ipkiss. He is dyslexic.

MICHAEL MASAOAY

Birth:	6/25/72	**Hair:**	Brown	**Missing From:**	San Francisco, CA
Missing:	1/25/89	**Eyes:**	Brown	**Age Missing:**	16 years
Race:	Asian	**Height:**	5'1"	**Age Now:**	26 years
Sex:	M	**Weight:**	160 lbs.		

Michael became missing under suspicious circumstances. Michael is Filipino. He has thick hair and white scars (spots) on his body.

JACOB WETTERLING

Birth:	2/17/78	**Hair:**	Brown	**Missing From:**	St. Joseph, MN
Missing:	10/22/89	**Eyes:**	Blue	**Age Missing:**	11 years
Race:	White	**Height:**	5'0"	**Age Now:**	20 years
Sex:	M	**Weight:**	75 lbs.		

Jacob's photo is shown age-progressed to 19 years. He was last seen at approximately 9:00 p.m. He was with his brother and another friend when they were threatened at gunpoint by an unknown individual. Jacob has a mole on his left cheek, a mole on his neck and a scar on his knee.

  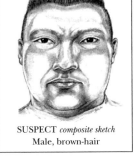

SUSPECT *composite sketch*
Male

SUSPECT *composite sketch*
Male, brown-hair

CHRISTINA WILLIAMS

Birth:	5/1/85	**Hair:**	Brown	**Missing From:**	Seaside, CA
Missing:	6/12/98	**Eyes:**	Brown	**Age Missing:**	13 years
Race:	Biracial	**Height:**	5'3"	**Age Now:**	13 years
Sex:	F	**Weight:**	80 lbs.		

Christina was last seen around 7:30 p.m. walking her dog in the Nijmegen Road area of Presidio of Monterey Annex, California. The dog was later found about a half block from Christina's residence. Christina is White and Asian. She has a mole on her cheek. The sketches shown are for the two male suspects who may have been involved in her disappearance. They are described as being Asian or Pacific Islander. The vehicle they were believed to be driving is described as a late '70s to early '80s gray Ford Granada or Mercury Monarch with gray primer spots.

KEVIN McCLAM

Birth:	4/2/82	**Hair:**	Black	**Missing From:** Goose Creek, SC
Missing:	3/30/97	**Eyes:**	Brown	**Age Missing:** 14 years
Race:	Black	**Height:**	5'7"	**Age Now:** 16 years
Sex:	M	**Weight:**	140 lbs.	

Kevin was last seen playing video games in his home during the early morning hours of March 30, 1997. He has not been seen or heard from since; however, his clothing was found at a nearby building site.

CAYCE McDANIEL

Birth:	7/14/82	**Hair:**	Lt. Brown	**Missing From:** Milan, TN
Missing:	8/17/96	**Eyes:**	Brown	**Age Missing:** 14 years
Race:	White	**Height:**	5'4"	**Age Now:** 16 years
Sex:	F	**Weight:**	120 lbs.	

Cayce was last known to be at her residence on August 17, 1996. Her family came home to find her missing and the back door left open. She has a strawberry birthmark on the underside of her lower left arm.

RACHEL MELLON

Birth:	10/13/82	**Hair:**	Black	**Missing From:** Bolingbrook, IL
Missing:	1/31/96	**Eyes:**	Hazel	**Age Missing:** 13 years
Race:	Asian	**Height:**	5'0"	**Age Now:** 16 years
Sex:	F	**Weight:**	65 lbs.	

Rachel disappeared from her residence on January 31, 1996. She was last seen wearing yellow sweatpants, a pink top, red house-slippers and was wrapped in a blue blanket.

LOUKTHAYOTH PHIANGDAE

Birth:	12/9/84	**Hair:**	Black	**Missing From:** Raymond, WA
Missing:	2/6/96	**Eyes:**	Brown	**Age Missing:** 11 years
Race:	Asian	**Height:**	4'5"	**Age Now:** 13 years
Sex:	M	**Weight:**	65 lbs.	

Loukthayoth was last seen near his residence on Crescent Street in Raymond, Washington on 2/6/96. He has not been seen or heard from since. His nickname is Luke.

ZACHARY RAMSAY

Birth: 12/18/85   **Hair:** Brown   **Missing From:** Great Falls, MT
Missing: 2/6/96   **Eyes:** Brown   **Age Missing:** 10 years
Race: Black   **Height:** 4'0"   **Age Now:** 12 years
Sex: M   **Weight:** 100 lbs.

Zachary was last seen leaving his residence for school at approximately 7:30 a.m. on February 6, 1996. He did not arrive at school and has not been seen or heard from since. Zachary is biracial. He has a scar between his eyebrows and on his arm. He has blotchy skin and dimples.

AARON STEPP

Birth: 9/24/93   **Hair:** Blonde   **Missing From:** Columbus, OH
Missing: 3/11/97   **Eyes:** Blue   **Age Missing:** 3 years
Race: White   **Height:** 3'2"   **Age Now:** 5 years
Sex: M   **Weight:** 39 lbs.

The photo shown was taken when the child was 17 months old. He was last seen on March 11, 1997, playing in a neighbor's backyard. He may be known by the name "Cody."

RICKY THOMAS

Birth: 12/21/83   **Hair:** Sandy   **Missing From:** Bristow, IN
Missing: 11/6/97   **Eyes:** Hazel   **Age Missing:** 13 years
Race: White   **Height:** 5'8"   **Age Now:** 14 years
Sex: M   **Weight:** 170 lbs.

Ricky was last seen at approximately 1:00 p.m. on Oak Ridge Road in Bristow, Indiana on November 6, 1997. He has small scars on both cheeks.

KE'SHAUN VANDERHORST

Birth: 7/17/93   **Hair:** Black   **Missing From:** Philadelphia, PA
Missing: 9/25/95   **Eyes:** Brown   **Age Missing:** 2 years
Race: Black   **Height:** 2'0"   **Age Now:** 5 years
Sex: M   **Weight:** 29 lbs.

Ke'Shaun was abducted from his residence by an unknown black female. Suspect is believed to be between the ages of 35 and 40 years old and uses the alias "Virginia Graham."

"This is a wonderful day," I said.

And I meant it.

"For people like myself," I said, "parents of missing children, and as you know, my son was abducted and found murdered—this is a positive day, to see people who have been recovered safe and alive. We are celebrating the fact that these children are here today."

One by one, I started mentioning some of the folks I saw in the crowd. Some of them just came running up to the stage, and we hugged each other, and sat down at the edge of the stage. Juanita Williams, a wonderful local singer, got up, and sang "Amazing Grace," and when she sang, "I once was lost but now I'm found," all the parents in the tent grabbed their children, and hugged them, and cried the happiest tears they could cry, until they couldn't cry anymore.

■　■　■

Afterward, we spend more than an hour taking pictures together, reliving, sharing, laughing, crying, hugging—it was an enormously emotional afternoon. I didn't let on that I knew something no one else knew—that this was not just our high moment, this was our swan song.

When I could finally break away, I went to call Lance Heflin first. While we were basking in the glow of this day, he was back at the shop, putting together the segments for the show. I thought, as the executive producer, he had a right to know before anyone else; and because Lance is my partner, I wanted him to hear it directly from me.

I really didn't know how I was going to break it to him. From the time, two years into the show, that he took over as executive producer, he's always shared my passion for the mission; he's been my partner, my confidant, my friend. It was he who created the missing-child alerts; and it was he, more than anyone else, who was responsible for keeping the show on the air so long. I knew he put his heart and soul into the show, every week. I knew this meant he'd have to uproot his wife and kids. I knew it meant that all our plans were kaput.

I knew I had to make the call.

"Lance," I said. "I talked to Chase."

"So? Are we an hour or a half-hour?" Lance doesn't beat around the bush.

"Lance, I hate to tell you this. We're not on the fall schedule."

He let go the hard, fast, two-note laugh we'd all come to know so well.

"Right. So, are we an hour or a half-hour?"

"Lance," I said. "You didn't hear me." He could tell then, from my tone, that I was serious. I told him again: We're not on the fall schedule.

He uttered one word, four letters, that expressed what we were all feeling.

Then, dead silence.

Lance is not the kind of guy who's going to express his emotions, but I knew he was devastated. He took on that grit-your-teeth, all-business tone.

"All right. We'll talk when you get back here."

He told me to tell Paul, and he would inform the rest of the staff. Then he hung up.

I pulled Paul aside. He was in that moment of exhausted exhilaration that comes after the curtain goes down. I said, "Paul, this was the best thing we've ever done."

And then I had to break the news.

"I have something I have to tell you. You're not going to believe it. I'm not going to New York. We've been canceled."

There was nothing else to say.

We both had tears in our eyes.

From the great emotion of the afternoon.

And from the impossible realization that it was all over.

■   ■   ■

Usually, when the hammer falls, the network will let you go on for a couple more shows, just to give you time to close up the shop. Lance managed to get another summer's worth of episodes, which meant our last show would air September 9; that would give the staff a little extra time to line up other work. Many, including Paul Sparrow, headed for Los Angeles; a few stayed around to help finish out the string.

We taped the show on the road all summer, and had just a skeleton crew left by the time Labor Day rolled around, and it was time to tape the last show. Our studio had already been dismantled, and turned over to the local Fox station to construct their new news set. So for that last show we hung an *America's Most Wanted* logo in a back studio, and did the best we could.

I knew what I wanted to say, when it was all over.

I just never knew how much trouble I would have saying it.

We were taping the last act, the last goodbye, and suddenly, for the first time in nine years, I began to choke up on the air. Each time we started, I found my eyes welling up and my throat catching.

I didn't want to cry on the air. I wanted to leave our viewers with a feeling of hope, not a feeling of doom; a feeling of accomplishment, not a feeling of despair.

I looked around at the dozen or so people in the room. No one wanted to catch my eye. Everyone was feeling too emotional.

I didn't know how I was going to get through this.

And so, for the first time ever, I asked that the set be cleared. There was just me, the cameraman, and a producer in the room. They started rolling the tape.

I thanked the people who made it possible for us to catch those 434 fugitives—where, apparently, our count would end. I thanked the Fox network, for having faith in us, the law enforcement community, for working with us, the tipsters, who had the courage to make the calls, and our staff, who always treated their duties as a public trust.

"*America's Most Wanted* may be ending," I said, "but the battle isn't ending. I believe the way we reduce crime in this country is if everybody fights back. So keep that battle going. Hope to see you somewhere along down the line. And for myself and millions of other crime victims, I want to say thanks for watching, thanks for caring, thanks for helping us make a difference. We couldn't have done it without you. God bless you."

And they stopped the tape, and turned out the lights, and we walked out of the studio, never to return.

■   ■   ■

That summer, an unusual phenomenon began to take place.

Law enforcement was the first into the fray. Dozens of police stations, sheriff's departments, state police, all started writing and phoning Fox, imploring them to reverse the decision, demanding it. The FBI told us they were not allowed to comment on a commercial venture—then went ahead and did it anyway, issuing a strong statement of support for the show. Suddenly, it was coming from everywhere—senators, congresspeople, state legislators, sheriff's departments, boys' and girls' clubs, state police; the letters came showering down.

Bob Miller, the governor of Nevada, a good friend of the show's, started a letter-writing campaign among governors. He got the governors of thirty-seven states to put their signatures to letters asking Fox to put us back on the air. Getting thirty-seven governors to agree on anything, even what time of day it is, is impossible enough; so getting them to agree with this was truly amazing. Then we got word that the attorneys general of all the states were doing the same—rumor had it that all fifty were writing letters to Fox.

Frankly, I think Fox was prepared for this part; they expected our political and law enforcement allies were going to protest, and I think they were ready to weather the storm.

But they weren't ready for the hurricane that followed.

Little by little, at first, then suddenly in a torrent, the letters from average citizens began to arrive. Every day, you'd walk into the office, and you'd have to step around the boxes and bags of letters that were pouring in. You'd dip your hand into the bag, and pull out a letter, and feel the fury: You *can't* take *America's Most Wanted* off the air, they were saying. This is the one show that makes a difference. What is wrong with you people?

Word was coming from the West Coast as well—the Fox offices in Los Angeles were being barraged as well.

It was turning into a cause célèbre. All the newspapers picked up on it—*The New York Times,* the *Washington Post,* the *Los Angeles Times,* all trumpeted the story. And there were plenty of stories to follow: The general manager of the Fox station in Washington, D.C., sent all the letters he'd received to Rupert Murdoch. Someone in Rupert's office—by mistake, I think—sent them back. Somehow this leaked into the press, as a big story: Rupert Murdoch wasn't even opening the mail from Fox viewers!

Things kept getting worse for Fox. A few months before we'd gone off the air, one of our producers walked downstairs to have a cigarette in front of the building, and ran into a woman in the lobby, crying. Security wouldn't let her upstairs, she said, but she had to talk to someone at *America's Most Wanted.* It seems that we had turned down the case of her brother's murder. So the woman, Crystal Porter, got five thousand people in her hometown to write letters requesting that we do the story; then she drove, with the five thousand letters, all the way from North Carolina to camp on our steps.

What could we do? We had to agree to do the story. But before we could do the case, we were yanked off the air. So what did Crystal do? She drove across the country, with her five thousand letters, and tried to deliver them to Rupert Murdoch.

Fox wouldn't let her on the lot—so she camped out on the sidewalk day after day, until everyone picked up the story. She appeared on *Entertainment Tonight, Extra,* and in all the papers, crying that her brother's killers would never be found unless Fox reversed its decision. It became another public-relations disaster for Fox.

For my part, I was staying out of it. Every day, reporters called me up, wanting me to say something terrible about Fox. I wouldn't. I believe you should take the high road. Fox had given me the chance of a lifetime, and we'd had a great run, and frankly, the reality had set in that the run was over. I thought, what an honor it is to have all these people writing these letters—spontaneously, unprompted by anyone; there was never any organization to the letter-writing campaign, it just happened—what a testimonial to the hard work of our staff over the years.

After the last taping, I had my last meeting with the staff. We went back to what used to be our set, now littered with the construction of a half-built local news studio. Everyone raised a glass of champagne, and we toasted nine great years.

I told them they had so much to be proud of. Not just the four-hundred-odd fugitives we'd brought to justice, but the seventeen missing children who were home asleep in their beds. A lot of you didn't get a chance to be at the Mall for the reunion, I said, but it was a testament to all the good that you have done.

I said the media always focused on the captures, but I've always thanked you for the justice and closure you brought to the badly damaged victims who came to our doorstep when they had nowhere else to turn.

You treated them with kindness, and dignity, and you have left behind a legacy that you will be proud of all the days of your life, wherever you go.

I'm not a TV host anymore. I'm just a father of a murdered child. And what you have done for us, for all the parents of missing and murdered children, is more important than anything that anyone has done for us before.

And I raised my glass one more time, and said, maybe we'll get a chance to do it again someday.

Who knew that chance would come so soon?

■   ■   ■

There had been a shakeup at the network. The new president was Peter Roth, a sympathetic, emotional, personable guy, and very passionate about what he believed in. And he believed in *America's Most Wanted*. Above him was a new chairman, David Hill, an Aussie who'd been around the block: He'd been a reporter, a producer, and an on-air correspondent, covering stories on the world stage for years. He'd done it all in the TV business, and he was all business.

Rupert had brought him on board to shake things up. And shake them up he did.

Whereas the pleas of the public had been falling on deaf ears before, Roth and Hill were smart enough to know that you don't ignore your customers when they complain. And no one had ever heard a complaint of this magnitude before.

We'd long since lost count, but a conservative estimate was that more than one hundred thousand people had written to Fox, to the stations, or to us, demanding that the show be brought back on the air, and that the switchboards had logged another one hundred thousand calls. Nobody keeps records of these things, but a lot of people said this was the biggest protest in TV history. All I know is, it was finally doing the trick.

Hill and Roth were willing to face down the network's spoon detectives, the bean counters who never really understood the show and what it meant to the network. They were willing to go to Chase and Rupert and fight for the show. It was by no means going to be an easy fight—but Hill and Roth were willing to fight it.

Lance and I flew out to his office.

We heard David Hill say the most amazing thing:

I'm willing to say we made a mistake, and to bring the show back, Hill told us.

To bring the show back.

I couldn't believe it.

But in the next moment, Hill was saying: I don't want the same *America's Most Wanted.*

What Hill was hearing in those letters and calls—because he did read them—was that America was sick and tired of crime, that they wanted to see someone stand up and speak the truth—not just about criminals, but about the revolving-door justice system that lets them back out on the streets, about the jelly-spined legislators who don't pass the tough laws needed to stop them, about the defense attorneys who get them out on technicalities, about the weak judges who let them off with a slap on the wrist. They wanted to hear someone speak out and fight back.

And that someone, Hill told me, is going to be John Walsh.

If we bring the show back, we bring it back in a new form. We take the gloves off, and speak our minds. This is going to be the show where America fights back, he said.

And the next thing we knew, we were back on the air.

As *America's Most Wanted: America Fights Back*.

"Be careful what you wish for," Lance was telling the staff, "because you just might get it." The elation around the office— among the few staffers still left to cheer—was muted. Yes, we're coming back, Lance told them. But the bad news is, Fox wants us back in seven weeks. We have no staff, no producer, no writer, almost no researchers; we have no camera, no studio, no director. We have no stories on the shelf. We have no stories in the pipeline.

Oh, and by the way, Fox wants an all-new *America's Most Wanted*—tougher, angrier, edgier.

No vacations, people. Be prepared to work every weekend.

"We're back on the air," he said.

"Congratulations.

"Now get back to work."

It was a mad scramble—trying to hire new staffers and train them, trying to come up with a new studio, trying to figure out how the new show would work. It seemed like there were endless meetings, floating ideas for "toughening up" the show.

One concept we hit on early was the idea of naming our own Public Enemy Number One—separate from the FBI's famous list. This would be some guy that we just decided we had to take off the streets. We'd just pursue him, relentlessly, until we found him. Do his story every week, if necessary. Someone in one of those meetings came up with the tag line for the segment: "We'll hunt him till we hunt him down."

But if we were going to do this, we knew we had to start off with the right case. Victims all our viewers could relate to. A criminal so heinous that no one would miss the concept—that this is why *America's Most Wanted* is back on the air. So that we can fight back against scumbags like this.

One of our reporters, Steele Bennett, came up with just such a case. As we listened to the details, we knew.

This was the worst guy out there.

This was the one we'd bring in first.

■ ■ ■

We got ready to rush the case into production. It was Saturday, just two weeks before we were going to air.

And in limped Steele.

In the wild scramble of getting the show back on the air, the producers had forgotten one little matter.

Steele had had a hernia operation less than twenty-four hours before.

But trouper that he is, he hobbled into the office, all hunched over. Phil Metlin, the news director, dropped his pencil when he saw Steele. "Oh, I'm sorry, man, I forgot," he said. We set Steele up in the conference room so that he could keep his feet up, with a computer, his notes, and a phone around him, and in eight hours he completed a case file on our first fugitive in our second life.

What made the case so important was not just that the bad guy was so evil—but that the victims were such wonderful people, so innocent.

"It was atrocious," Steele remembers. "We get tons of awful, awful things. But not always do you have the truly innocent victims. You'll get a call and the caller will say, 'My daughter was killed,' and you'll say, 'Oh, that's awful, how did it happen,' and she'll say, 'Well, she had fallen off the wagon and she was back on crack cocaine and she was hooking.' But you don't get the kid who's gone to visit Grandma in Kansas."

■ ■ ■

Christopher Abercrombie, five years old, was a bright, beautiful child whose only concern was the trouble he got into at school—for kissing his classmates because he loved them. He liked to sing songs from *The Lion King* and aspired to be a rock star.

The facts of the case were simple. Chris's parents, John and Leah Abercrombie, were in the process of moving. So Chris's grandmother Carol Abercrombie decided to take him on a little trip to visit relatives in Salina, Kansas.

It's almost a cliche to say that Salina is the kind of place where kids ride their bikes everywhere and no one locks his doors—but to give you an idea of what Salina is like, this is one of the crime tips you hear when you call the police department and get put on hold: "We've had a seventy-seven percent increase in car theft since 1995, and many of the 193 cars stolen had the keys in the ignition. Please help prevent this crime of opportunity—don't leave your keys in the ignition."

It was a great visit, three people who spanned four generations: little Christopher; his grandmother Carol; and his great-grandmother Delores McKim, the matriarch of the family.

Delores, eighty years old but full of life, was delighted to get a chance to see her daughter Carol and her great-grandson Christopher, and they all had a wonderful time. Christopher loved climbing the apple trees outside his great-grandma's house.

On the morning of Sunday, July 21, 1996, at 9:15 A.M., another daughter of Delores's, Kathy Melander, who lived just outside of town, called Delores's house to arrange plans for the day. It was Christopher's last day in town, and the women were planning to take him to the community theater. There was no answer, but Kathy was not concerned. *Oh, I'm sure they're just sitting outside,* she thought. *It's such a nice morning.*

But when she called back half an hour later, and at fifteen-minute intervals after that, and still got no answer, she was worried. By noon, she decided to drive into town to see if everyone was all right.

She walked up to the closed garage door.

"I had to stand on my toes to look in, and I saw that the car wasn't there, so I was real relieved," she said, thinking they must have gone off somewhere. Kathy had her mom's garage door opener, so she opened the door. And something wasn't quite right.

For one thing, the door to the house was open. Two other doors into the garage were also open, doors that were usually closed. And the window was open.

"It was like somebody screamed at me, 'Don't go in,'" Kathy said. "When the garage door was down and the car was gone, and those doors were open that are never, never, never open, and the door to the house was open, it just was wrong."

Kathy ran to a neighbor, who called 911. Officer John Krenowicz from the Salina Police Department arrived quickly. He found no signs of forced entry—but he did notice a trunk under the window, and a footprint in the dust clear enough to make out the size, thirteen.

He called for backup, and entered the house.

The officers noticed a desk in the kitchen with the drawer open, and a pile of papers on the floor.

The officers opened a hallway door, looked in a closet, the bathroom, nothing.

Then they came to the end of the hall, with a door on the right and one on the left.

They looked inside the room on the left.

Krenowicz turned to his partner and said, "Mac, we just gotta lock this down." And they walked back out of the house, to call for an ambulance. Kathy saw them emerge.

"I immediately knew what happened," Kathy said, "When I saw their faces."

■ ■ ■

What the officers saw:

Eighty-year-old Delores McKim was lying on the floor, on her left side, with her arms under her body. At first officer Krenowicz thought she had fallen. Then he noticed the large amount of blood under her head.

As Krenowicz reached for his radio, he turned, and saw the

other body in the room across the hall. It was Carol, Delores's daughter, on the floor, in her pajamas, face up. She was also lying in a pool of blood, beaten severely in the face.

It would later be determined that she had been raped, as well.

Krenowicz walked into the room where Carol was lying, and turned on the light.

He noticed little five-year-old Christopher, lying face down, on the bed.

He had also been beaten to death.

■ ■ ■

What the officer did not know:

In the dark of night, at about 1:30 A.M., a mysterious figure had parked his car at the Heather Ridge Apartments, about a half-mile away. His intent was to rape and kill someone. Nothing more, nothing less. He had targeted an old woman he knew lived alone.

He did not know she had company.

When he approached the old woman's home, he hesistated. Then circled. Slowly, deliberately. With something like side-cut pliers that he'd brought along, he cut wires that led to the house—the telephone, the electricity.

Little by little, he was isolating his prey, leaving her no way out.

He tried the back door, but it was locked. He walked around front, and noticed that the garage window was slightly ajar, and did not have a screen. As he began to enter, a car drove by. The man crouched in the bushes, and noticed a bright landscaping light next to him. He unscrewed the bulb, leaving the front of the house in darkness.

He managed to make his way through the garage window, stepping on the foot locker inside to balance himself. He headed for the room of his prey.

The intruder had been in this home before. He and his father had helped the family move in. And he'd attended the big ham radio meetings that Delores McKim's husband used to hold here. So he knew his way around.

Carrying a pipe wrench, he headed straight to the back of the house, where the bedrooms were. He knew the master bedroom was at the end of the hall on the right, but he thought he'd check the other rooms first.

That's when he saw Delores's daughter, Carol Abercrombie, sleeping.

He opened the door to her room, and stepped in.

Bumping into a table.

The noise woke her up, and she saw the strange man, towering over her.

Maybe she saw the pipe wrench in his hand, as it came down, forcefully, on her head.

As she lay there, blood pouring from her forehead, she may have heard the screams of her grandson Christopher, lying next to her, as the man began beating the child as well, and then the screams of her mother, next door, already out of bed and standing, as the intruder entered her room and beat her too.

Maybe Carol saw and heard all this, because the autopsy showed that all three family members survived, for a time, after they were brutally beaten.

Which, of course, also means that poor Delores and Christopher were alive, and possibly aware, when the intruder put down the pipe wrench, walked over to the place where Carol lay bleeding to death, and raped her, the final, horrible, brutal act of a madman. When it was all over, he washed his hands in the hall bathroom, and walked to the refrigerator, leaving his three victims, three generations of a family, to bleed to death in the dark.

The intruder took a soda, sat down, and thought about how to get rid of the bodies.

Then he figured, oh, the hell with it.

I'll just leave them here.

He found the women's purses, and took a couple of hundred dollars and a credit card.

And he drove to the Flying J truck stop, and ate a big breakfast of ham and eggs.

■   ■   ■

The people of Salina were horrified. Never had there been such a horrible, gruesome murder—three generations, wiped out in one moment. And in a house right across the street from the governor's parents, no less—a neighborhood everyone considered one of the safest. It was beyond belief. What monster could possibly commit such a frightful act?

Except for some excellent police work, we might never have known.

Here's how it all came together.

The credit card that the intruder stole from Carol was used just before 5:00 P.M. on the day of the murders at the Kwik Shop in Salina to pay for gas at the pump. It was also used unsuccesfully at an ATM—which snapped a partial photo of the user. The quality was poor, and the face unidentifiable; one could make out that the subject was a man, about six feet tall, and of stocky build.

Four days later, a funeral was held for Delores in Salina. On a hunch, police set up surveillance cameras at the church, and asked family members to keep an eye out for suspicious people. The town was in shock; many who knew Delores came to cry and pray; many who didn't came as well, in a pilgrimage of shared grief. A hundred people filled the small church.

Sheriff's deputy Brent Melander—stepson of Kathy Melander, the daughter who first called the police that awful day—was one of those in attendance. He spotted a guy he knew—because the guy had done time at the Salina County jail. His name was Alan White.

Brent thought it was odd to see him there. The two men locked eyes—just for a second—then White, appearing nervous, headed into the rest room. He later took a seat at the rear of the church for the ceremony.

Quietly, Brent went up to his stepmother. Do you know why that guy would be here? he asked. No, she said, no idea—although she remembered later that White's father and Delores's late husband had been in a ham radio club together. Still, that's a pretty tenuous connection. Brent had an officer radio the dispatch, to run a check on him. They found out he was serving weekend jail time as part of his parole on a residential burglary.

In the coming days, they questioned Alan White's girlfriend—who lived next door to the apartment complex where Delores McKim's car had been recovered. They questioned Alan White, whose story seemed a bit shaky.

Police definitely had zeroed in on a suspect. But the good break was followed by a bad one. The newspapers printed a story that the police had a surveillance-camera photograph of the possible suspect. It was enough to spook Alan White. He took off.

A month later, White jumped on a Greyhound bus headed from Lincoln, Nebraska, to Cleveland. From there, the trail went cold.

At that point, White was only wanted on his parole violation; there was still not enough evidence to tie him to the crime. But the rape examination on Carol Abercrombie had revealed semen in her vagina. One way to tie White to the crime—or exonerate him—would be a DNA test.

Alan White's parents, Larry and Jo White, were certain of their son's innocence and would do anything to clear his name.

They were asked for a blood sample.

His parents turned out to be two of the most upstanding people we had come across. So many parents of fugitives just stonewall the cops, they stonewall *America's Most Wanted,* but here were these people, willing to come forward and let the chips fall where they may. What a gamble they were taking!

On October 21, 1996, lab reports from the Kansas Bureau of Investigation laboratory in Topeka confirmed a genetic match between Alan White's parents' blood and the semen found in the body of the victim.

Six days later, Alan White was charged with a triple murder.

Jo White took the news stoically. "We totally had no qualms about donating our blood, because we knew it would clear him," she said. "I guess we fried our own son."

The family was forthright with us. "Like it or not, if it does convict him, then that's what has to be," said White's father, Larry.

"We have to live with that," said Jo. "We'll always know we did what we thought was the right thing."

"I can love him," said Larry. "I don't have to love the things he does."

But no one could make Alan White pay for the crime. Because no one knew where he was.

And it was still eleven days until *America's Most Wanted* was coming back on the air.

■   ■   ■

All I could think of was, we've got to catch this guy. How do you take away three generations of a family? Who could do such a thing? The motive was probably robbery; maybe robbery and rape; but why, in the name of the Lord, do you kill everyone in the house? And the family—how do they live with that, ever? How do they go on? When Adam was killed, I went into the darkest hole, a place I never thought I would come out of. It was almost the end of me on this planet. Here's a young man, John Abercrombie, who not only lost his only son—a beautiful little boy, just a little younger than Adam was—but also his mother, and *her* mother. I thought, what must this man be going through? What must his wife be going through? She was the first to get the call—can you imagine trying to tell your spouse that his son, his mother, and his grandmother have all been killed?

The police were happy to see Steele when he landed in Kansas. So was Kathy Melander. They wanted the bastard caught, and were going to do anything to find him. Kathy gave us the keys to the house where the murder took place, so that we could use it to film the reenactment. She even gave Steele the keys to her mom's car— the one Alan White had used for his getaway car, and then abandoned—so he could have it to drive around. It was still covered with black graphite from the police going over it for fingerprints. "I ran it through the car wash to clean it up," he remembers, "and got a little spooked driving it—because the last one to drive it before me was Alan White—so I took it back."

It fell to a freelance producer to interview Christopher's

parents, Leah and John Abercrombie, back home in Greenville, North Carolina. That was the heartbreaker. These people had lost so much. We made it clear to them that we could do the case without them—but they wanted to do their part. "You want this man caught so bad, and if you don't do it, what might happen?" said Leah Abercrombie. "Even if there's a slight chance he could be caught, you want to do it."

While all that was going on, we were back home, going crazy, trying to reassemble the show. It was like a jigsaw puzzle that had fallen on the floor, and a lot of pieces had disappeared under the rug. Sharon Greene was training her replacement on the hotline— Wanda Witherspoon, who'd just a few months earlier put together the celebration on the Mall—and desperately trying to get the hotline phones reinstalled, because they'd already been torn out. Next door to our old set (from which they were now broadcasting the local news) a Fox team scurried around madly putting up a new set for us. They were led by George Greenberg, David Hill's right-hand man. Lance knew George from the days they'd worked together at a news station in Miami, but now we couldn't believe he was here. George was in the middle of launching Fox SportsNet. He was in the middle of producing Fox's first World Series broadcast. And he was sweating every detail of the new *AMW*. His passion, his respect for the show, and his belief in our mission were a great boost.

Somehow, everything fell into place.

Everything was ready.

The Alan White case was set to go.

Now all we gotta do is catch the guy.

■　■　■

"*America's Most Wanted* is back—and man, it feels great to say those words." With that line, we started our second life, show number 428, just seven weeks after we'd said our last goodbye. I sat on that new set, looking around at all the new faces, and thought, how incredible it is that we're back. "Our new mission is simple," I said on that show. "Take a look at crime in this country, and say—

enough is enough. Well, let's get busy. Because from this day forward, *America's Most Wanted* is where America fights back." I introduced the first case—and for the first time, got to start saying what I was really feeling about these characters. "This coward's name is Alan Eugene White," I said as they flashed his picture over my shoulder. "He's our first Public Enemy Number One. Let's track him down."

After we aired the piece, I wanted to do a little tag. I remembered what David Hill had said about taking the gloves off. I thought, that's what the man wants, that's what he's gonna get.

"This is one of the most heartbreaking cases we've ever been involved in. Police say Alan White is capable of anything. This guy has gotta be taken down. Justice for this devastated family starts with you. So let's get busy. The next time I see Alan White's face, I wanna see bars in front of it."

It was the tone I wanted to set for the new show. Stop pretending to be objective about these cases. Let's get the scumbag.

(The producers spent about two weeks arguing over whether I could say "scumbag" on the air, by the way. We decided it was okay—but then our viewers objected. They thought it wasn't dignified. So I mostly stopped using it.)

(But I really wanted to get the scumbag.)

■   ■   ■

It was a bit chaotic on the hotline that Saturday night, our first hotline operation in the new studio. The phones were working, and enough of our old hands had come back that we weren't starting totally from scratch. But we'd never had a night with so many newcomers manning the phones. Sharon Greene, the outgoing hotline supervisor, and Wanda Witherspoon, incoming, were both trying to keep order. But when the tips started coming in on Alan White, there was a bit of a problem.

Understand that answering the phone on the hotline is a little like being a firefighter: long periods of relatively dull routine, interrupted by moments of intense excitement. The first time you answer the hotline, taking all those calls from people who have very sincere but not very specific information, you get lulled into a fairly efficient, fairly low-key mindset—like Jack Webb on *Dragnet.* Just the facts, ma'am. Where did you see him? Uh-huh. And that was how many years ago? Okay.

But then you get one of those calls.

Where it slowly dawns on you.

This is it.

Well, one of our first-time operators got that call.

And she freaked out.

Fortunately, Wanda was right there. Quietly, so not to embarrass the operator—but so not to lose the caller, either—she took over the call.

It was right on the money.

■　■　■

"My boyfriend and I were watching *America's Most Wanted,* because it had just come back on the air and we couldn't wait to see it."

But Mary King, a counselor at Boston-area homeless shelters, with the light Irish features to go along with her thick Boston accent, couldn't believe what she saw.

"They featured the story on Al White," she continued, "and I looked at the picture and said, 'That's the Al White from my program!'"

It seems that an Al White was staying at one of Mary's homeless shelters while doing odd jobs around town. She immediately got on the phone to *AMW.*

Back on the air for all of twelve minutes. And here came our first hot tip.

Wanda and Sharon relayed the tip to the Boston P.D., and faxed them White's picture. They headed for the homeless shelter, looking for our first Public Enemy Number One.

At ten-thirty that night—just half an hour after we went off the air—they found him.

Unbelievable.

Alan White.

On the run for ninety days.

Captured in ninety minutes.

■   ■   ■

We know the details of what happened in the house on the night of the crime because, while waiting in jail, Alan White, to pass the time, told the story to a cellmate. The cellmate told it to the prosecutors.

Shortly afterward, Alan White pleaded guilty and was sentenced to 157 years.

■   ■   ■

So it had all come full circle. It seemed like a million years since I was sitting in that car, listening to Chase Carey tell me that we were going off the air. A million years since I stood before all those parents, who'd come to Washington to say thank you to the tipsters who'd saved their children's lives, and thought it was all over. What a long, strange trip, from that burning hot spring day, to this cool fall evening.

And how appropriate, how important to me, that the first— allow me—the first scumbag that we caught was a man who took among his victims a beautiful, blond little five-year-old boy. When I think of all the twists and turns and coincidences that had to take place to get this story on the air, and I think of how it all wound up, I can't help but get a little wistful, and allow myself to think, well, well, Adam, my little angel, you are still watching out for me, aren't you.

■   ■   ■

The parents of little Christopher Abercrombie brought us full circle as well. Steele Bennett had taken the cops on the case out to dinner in D.C., that night, then they all headed down to the hotline for the show. He was there when the call came in that White was in custody. His first call was to Christopher's parents, John and Leah. They were stunned.

"Steele called us right at the end of the show," Leah said. "At that point we felt like he was a friend more than a professional working with us. When he called, it was an incredible feeling. You thought all along, 'Where is this man who has done this, is he doing it again to someone else?'—and then he was off the street."

Steele thought his life was going to finally become normal again. Eight days after his hernia surgery—eight days of mad, fly-by-the-seat-of-your-pants production—were over. Alan White was in custody in Boston. Steele could finally relax. Some old friends were playing poker later that night, and he was planning to join them.

His supervisor, Phil Metlin, who was in the studio that night as well, walked up to Steele.

"Need somebody to do the capture report," he said. "You want to go to Boston?"

Why not, said Steele. Followed it this far, might as well follow it to the end.

So he stopped by the poker game—"Hi, bye, gotta go to Boston"—then headed to the airport.

He was not the only one who would make the trip.

A few days later, Alan White was finally being moved, and we wanted to pick up a "grab shot"—the shot of the perp in cuffs, the payoff shot for our viewers. While arranging the shoot, Steele checked back in with John and Leah, to see how they were doing.

He had heard rustling going on in the background, and asked what was happening.

"We're packing," Leah said. "Promise you won't tell anybody? We're going to Boston. We want to see this guy's face."

■　■　■

And that's how it came to be that, in the wee small hours of a Thursday morning, the survivors of a massacre that took three generations of a family stood on misty street corner, hugging the reporter who'd brought in the killer.

And they went to the police station, and waited for dawn, when Alan White would be brought down the steps, and out to a waiting car, to be driven to his arraignment at the courthouse.

Just after dawn, he emerged.

"Oh, my God, there he his," Leah whispered.

"I knew that he was caught," she said, "but to see him in handcuffs makes it so real."

Alan White looked up, and saw Leah, across the street. Their eyes locked for a moment. Then he looked down. "He couldn't even face me," Leah said. "He couldn't even face me."

White was whisked away, and it was time for one more meeting. The other reason John and Leah had come to Boston.

Steele had the telephone number of the tipster, Mary King. He called her, and they arranged to meet on the Boston Common at noon. There were still a few hours to kill, so Steele took the Abercrombies to Cheers, bought them a souvenir glass, and then they headed on to the Common.

From across the open expanse, Steele spotted the woman fitting the description she'd given on the phone. And she spotted them.

There were no words exchanged, as Mary approached John and Leah. Only tears, and hugs.

"Thank you," they said, their faces buried in Mary's hair.

"Your story tugged at my heart," she told them. Then she handed them a bundle she was carrying, something wrapped in tissue paper. "This is for you. This is for Christopher. Maybe it will help."

And the Abercrombies took the bundle, and unwrapped it.

Inside was a small glass figure.

It was a figurine of a little boy.

A cherub. An angel.

A little tow-headed boy, smiling down on the world below, floating on crystal wings.

EPILOGUE

You Can Make a Difference

One of our producers estimated, a little while back, that we had passed our one millionth call to the *America's Most Wanted* hotline. It's a staggering notion, when you think about it: more than a million people, sitting home watching TV, seeing someone in pain, and saying: I can do something to ease that pain. And I will.

In each of the cases in this book, you have met the victims of crime, anguished souls ripped violently from the fabric of their workaday lives, thrown mercilessly into a dark pit of despair, searching desperately for some way to make sense of their lives again. And in each of those cases, someone has tried to reach out a hand and help those victims back into the light. It is a pure, selfless act of mercy, one that ennobles us all for its grace and kindness.

And now it's your turn.

There are so many families out there, waiting for the justice and closure that our viewers have brought to more than five hundred others over the years. Each of these families waits, patiently, for the miracle to come.

I want to tell you about four more cases. These cases have not been solved.

Yet.

Each case involves a fugitive we have not been able to find.

Yet.

In the photo section of this book, you will see their faces. They are the people we need you to find. These are the reasons I need you to find them.

I want you to look closely at their pictures.

I want you to pay close attention to these stories.

If you know where these fugitives are, I want you to call 1-800-CRIME-TV. We understand that a lot of people don't want to talk to the police, so remember: You can ask to remain anonymous, and we will honor that request.

But I want you to do the right thing.

And I want you to remember:

You can make a difference.

JAIME "SIX FINGERS" EDWARDS

The streets of Stamford, Connecticut's, South End are a melting pot of nationalities and personalities. The area is home to thousands of hard-working people. It is also the home to a chapter of the gang known as the Nation, a violent group born in the prison system but spilling out onto the streets of America. Many gang members ruled the drug trade on Stamford's South End.

Bennie Perez didn't like them one bit.

Bennie had come from Puerto Rico as a teenager, with a dream of becoming a pro boxer. But his toughest fight took place outside the ring: He made it his personal mission to take on the drug dealers that were the scourge of his neighborhood. He was determined to raise his two children without the specter of gang violence looming on every street corner.

So he took them on.

When he saw a drug deal go down, he'd honk his horn, and flash his headlights, until the cops came.

Or, more often than not, he'd get out of his car and take on the dealers himself. Confronting them, demanding that they leave the neighborhood.

"Bennie chased them down the street," his wife, Iris, remembers. "He was very against drugs. He thought he could do something about it."

Bennie's one-man war on drugs got the attention of the cops—who begged him to be more careful, and leave the policing to them.

He also gained the attention of a particularly dangerous member of the Nation, twenty-five-year-old Jaime Edwards. Edwards became one of the targets of Bennie's anti-drug crusade—and he did not appreciate Bennie's interference in his business. The two men had known each other years earlier, back in high school. They raced cars once—and Edwards lost.

This time, he would not lose.

On the evening of February 4, 1995, Bennie was going to take his first step on the road to professional boxing glory. His cousin, an ex-prizefighter himself, had wrangled Bennie his first pro fight. That evening, before the fight, Bennie was driving to his cousin's house.

He passed Jaime Edwards.

Police say Edwards took out a nine-millimeter semiautomatic pistol and fired into the car, striking Bennie, who fell across the seat. With the car in gear, it kept moving, slowly, and police say Edwards walked along, firing again and again, emptying his pistol into the dying fighter's body.

The car came to rest against a snowbank.

And Edwards disappeared.

The newspapers eulogized the fighter who dared to take on the gangs. But the man who took his life remains at large.

We've got one great clue. He is known as Jaime "Six Fingers" Edwards because of a strange characteristic: He has two thumbs on his left hand. We've even got his extra-digit fingerprints to prove it.

Bennie's wife, Iris, left alone with their two children and her memories of a fighter, believes that you can carry on Bennie's fight by bringing Edwards to face justice.

His son Angel, who was four when Bennie was killed, has a simpler request.

He just wants someone to find "the bad man that killed my daddy."

MARGARET RUDIN

It was the kind of marriage you read about in the society columns.

And the kind of crime they make movies of the week about.

Ron Rudin was a millionaire developer, taking high risks in a town that lives for high risks, Las Vegas.

His new wife, Margaret, was the beautiful owner of an antique shop. For both, it was marriage number five.

We got two different pictures of this pairing:

"Ron and Margaret had such a fairy-tale romance," a cousin of Ron's told us. "We thought that she was the best thing that ever happened to Ron."

"Margaret Rudin's a gold digger," Las Vegas detective Jimmy Vaccaro told us, "and has been one all her life. She's always in quest of the big dollar, and she thought she'd found that in Ron Rudin."

Turns out the cop's picture was a little more accurate than the cousin's.

A month before their wedding, Margaret wrote in her diary, "The most important priority is having Ron to share in a happy exchange the rest of our lives." But not long after they were married, she logged a more ominous entry: "I'm good at being a bed partner, cook, decorator, housekeeper . . . Ron has been a liability to me . . . Ron has not fulfilled my life."

No one knew how bad things actually were until Ron failed to show up for work on December 19, 1994. Three days later, his car was found at the Crazy Horse Too Topless Saloon, the sort of place the millionaire developer never frequented. It would be a month later before fishermen at Lake Mohave would make the discovery that told the world what happened to Ron Rudin.

They found his skull.

Ron had been shot, decapitated, stuffed in a trunk—an antique trunk, it was duly noted—and dragged to the lake. The trunk was set on fire.

The charred head rolled away.

Police, called to the scene, found Ron's burned remains. Ron, reportedly suspicious of his wife's motives and plans, had left behind a signed statement that if he died by violent means, anyone found responsible for causing his death would be cut out of his estate. But with no evidence to link anyone to the murder, the settlement of Ron's estate moved forward. Margaret was expecting sixty percent of Ron's $11 million trust—but for some reason, agreed in an out-of-court settlement to accept $500,000. She took the money and ran.

Later, police would determine what they believed to be the reason.

They found the gun that they say linked Margaret to the murder. Eventually, a grand jury found enough evidence to charge her with the crime.

But no one ever found Margaret Rudin.

The clues: She's gone by the names Margaret Frost, Margaret Mason, Margaret Zumbrunn, Margaret Brown, and Margaret Krafbe. She has relatives in Palm Springs, California, and in the Chicago area. She's dyed her hair both red and blond, but it's probably black now.

She talks and acts like a rich woman.

But she's just a black widow.

She's probably spent a lot of her money by now.

Meaning she's probably hunting for her next prey.

VERNON HENRY

He wasn't the kind of kid you'd peg to become a militia-loving, government-hating, gun-toting survivalist: He was a long-haired marijuana-smoking sixties hippie. His puppy love for his childhood sweetheart, Connie, grew into a true romance, and they got married.

But after they started raising their children, Connie started seeing a different side of Vernon Henry coming to the fore.

He was increasingly distrustful. He was intensely controlling.

And he was becoming more and more jealous.

When Connie went out for a drink after work, he'd become ballistic—eventually getting so angry that he forced her to quit her job and stay home, where he could keep a better eye on her.

And it wasn't just Connie. When their four children started growing up, he went into the same rage when they'd go out. It infuriated him when the oldest, Juston, decided he'd had enough, and left home to move in with the neighbors. Vernon Henry saw the neighbors as he saw the government, as a meddling interference in his life.

So the night his teenage daughter Heather went out on a date with the neighbors' boy, it was too much for Vernon. First he tried to stop her; failing at that, he launched into an argument about it with Connie, which lasted most of the evening.

Just before midnight that night, August 12, 1996, the neighbor boy dropped Heather off at the house, kissed her goodnight, and made a date for the next evening. "Yeah, I'll pick you up after work," he called out.

But he would not get the chance.

Heather walked in the front door, and found her parents, still awake.

From her room, Heather's younger sister Casey heard fragments of the shouted arguments:

"Don't treat the kids that way!" her mom was saying. "You shouldn't be striking them! You shouldn't be pushing them around!"

Then:

"Don't point the gun at us! You could hurt somebody!"

Then:

"Run! He's getting bullets!"

Then, Casey heard three shots.

Police say Vernon had taken a .45-caliber handgun from a bedroom drawer, then went to his workshop in the garage to get some bullets. He came back into the living room.

They say he shot his wife and daughter in the chest.

They fell to the floor.

Casey ran to the phone.

"911, What's your emergency?"

"Hello. My dad just shot my mom and sister . . ."

"Where are you?"

"I'm in the house. My dad left. He took the car and left."

By the time paramedics arrived, Connie and Heather were dead.

Vernon Henry will not be easy to find. An intelligent man, not well schooled but very well read, he is a trained survivalist. He loves going up to the mountains, and could survive with very little. He is a good fisherman.

Before he left, he had three guns, including, police say, the murder weapon.

None of those guns was recovered.

He most likely still has them with him.

DENNIS MELVIN HOWE

He was a loner. A chain smoker. Quiet and precise. He came from Saskatchewan, where he had served time for burglary, and for assaulting two women and a child. In January of 1983, he ditched his parole officer, and began living under an alias in a Toronto rooming house.

She was a beautiful child: always sunny, always smiling, always positive, always bringing out the best in people. Her name was Sharin Morningstar Keenan—Sharin, her parents said, as in sharin' the load, sharin' the sunshine, sharin' the joy: "A wise, bright, old spirit," her mom called her.

That night, January 23, 1983, when she did not come home from the park, the alert went out: She is nine years old. She is four-feet-eight. She weighs seventy-five pounds. She has dark, shoulder-length hair. She is wearing a brown quilted coat, a cotton skirt, and a white blouse.

She is gone.

It became the biggest manhunt in Toronto's history—some said in the history of Canada—involving literally thousands of citizens, and hundreds of police officers.

Her friends said that just before she disappeared, they saw Sharin talking to a man. He was chain smoking. He had yellow teeth and wrinkly skin and hairy arms and a deep laugh.

Police went door-to-door with the description, and eventually came upon a house, 482 Brunswick Avenue, not far from the park where little Sharin had been playing before she disappeared. In that house was the room that Dennis Melvin Howe had been renting. They searched the room.

"Nobody actually came out and said, you know, 'We found her,'" her mom said. "What the officer said, who was there, was, um . . . 'We found a child.'"

What the officer did not say in that moment:

They found the child in the refrigerator.

An autopsy revealed that Sharin had been sexually molested, and strangled to death.

Police charged Dennis Melvin Howe with the murder.

And he has remained at large for nearly sixteen years.

Of all the cases that we have not been able to solve, this is the one that haunts us all the most deeply. So many of these child predators are off the streets, thanks to our viewers, and I am so grateful for that. But the fact that this man has eluded us all these years seems almost impossible.

Some staffers have speculated that he is no longer alive.

I am not ashamed to admit that I hope that is the case.

But my gut tells me it is not.

That he is out there.

And if he is out there, I guarantee he is still preying on other children, somewhere.

And he will continue to do so.

Until you stop him.